Battersea Dogs & Cats Home

CHOOSING
the
RIGHT DOG
for you

Gwen Bailey

Includes profiles of over 230 breeds
Completely revised and updated

hamlyn

Produced under licence from
Battersea Dogs Home Ltd

® Battersea Dogs & Cats Home

Royalties from the sale of this product
go towards supporting the work
of Battersea Dogs & Cats Home
(Registered charity no 206394).
battersea.org.uk

Battersea Dogs & Cats Home has
been caring for and rehoming
abandoned, stray and neglected
animals since 1860. We have looked
after over 3 million dogs and cats
since then, and we aim never to turn
away an animal in need of our help.
To find out more about our charity
visit **battersea.org.uk.**

An Hachette UK Company
www.hachette.co.uk

First published in Great Britain in 2004
by Hamlyn, a division of Octopus
Publishing Group Ltd
Endeavour House
189 Shaftesbury Avenue
London
WC2H 8JY
www.octopusbooks.co.uk

This revised edition published in 2014

Copyright © Octopus Publishing
Group Ltd 2004, 2014

Text copyright © Gwen Bailey 2004,
2014

ISBN 978-0-600-62678-7

A CIP catalogue record for this book is
available from the British Library

Printed and bound in China

10 9 8 7 6 5 4 3 2 1

Contents

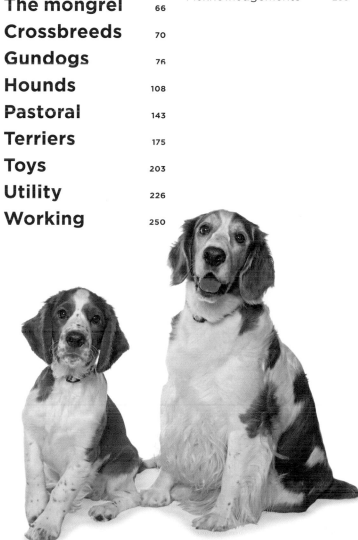

Getting a dog

Things to consider
Choosing your dog
Finding your dog

Are you ready for a dog?

Deciding to take a dog into your home is a big step. You need to be ready for all the responsibilities involved, not just now, but for years to come. Being prepared and informed will help you make the right decision. Below are some things to consider when assessing your current lifestyle to help you decide whether you have the resources to take on a dog.

Time

Owning a dog will take up a lot of your time. You will need to put aside time for walking, playing, training, grooming, visiting the vet, feeding and giving affection, as well as more mundane duties such as buying dog food, drying their coat after a wet and muddy walk and cleaning up dog hair, mud and drool. Do you currently have lots of time on your hands? If not, what will you give up to take care of your dog?

Do you have an active social life? If so, are you prepared to give some of this up to be at home with your dog? If your children enjoy activities such as swimming or dance classes throughout the week, there may not be time to walk and play with a dog every day. Do you work full time? If so, are you in a position to offer a dog all it needs to feel fulfilled and content? You will need time to settle a new dog in before leaving it for full working days.

Cost

Make a realistic assessment of your current financial status to find out how much spare money is available once all household bills and expenses have been paid. Estimate the likely costs per week of the type of dog you are considering (see pages 20–21). Would owning a dog mean that you would have to make savings elsewhere?

Mental and physical energy

Dogs need play, companionship and physical exercise every day to feel content. Younger dogs

Below: The time needed to look after a dog can be considerable. Before taking on a dog, make sure you have time to care for all its needs.

and those from working breeds need the most. Think about your current lifestyle and commitments. Do you collapse exhausted on the sofa at the end of a long day? If so, taking on a young or active dog could be a disaster for you both. Trying to provide for an active animal's need for physical and mental stimulation can be very taxing when you are tired, so be realistic about how much extra energy you have to devote to a dog.

Allergies and health

Could anyone in your family or living in your household suffer from an allergy to dogs? Make sure that everyone spends some time around dogs before you make your decision to get one.

Is your general health good enough to allow you to care for your dog every day? Are you mobile enough to scoop the poop? Who would care for your dog if there is a sudden deterioration in your health or you had to be hospitalized?

Accommodation

If you live in rented accommodation, are you allowed to keep pets? If you own your own home, are you prepared for any damage to the property or fences that may come as a result of dog ownership? If you live with other people, are they fully prepared for life with a dog and are they happy to accept any additional work or responsibilities that living with a dog might bring?

Do you live near a park or a safe area where a dog could run freely? If not, how will you exercise your dog adequately? Sufficient daily exercise is essential to keep a dog quiet and calm in the house. Do you have a fenced garden where you could safely allow a dog to exercise and play? If not, how will you manage the process of housetraining? If you don't have a garden, you will need to set aside time to take your dog out for toileting, exercise and play many times a day.

Below: Providing your dog with sufficient exercise will get you outside in the fresh air too, but be prepared to go out every day in all weathers.

Experience and knowledge

Do you have sufficient experience and knowledge for the type of dog you want to own? Some dogs are easier than others to train and look after so the more you find out in advance, the better. Talk to other owners to help you decide if the type of dog you are considering would actually be right for you.

Looking to the future

Although it is impossible to look into the future, it is important to consider your future plans and how a dog would fit in.

- **Partners** If you are single, what will happen if you find a partner who doesn't like or appreciate your dog? What if they have a dog too? How will your dog adapt to having another dog in the household?

- **Children** If you are considering having children in the future, how well will your dog cope with the sudden competition for your attention?

Above: School-age children are old enough to enjoy a new dog in their lives and will also be able to help care for it.

Right: A dog can be a lovely addition to a family, but make sure you have sufficient time, energy and resources to care for the dog properly.

Can I afford the daily expense of owning a dog?

Do I have insurance or savings to pay for unforeseen expenses, for example if my dog causes an accident, damages someone's clothes by jumping up with dirty feet or becomes ill and needs medical care?

Do I have sufficient time every day to provide for all my dog's needs?

Will I have enough mental and physical energy to make sure my dog is adequately stimulated and cared for?

Does anyone in the household suffer from allergies to dogs?

Will my state of health allow me to care adequately for a dog?

Does my accommodation make it easy for me to own a dog?

Do I have enough knowledge about the type of dog I want to own?

Will a dog fit into my future lifestyle?

You would need to choose a child-friendly dog and socialize a puppy with different children of all ages from the beginning.

- **Work and travel commitments** What would happen to your dog if you are promoted at work or lose your job, and your new job involves extensive travel or longer hours? Are you hoping to travel in the future? If so, who would look after your dog and is it fair to leave it if you are planning a long trip?

Reasons for owning a dog

Different people have different reasons for wanting to have a dog in their lives; it might be to get them out in the fresh air for a walk every day, it might be for companionship. Understanding your own reasons for wanting to own a dog will help you decide whether in fact to get one, and if so, what type of dog would be best suited to you. Be honest and examine your motives carefully.

Companionship

Many people want a dog for companionship. There is nothing quite like a happy doggy greeting when you get home, or a warm dog's head asleep on your slippers in the evening. However, dog companionship is no substitute for human company and if you are lonely, don't expect a dog to meet all your social requirements.

Below: Many owners buy a dog for companionship and to play with. Finding the right type of dog that can fulfil expectations is essential.

Exercise

Dogs need exercise every day, the perfect motivation for you to get out and exercise regularly too. Don't forget, however, that if you are getting a dog to help you exercise, you cannot stop once you think you are fit enough or if you lose interest.

Dog sport competitions

Some owners get a dog to participate in a specific dog sport, such as agility, field trials or dog dancing, and will usually have a good idea of what breed they want. If you want to take part in one of these activities, it is essential to create a strong bond with your dog and spend a lot of time training. Remember, your dog will require plenty of exercise on the days you aren't training or competing if it is an active breed.

Fun

Dogs do funny things that entertain and amuse us and their sheer exuberance for life can be infectious. Some owners choose boisterous dogs with big personalities to make an extrovert and engaging companion. However, even if you enjoy a boisterous dog, others may not, so training calm manners is essential.

As a child substitute

Many childless couples, or older parents whose children have grown up and moved away, get dogs to fulfil their need to nurture. These dogs are often lavished with lots of care and affection, although problems can arise if owners treat them too much like children instead of members of a different species with needs of their own.

For the children

Many parents buy a dog to help complete their family or because their children keep asking for one. However, at least one adult in the household should be happy to be totally responsible for the dog's daily needs, and to teach the children and the dog to interact successfully with each other. Parents need to make sure that at least one of them

Above: Sociable dogs can have a very happy life with owners who have a strong desire to nurture.

has sufficient time for the dog each day, as children may not be able to walk the dog alone when they are young and may move out to somewhere that they can't take the dog when they leave home.

To bring human social contact

Meeting other dog owners brings an extra enjoyable dimension to dog ownership for many. If this is your reason for getting a dog, make sure you choose a dog that also enjoys socializing, with both humans and with other dogs.

Status dogs

Large or bull breeds are often purchased by insecure humans in the hope that the dog will enhance their image or status. Sadly, such dogs are often encouraged to be aggressive, which is dangerous for both owner and dog, and their needs may be neglected by owners that lack the knowledge and resources to care for them properly.

Protection dogs

Owners that live in scary neighbourhoods may buy a dog for protection. This can lead to dangerous situations for passers-by and the owner, particularly if the owner doesn't know how to control the dog. The dog's welfare can also suffer if it doesn't get enough exercise or understanding. Wanting a dog to provide you with protection is not a good reason to get a dog.

Replacing a previous dog

When a dog dies, it usually leaves a big hole in its owner's life and it is tempting to get another straight away. However, if you get a replacement dog too soon, you may find it hard to bond with the new one. Try not to expect the new dog to be just like your previous one, even if it looks the same. Sometimes it is better to go for a completely different sort of dog so you don't have any expectations.

Right: Meeting up with other friends who have dogs is an essential part of dog ownership for some people. They will need a dog that is sociable with both people and other dogs.

Below: Gentle, sociable dogs that are not too boisterous make good pets when there are younger children in the household, especially for families who have not owned a dog before.

THE BENEFITS OF A DOG

- **Companionship** Dogs bring unconditional love into a home. They don't judge and are always there when we need them.

- **Warm greetings** Dogs are always ready to greet us with enthusiasm and a wagging tail, even if we have only been away for a short time.

- **Fun** They can make you laugh and play, even when you are an adult.

- **Exercise** Dogs get us out and about in all weathers, off the sofa and into the park or countryside.

- **Helps you make friends** Many dog owners enjoy meeting other owners when out for walks, at training classes or shows. Some people have even met their life partner while out walking the dog.

- **Doggy interests** Dogs allow us to take part in dog sports and other competitions.

- **Lessons in life skills** Dogs can help parents teach compassion, thoughtfulness, respect and responsibility to their children.

When not to get a dog

There are times in life when the desire to get a dog is strong, yet it is not a good time. It is much better, for both you and the dog, to resist the urge and wait until your circumstances are more favourable. When the time is right, you will be much more likely to build a successful and rewarding partnership with a new dog or puppy.

When expecting a baby

During pregnancy, the need to nurture is strong and families are often drawn to the idea of getting a dog to complete their family. Unfortunately, when the baby arrives, there is often limited time and energy to care for a pet, so unless the dog is already settled in and well behaved, problems can quickly arise.

Getting a puppy during pregnancy is a potential disaster as it needs close care and attention for a full year after purchase if it is to grow up successfully. Even an adult dog takes at least six months to settle in fully, and possibly longer if there are any behaviour issues. It is unwise to try to tackle this as you go through the tiring end stages of pregnancy and caring for a newborn. It is better to wait until the children are at an age when they can enjoy a dog's company too.

When working full time

If you work full time, it is not a good idea to get a dog unless you can make arrangements to have it well looked after during the day, such as employing a dog walker. This is especially true of puppies, who need someone to be there to feed, educate and provide them with company. All dogs prefer to be with someone, and leaving them alone for eight hours or more while you are at work can result in considerable welfare issues for the dog. It is better to wait until someone in the family is home for most of the day, or you find a job where you can work from home or take your dog to work with you.

Below: During pregnancy, a strong need to nurture can increase the desire to take on a pet that there may not be enough time for once the baby arrives.

Left: Dogs left alone all day can be bored and lonely, especially if they are young, active, sociable or prone to being worried when separated from their owners.

When you've just moved in with a partner

Couples that have just got together often consider getting a dog. This can sometimes work out well, but if you have only been together a few months, it may be better to wait until you are sure your new partnership will work out. Otherwise, one of you may end up caring for the dog alone, which may not be easy or possible. Once your relationship is established and you have started going out less and being at home more, a dog will be a welcome pet.

When you are feeling unhappy

Getting a dog to make yourself happier rarely works. Feelings of loneliness, insecurity or anxiety will not be made better by the addition of a dog. People often get dogs when, for example, they have just moved to a new area and are yet to make friends, they are lonely, they feel they are not respected or valued by others, or if they are worried about going out alone.

Dogs need emotionally strong, supportive owners if they are to flourish. Getting a dog when you feel down may result in an unsuccessful relationship with the dog, too, which will cause more upset. Dogs that are not supported by their owners may develop behaviour problems that are difficult to overcome, so it is better to wait until you are feeling emotionally strong and can offer a dog a secure and stable home.

More than one dog?

If you enjoy living with one dog, then having another dog has to be even better, doesn't it? The answer is yes in many cases, but there are exceptions. There can be some unexpected consequences of owning two or more dogs so think carefully before you introduce another into your life. It could be twice as much fun, or twice the trouble.

Life with a pack

Two or more dogs, once they know each other well, will behave as a pack. They will follow each other and learn from each other, and if one dog has any unwanted behaviour issues, these can quickly be transferred to the other dog. Barking and boisterousness can become a big issue when there is more than one dog, especially when visitors come to the door. One dog may stay close to you on a walk, but if there are others to run off with, it may have more confidence to do so. Chasing and predatory behaviours are also more likely to occur if there is more than one dog.

Before taking on two or more dogs at the same time, make sure that they have been introduced to each other and that they get on. You should also make sure they are well behaved, or that you can cope with any problems they may have. If you already own a dog and are thinking of getting another, it is wise to train your existing dog well first so it can set an example to the new one.

Right: Many dogs will tolerate a new puppy, but it is important to make sure the puppy plays more with people so that it prefers to play with humans and doesn't learn to pester the older dog.

Below: Unless prevented from doing so, two puppies raised together will spend a lot of time playing. This can have a detrimental effect on the relationships they build with people.

Two puppies

It is never a good idea to get two very young puppies together. The bond between them will be strong and they may never learn to relate to humans in the way that a puppy on its own will do. Two puppies left to play together will be unresponsive to training and interaction with their owners and often make unsuccessful pets. To raise two puppies successfully, you will need to separate them and give each puppy lots of time on its own with you for training and education, which is not easy unless it is your full-time job.

A puppy to replace an existing dog

Owners often buy a puppy when their dog is getting older. This can be successful if the older dog is happy to have the puppy around. Keeping the puppy mostly separated from the older dog during its first year will help ensure it does not pester the older dog, but also, more importantly, that the puppy will learn to play and relate well to humans.

Can you have too many?

Owning more than two dogs makes it more challenging to take them on outings. Much will depend on how well behaved they are, but it is harder to keep more than one dog quiet and under control. Walks with multiple dogs can also be more of an adventure, and you may find that friends visit less often as you begin to own more dogs.

Generally, dogs of the same breed or those bred to do a similar job will get on with each other better than those from very diverse breeds. This is because they will play in a similar way and have similar ways of behaving. Two dogs of the opposite sex will tend to get on better than two of the same sex, especially if they are young. Be careful to choose dogs that are similar in size, energy and strength of character so that one isn't likely to be damaged by the other during play or in times of excitement.

The cost of ownership

Owning a dog can be expensive and it is best to be prepared, in advance, for all the money you will be expected to pay out once you own one. Use the list below to help you assess how much your chosen dog will cost you per week and check that you have enough spare money to cover all eventualities.

Below: Insurance costs vary and may be higher for breeds that are known to have a lot of inherited diseases and conditions.

Expenses	Notes	Cost per week
Food	Investigate the different types of dog food available and decide what you would feed your dog. Find out how much a dog of the size you intend to buy will eat each week.	
Routine vet treatment	Ask your local veterinary surgery about routine veterinary treatments (for parasites such as fleas, ticks and worms, nail clipping and routine vaccinations), how often you need to give them and their cost.	
Pet insurance	You will need veterinary insurance in case of accident or disease. Check out the various policies available, their cost, the excess and how much they will cover you for. Which policy is best for the type of dog you have chosen?	
Third party insurance	Most pet insurance covers third party liability, which you will need if your dog causes an accident or damage, or injures someone. Some house insurance will also cover this. If not, you will need a separate insurance.	
Equipment	You will need to purchase a good-quality dog bed, lead and collar or harness, an ID tag, a crate and/or seat belt, bowls and toys when you first get a dog. An old or thin-skinned dog may need a coat. All of these will need replacing from time to time if worn or chewed.	
Chews and treats	Chews are needed to keep your dog's teeth in good condition, and to save household items from being chewed if your dog is less than a year old. Treats are needed to allow you to train and entertain your dog. How much will sufficient chews and treats cost?	
Dog walker	If you work all day or are likely to be away from home for long periods, you will need the services of a dog walker to give your dog exercise, a chance to toilet and a break from the monotony. How much will it cost to hire a dog walker per week?	
Kennels or dog sitter	Unless you take your dog away with you, you will need to find a good kennels or dog sitter when you are on holiday. How much will this cost, spread out into weekly payments?	
Total cost:		

Whose dog is it?

Dogs, just like children, are totally dependent on others so it is important that they have at least one person who can take responsibility for them and make sure they have all they need throughout the day, every day. Every member of your household should know, and respect, who that person is to make sure the dog's needs are never overlooked.

Daily needs

To make sure a dog is content, it needs to have all its needs met daily. A dog's daily needs include:

- Food
- Water
- Exercise
- Toilet breaks
- Play
- Companionship
- Training
- Grooming
- Veterinary treatment if unwell

Routine care

When you take on a new dog or puppy, you need to get used to actively thinking about your dog many times a day and deciding what it may need at that moment in time. Providing for your dog's needs before it has to remind you, or even begin to misbehave because it needs something it is not getting, will lead to a much calmer life for you both. Getting into a routine of care will help you remember, as you will get used to providing certain things for your dog at set points throughout the day. Gradually, as you get to know your dog, you can provide appropriate care without thinking too hard about what you need to do, but, initially at least, you will need to remember to think of your dog at intervals throughout the day and decide if it has all it needs.

Below: Busy families need to decide who is going to meet each of the dog's needs each day, and it is best if one person checks that everything has been done.

Partnerships

It is usually easy for partners who are living together to decide who should be allocated which part of their dog's daily care. Try to discuss who will do what task before you get a dog to iron out situations where there may be difficulties in providing adequate care or where both partners may want to do it.

Families with children

Parents with children may be very busy and it is easy to forget or not have time for all aspects of the dog's daily care. For this reason, it is important for one person to take full responsibility for making sure the dog has all it needs each day, even if he or she asks someone else to do it.

Older children in a household may want to, or be asked to, take over the dog's care and this is a good way to teach responsibility. However, it is really important that this is supervised on a daily basis by an adult who can remind the child of anything left undone, especially if the care is split between more than one child.

Extended family and friends

In addition to those who look after the dog on a daily basis, it is good to have a larger network of people, consisting of family and friends, who know the dog well and can look after it from time to time. This gives a good fallback position should there be a reason why the owners cannot care for it at any time, especially important if the owner lives alone or is elderly.

House-share dogs

If a dog is to live in a house with multiple occupants, the dog's owner needs to be fully responsible for the dog's daily needs and able to provide for those needs, rather than being reliant on other members of the house to play a role. This ensures that the dog is fully cared for at all times.

Above: Walking the dog can be a delight or a chore, depending on the weather, but someone needs to make the effort to do it every day.

Checklist for ownership

This section of the book will have given you a lot of things to consider before you decide whether to get a dog. To make sure the dog is able to stay with you for the rest of its life as a much loved and cherished pet, ask yourself the following questions and consider the answers carefully. Try not to let the emotional desire to get a dog blind you to the possibility that this may not be the right time. If you do decide to go ahead, the rest of the book will help you choose the perfect dog for your lifestyle and family.

Right: Make sure that you factor in all the costs of dog ownership, from pet insurance and veterinary bills to equipment, food and treats.

Are you ready for a dog?

☐ Do I have insurance or enough savings to pay for unforeseen expenses, such as veterinary fees after an accident, cleaning bills if my dog jumps up on someone with muddy feet or boarding kennel fees if I have to go away unexpectedly?

☐ Do I have sufficient time every day to provide for all my dog's needs?

☐ Will I have enough mental and physical energy to make sure my dog is adequately cared for every day?

☐ Does anyone in the household suffer from allergies to dogs?

☐ Will my state of health allow me to care adequately for a dog?

☐ Does my accommodation make it easy for me to own a dog?

☐ Do I have sufficient knowledge about the type of dog I want to own?

☐ Having considered all my plans, will a dog fit into my future lifestyle?

Reasons for owning a dog

☐ Do I want to own a dog for the right reasons, such as companionship, exercise and fun?

☐ Do I have other reasons for owning a dog and expectations that dog ownership will not fulfil?

- If you are pregnant.

- If you work full time.

- If you are in a new relationship.

- If you think you are in need of a dog because you feel unhappy.

- If you want a dog for protection or to enhance your status.

- If you are planning to move house or go on a trip in the near future.

More than one dog?

Is it a good idea to get more than one dog?

Cost of ownership

Can I afford everything my dog will need?

Whose dog is it?

Who will provide for all the dog's needs each day?

....

....

....

What will happen to my dog if I cannot care for it for a while?

....

....

....

All dogs are different

Dogs are one of the only species to come in such a vast range of sizes, shapes, coat types and colours. Different breeds have been created with different characters and personalities to fulfil a wide range of different roles, such as guarding, tracking or herding. Individuals within these breeds are fairly consistent in appearance but it isn't enough to like the look of a dog. It is vital to find out about the job for which the breed was created, and learn all about its traits, before deciding whether it suits you and your family.

Wild ancestry

Wolves are the most likely ancestors of our pet dogs. Although wolves are very different from domesticated dogs, they provide a blueprint for our pets. Since our dogs show similar behaviour patterns, it is useful to look to wolves to give us an idea of why dogs are like they are.

Wolves evolved to track, chase and bring down large deer-sized animals. To do this, they have to hunt as a pack and live in family groups with strong social bonds. These bonds are strengthened by their ability to display and understand an intricate system of body language signals. Consequently, dogs are intensely social, something they inherited from their ancestors, and which man later accentuated through breeding.

Left: Generations of breeding give Collie puppies the propensity to herd and chase, which will need to be channelled into toy play to prevent unacceptable chasing as they mature.

Wolves are perfectly suited to their environment and many of their behaviours, such as turning round and round to make bedding comfortable before lying down, burying excess food, rolling in smelly substances and chasing have been handed down to our pet dogs.

When early humans began to settle in villages, waste dumps provided a new food supply for wolves. It is thought that the more confident wolves would have risked encounters with humans to feed from these dumps. These wolves, with less reactive and more 'friendly' genes, would have thrived and passed their genes on to future generations. These animals gradually evolved into 'village dogs' with weaker jaws, reduced reactivity, reduced predatory desire and probably less intelligence. Our modern dogs were created from these 'village dogs', resulting in the wide array of breeds we see today.

Dogs with jobs

People soon realized that they could affect the body shape and characteristics of dogs by selecting which individuals to breed with each other. Since there were a variety of jobs that dogs could do to help people survive and prosper, dogs of different shapes and sizes were bred for different useful activities. For example, dogs that would pick things up in their mouths were bred to help with hunting; large dogs with thick coats were bred to help fishermen in Newfoundland haul in nets and retrieve fish; elegant dogs with spotty coats were bred to run alongside the carriages of the rich, and small active dogs were bred to catch and kill vermin. Since many dogs were bred for similar functions in different parts of the world, we have ended up with many different breeds, some of which were bred to do similar jobs.

As well as physical characteristics, personality traits can also be chosen by selective breeding. Consequently, dogs bred to herd not only are physically adapted for chasing, but they also have an intense reactivity and a strong inherited desire to chase, which can then be honed to perfection by the trainer. Similarly, dogs bred to guard not only are large and powerful, but also have strong characters and the confidence necessary to see off a threat. Dogs bred to be companions, on the other hand, are generally sweet-natured and enjoy the company of people.

Above: High-energy dogs that are not given a job to do tend to invent their own, investing their energy in behaviours that are often less than acceptable to owners.

Breed groups

For simplicity, purebred dog breeds are categorized into seven different groups, according to what they were bred to do. These groups are terriers, gundogs, hounds, pastoral, toys, utility dogs and working dogs. Below is a summary of their origins and personality traits. If you are not sure which specific breed to choose, begin by choosing a group and then try to narrow it down.

Categorization

The groups used in this book represent the most common categorization around the world. However, different Kennel Clubs categorize dogs in different ways. For instance, the American Kennel Club has a 'Miscellaneous' group containing six breeds which European Kennel Clubs do not have. There are also some differences of opinion as to which dogs are in which group – in the United States, for example, a Bichon Frisé is classed as a 'Non-sporting' dog, but in the United Kingdom it is in the 'toy' group.

Terriers

Terriers are dogs that were originally bred to catch and kill animals considered to be vermin, or for sport. Most were bred to 'go to ground' to dig out animals from their lairs and so are natural diggers. Usually small in height, they tend to have strong predatory instincts and may pose a danger to small pets unless they have grown up with them and view them as a member of their family. Most will chase and may possibly injure cats unless they have been raised with them.

Terriers are usually tenacious, rough players with a hard bite, but many do have small mouths. They often have strong characters and a busy, excitable nature, which can be very charismatic. They are easily alerted and can make good watchdogs, although for some owners, their inclination to bark can be annoying. Terriers are feisty and quick-tempered and tend to react first and think later if something upsets them.

Below: Gundogs, such as Pointers, are energetic, busy and playful. They are usually easy to train and willing to please, making them good family dogs for active families.

Opposite: Terriers tend to be small and full of character. Their ancestors have passed down genes that give them the propensity to be feisty and quick to react.

Terriers tend to be quick to react if something upsets them and are not always willing to do what you want them to do, but they are usually affectionate and outgoing and many owners enjoy their extrovert, independent nature.

Gundogs

Also known as 'Sporting dogs', gundogs have been bred to help people hunt by flushing game, pointing to game and retrieving the animals that are shot. They need to work closely with people and so they are usually sociable, willing to please and easy to train. They often have a soft bite so they do not damage the game they retrieve, but their desire to use their mouths can make them great chewers when growing up.

The upside is that they also play enthusiastically with toys. This makes them fun to be with, especially for children, and makes training easier as it gives you something other than food to reward them with. They usually enjoy close contact with their owners, but can be boisterous if they do not get enough exercise. Most gundogs have the energy and stamina to be on the move all day, so plenty of exercise is essential. They usually make very good dogs for an active family, as they tend to be tolerant and playful with children if raised with them and children are sensible.

Hounds

Hounds were bred to track and hunt prey with humans on foot or on horseback. Some were bred to bring down prey and many are not good with small pets unless they have grown up with them. Hounds often have deep, resounding voices to let the hunter know where they are, but they do not usually bark unnecessarily. Hounds are mostly very amiable and relaxed. They were not bred to work closely with humans so can be independent and uncooperative. They are not really interested in toys and can be difficult to train, tending to run off when they see something to chase.

Most hounds were bred to live in packs and, as a result, are usually sociable and friendly to humans and other dogs. They do not mind close physical contact but they are also happy with people who prefer to be less tactile. They are usually content to relax at home, appearing lazy when there is nothing to do, but need long, energetic walks to use up their tremendous energy and desire to run.

Pastoral

The American Kennel Club calls this group 'Herding'. The group can be roughly divided into two categories – dogs that were bred to round up flocks of sheep or herds of cattle, and dogs that were bred to live with and protect flocks of sheep from predators.

Herding breeds were bred to herd domesticated animals. They are hard-working and need plenty of exercise for their minds and bodies. Herding breeds usually love playing with toys. Their excellent hearing makes them alert, active watchdogs, but it can also result in noise phobias if they are not accustomed to loud noises early in life.

Herding breeds are usually sensitive and quick to react, and can be nervous if not socialized or used to dealing with different experiences as puppies. They are usually very responsive to commands once they have learned them and are easily trained. They were bred to work closely with humans and prefer to have a close, strong bond with their owner, often enjoying close physical contact with plenty of stroking and fuss. A few breeds prefer a strong bond with one person, sometimes at the expense of other people in the house.

Above: Hounds, like the Whippet, are sociable and tolerant, and like to run and sniff when outside, sometimes becoming so engrossed that they ignore their owners.

Below: Herding dogs are reactive and sensitive with a tendency to chase. They need gentle families and lots of socialization when young.

Some of the larger, more powerful breeds in the pastoral group were bred to live with flocks to protect them from wolves and other predators. They can have strong guarding instincts and need adequate socialization in order to prevent aggression. They tend to be large animals with heavy coats and are less energetic and reactive than the herding dogs.

Toys

Toy dogs were bred to be companions. Usually small in height, most make excellent pets as the working traits have mostly been bred out of them. If treated properly, like dogs rather than babies, they are usually very agreeable, mild-mannered and enjoy companionship. They are willing to please but may not be as quick to learn or responsive as the working dogs.

They are usually very keen on close contact with their owners and enjoy plenty of fuss and attention. This makes them a good choice for novice owners. Their small height makes them ideal for people without much space, but renders them prone to health problems so check puppies and adult dogs very carefully before buying to reduce the risk of inherited diseases.

Utility dogs

This group is a mixture of breeds that are not traditionally placed in other groups. Also known as 'Non-sporting dogs', they were bred to do a variety of different jobs from herding to guarding, and it is necessary to look at each breed individually to find out what traits they have, so you can decide if they fit the requirements for your lifestyle.

Below: Ancestors of the utility group did jobs that do not fit easily into the other groups. To find out the character traits of each breed, it is necessary to find out what they were bred to do.

Below Left: Dogs in the toy group have been bred to be companions over many generations. They are sociable and enjoy a close relationship with their owners.

Inherited traits

When choosing a dog, it is important to know and understand the different behavioural characteristics of different breeds. You will then be able to make an informed assessment of whether those traits will suit your home and lifestyle. Being prepared for strong genetic predispositions will allow you to recognize these traits and to train and educate your dog accordingly.

Ancestors' characteristics

Many of today's pet dogs come from parents who were bred to do a job, and consequently they carry genes for character and temperament that would have made them a good worker. Behaviour traits that make dogs good workers do not always make them good pets. Since pedigree dogs breed true to type, it is possible to find out about these traits in advance and either avoid them or learn how to deal with them so they are less likely to become an issue.

Below: Many terriers enjoy digging. Does this fit with your lifestyle, and will you be upset if they uproot precious plants in the garden or dig holes in the lawn?

Behaviour	Breed	Things to consider
Barking	All dogs, especially terriers and those bred as watchdogs	A barking dog can be useful if you need to know about intruders, but can quickly become a nuisance to you and your neighbours if barking is excessive.
Chasing and hunting	All dogs, but particularly hounds and herding dogs	Hunting and chasing can lead to control problems on walks. It needs to be channelled early on into games with toys instead.
Catching and harming small animals	All dogs, but especially terriers and Husky/Akita types	This can be a problem if you or your neighbours keep small pets. Some terriers have an innate desire to be predatory with small animals unless they have been carefully socialized with them and know them well.
Digging	Any dog, but particularly terriers	This may not be a problem unless you enjoy gardening or they tunnel under fences. It is easy to teach them to dig in one area of the garden only.
High energy levels and exuberance	Large dogs, especially gundogs or sporting breeds, and dogs like Boxers	Matching your dog's energy levels to yours is important. Care needs to be taken with large exuberant dogs if you have young children or elderly or infirm family members.
Possessiveness	All strong-willed dogs, but especially some gundogs	A strong desire to possess can make a useful retriever, but it can also lead to problems unless the dog is taught to enjoy giving objects back to people.
Chewing	Most young dogs, but especially gundogs	Dogs bred to use their mouths tend to chew a lot when young. Offer plenty of chews and toys to save household possessions.
Swimming	Dogs bred to help fishermen or hunters, particularly Newfoundlands and Labradors	Usually not a problem unless they plunge into lakes and ponds, or sometimes a water dish on a hot day.
Tenacious and hold on when biting	Dogs originally bred for fighting or baiting	Bull breeds have a tendency to hold on when biting if they are in an aroused and excited state. With their strong jaws, this can be a big problem if they get into fights or are aggressive.
Reactive to situations	Herding dogs and terriers	Reactive dogs make great workers, but they can also be fearful and have a low threshold for aggression. They need careful socialization when young as they can be trained to be responsive to cues.
Guarding and territorial behaviour	Dogs bred to guard	Guarding and territorial traits are useful if you live in an isolated property but can become an issue in built-up areas. These dogs need careful socialization when young.

Individual personalities

Although we can get a broad idea of a dog's behaviour traits from knowing about its breed, all dogs are different and even dogs from the same litter will exhibit differences in character and temperament, just as they may exhibit slight physical differences. Added to this, the personalities of adult dogs will also have been shaped by their upbringing and experiences.

Variation within a breed

Although you can be reasonably sure that you will get a dog that looks and acts like the breed you have chosen, you need to be aware that there will be variations between dogs of different lines within the breed. If you look at the pedigrees of different dogs from a particular breed, you will find that breeders often select certain types they like, repeatedly breeding from dogs within a small, related group. Their puppies may, therefore, be slightly different to puppies from a breeder that selects from different stock. Some breeders will also occasionally import 'new blood' from overseas and this can bring in variations in temperament as well as slight physical differences.

In addition to variations due to line breeding, all dogs will vary because their particular set of genes will be different to those of all other dogs. This will produce differences in character and temperament as well as in the strength of behaviour traits. Some will have stronger traits than others and, in a home environment, this will require extra work and training to ensure their behaviour stays within acceptable boundaries. Others may have less pronounced behaviour traits and so be easier to raise and manage.

Upbringing

All dogs are a product of the interaction between their genetic make-up and the experiences and situations that they find themselves in while growing up. They will be a mixture of the effects of nature and nurture, both of which have an influence on the character of the dog.

If you are acquiring an adult dog, take time to get to know that particular dog to find out if it is right for you. It may be a perfect example of its breed, but early experiences will have acted on its inherited personality traits to make it the dog it is now.

Above: No two puppies will be the same, even those from the same litter, as each will have a slightly different genetic make-up and different experiences that will shape its character as it grows.

If you are getting a puppy, remember that no matter how carefully you have selected the parents, its character will be heavily influenced by the people who raise it and the environment in which it is brought up. Make sure you know how to raise a puppy well so that you can give it the best start in life.

Above: The parents of the puppies, as well as their grandparents and great-grandparents, will contribute genes that will affect the puppies development and characters.

Choosing a puppy from a litter

No two puppies in a litter are the same. Some may be confident and bold, others shy and retiring. Since they are all slightly different and it is difficult to get to know each of them in the short time you spend with them to make your choice, it makes sense to ask the breeder's advice on which one is best suited to you and your family. If you are in doubt about the breeder's knowledge of the puppies, take along an experienced friend to help you, or go elsewhere. If your chosen breed is rare, you may have to join a waiting list and have less choice about the puppy you get, in which case you may have to trust the breeder to get it right for you.

Mongrel, crossbreed or purebred?

There are many different types of purebred dog, which have been bred by man to conform to certain standards. Some dogs, however, escape man's management and breed by themselves to produce mongrels. In addition, there are crossbred dogs, the result of a mating between two purebred parents of different breeds. All three have their advantages and disadvantages.

Mongrels

While man has been busy deciding which dog to breed with which, other dogs have been choosing for themselves for centuries. As the human population increases and there is less freedom and space for dogs to run loose, fewer dogs are allowed to wander. Consequently, it is getting harder to find a true mongrel, a mixture of all breeds. Although it is hard to predict how a mongrel puppy will turn out, there are many health advantages due to the wide gene pool from which these dogs originate.

Crossbred dogs

Crossbred dogs are the result of a mating between two purebred dogs of different breeds. If the dog is an adult when you acquire it, you can see what you are getting. However, it is a little more difficult to predict the size, shape and nature of crossbred puppies and you often have to

Left: Purebred dogs will develop in a predictable way but may have inherited conditions due to the interbreeding that is necessary to keep lines pure.

take a chance on what they will be like once they grow up. Crossbred dogs usually have fewer health problems than purebred dogs as the genes that cause problems are diluted by a bigger gene pool.

Below: Crossbreeds and mongrels are less predictable in the way they will grow and develop but are likely to have fewer inherited conditions.

Purebred dogs

Purebred dogs are produced by breeding dogs of a similar type, size and character. Once there are enough dogs of a certain type, the gene pool is closed and dogs cannot be out-crossed with other dogs. This allows for a breed to be created where all dogs are closely related and breed true to type.

The advantage of a purebred dog is that you know what to expect. All adults of the breed are likely to have a similar look and character. Therefore, you can choose one to suit your family and it is likely that the dog you choose will live up to your expectations.

The big disadvantage is that inherited defects and diseases abound in purebred dogs (see page 62). This is due to inbreeding within a relatively small group of dogs which concentrates faults in the genes and causes abnormalities or leaves a dog vulnerable to disease.

Line breeding (see page 34) can make this problem even worse as breeders frequently breed from even smaller groups of individuals in an attempt to breed a dog that conforms exactly to a list of physical standards set by the Kennel Clubs.

Because inherited conditions and diseases are common in purebreds, it is vital to know about the inherited problems associated with your breed and to make sure you find a healthy dog. If you are buying a puppy, this can mean a lot of work and perseverance. It is possible to test for some of the more common inherited conditions, so it is essential to know which conditions are problematic, how they are tested and what a good test certificate looks like.

Choices of age and gender

It is possible to acquire puppies, adolescent dogs, adults and elderly dogs. There are advantages and disadvantages with every age group, so it is important to consider each carefully and decide which will fit best into your home and family life. You also need to decide whether a male or female dog would be best for you.

Below: Puppies are easy to train and mould to your way of life, especially if you start with positive training at an early age.

Puppies

Puppies are impressionable and you can mould them to suit your family's character and lifestyle. Bringing up a puppy is also a lot of fun and watching it as it grows, learns, plays and develops will be enjoyable for all the family.

Raising a puppy is a job for someone with lots of time on their hands as it is important to be with the puppy for most of its first year so that you can educate it properly. If you have not got the time or you go out to work, consider getting an older dog instead. Chewing and housetraining can take their toll on the furnishings and someone needs to be there most of the time to teach a puppy right from wrong and to take it out to get used to the world.

If you had an old dog that has now passed on and you are thinking of getting a puppy, try hard to remember how much hard work they are. You may be 15 years older than you were when your last dog was a puppy and may not appreciate how much extra work is required to raise one.

Adolescent dogs

Adolescents and young adult dogs abound at rescue centres. Owners often give them up at this time, once the cute puppy stage is over, but training requirements are still high. Adolescents still have their youthful exuberance, and often make lovely pets if you have time to train and educate them as they often come from people who haven't done this. Adolescents will need love and patience to help them learn good manners.

Adult dogs

An adult's character will already be formed so it is important to choose wisely. They are usually past the housetraining and chewing phases, but expect them to take some time to settle into your home and routine. Adults often come ready trained and you have the satisfaction of knowing that you have rescued a dog with an uncertain future and given it a loving home.

Elderly dogs

Older or elderly dogs are often well behaved and may have been given up reluctantly by an owner in reduced circumstances. They usually make lovely pets, past all the difficult stages and content to rest and be peaceful for most of the time. They can make good companions for busy owners who have a lot of love to spare, but will often need nursing through the illnesses and conditions that can occur at the end of life.

Male or female?

Although individual dogs vary considerably, some broad generalizations can be made about the different sexes. Generally, females are more placid, less competitive and can be more timid than males. Males are usually more boisterous, more confident and are slightly more likely to have behaviour problems in later life, although neutering does have some effect on this.

Male dogs cock their legs and females squat (important for keen gardeners – male dogs can cause burns on the leaves of plants or trees they urinate on, whereas females tend to leave circular yellow patches on the lawn where their urine burns the grass). Both males and females make good pets, and it is really just a matter of choosing the type of personality you prefer. If you already have a dog, it is best to chose one of the opposite sex since a male and female are more likely to get on well together than two of the same sex.

Above: Adult dogs are good at adjusting their behaviour to fit their new lifestyle, although they will need help to learn the new house rules.

Choosing physical characteristics

The physical characteristics, such as the overall size, stamina, face shape and coat type of your dog can have a big impact on many aspects of your life together. Different breeds of dog have different attributes, so it is wise to carefully consider their effects and which are best suited to you and your circumstances before you choose a breed.

Energy levels and exercise requirements

Some dogs have the energy and stamina to be active all day, whereas others are more lazy. Choosing a dog to match your activity levels is essential or you could find yourself living with an overactive, discontented exercise junkie, or have to coax a reluctant layabout to go for long walks. Consider where you live and how easy it is to get to a suitable place for off-lead running of the type that your dog needs.

Busy, boisterous or lazy in the house

Dogs that are energetic out on a walk are not always busy or active in the house. Generally, smaller dogs are livelier indoors while larger dogs are content to lie around until there is something interesting to get up for.

Size and strength

Choosing the right size of dog is essential. Take into account the size of your house, car and garden, as well as the people that it will be in contact with on a regular basis. Getting the right size of dog is particularly important if you have to consider small children or elderly or infirm relatives. Consider how strong the dog will be in comparison with the person walking and controlling it. When getting a second dog, consider the consequences when playing or fighting if there is a large difference in their sizes. Also consider how you will control two dogs of that size on a walk. Think about the effect of the size of the dog you choose on friends and family that may visit, as well as on neighbours and people you meet.

Below: Your dog's coat type will affect how much time and energy you spend grooming and bathing it. Find a coat type to suit the time you have available.

Coat type

A thick, profuse coat means that a dog is likely to shed continuously in a centrally heated house and may be uncomfortably hot in summer, leading to constant panting and bad temper. Daily brushing will be needed to remove loose hair, which will otherwise collect in drifts around the house.

Fine, long coats will need careful daily brushing to prevent mats from forming. Long-coated breeds often have a covering of hair over their eyes, which may cause them to be more jumpy and nervous unless it is tied back or cut off. Feathers (strands of hanging fur) on the legs and tail can bring in mud and dirt from outside. Dogs with long hair on the face can get smelly through food and dribble and will need regular washing to keep clean.

If you have allergies, a dog with hair that grows continually and does not shed may help, but some people are allergic to the skin dander rather than the hair. Dogs that do not shed will need regular clipping and visits to the groomers.

Snoring and dribbling

Dogs with very short noses and squashed faces can be permanently short of oxygen and cannot exercise adequately, and they can also be prone to snoring. Dogs with loose skin around the face and mouth may dribble excessively and mopping up may be needed.

Long tail, short tail

Some breeds are 'traditionally docked', which means that part of the puppy's tail is cut off during the first few days of its life. Whole tails are preferable as they enable the dog to signal its intentions and mood more easily. If you want a puppy from a docked breed with an intact tail, ask your breeder to reserve one for you and look elsewhere if he or she refuses. In some countries, such as the UK, tail docking is illegal.

Above: Plenty of exercise and mental stimulation is important for young and active dogs, and will result in a calm and contented dog when it is at home.

Choosing a suitable character

As well as taking the time to choose a dog's physical attributes, it is very important to think about what kind of personality and character would suit you and your family best. Do you want a friendly dog, an independent dog, one who enjoys meeting people or one who is good with children? Get to know the 'personality' of your chosen dog and ask yourself if you would really enjoy living with such a dog.

Strength of character

If you have a gentle nature, choose a dog that is relaxed and happy to fall in with your plans. Dogs with strong characters can be pushy about trying to get their own way and will need someone with a strong character and plenty of rewards to persuade them to follow an alternative path.

Extrovert or introvert

Finding a dog to match the character of those in the household is important. Sensitive, gentle people may prefer a shy, retiring dog, whereas a lively, enthusiastic dog may be a better choice for a more extrovert family.

Think about whether you want your dog to be calm and relaxed, or if you would prefer one that is excitable and exuberant.

Left: Choosing a dog to suit your character and that of your family will result in a compatibility that will make everyone, including your dog, happy.

Loner or socialite

Some owners prefer a dog to bond closely with them and to largely ignore other people. If you enjoy close bonds, chose a dog that likes to connect rather than one that is aloof or independent, but be prepared to always be there for your dog as it will need you. Other owners prefer their dog to be friendly to all, especially if they have a family or many friends, so choosing an affectionate, outgoing dog will be essential.

Body contact

Some dogs like to be touched, stroked and cuddled, while others are not so keen. Finding a dog to match your desire for contact is important.

Lonely or able to cope alone

All dogs need to get used to being left alone from time to time during puppyhood, as those who have not been trained to tolerate isolation may become destructive, noisy or lose toilet control when left. This problem can be solved but it will take commitment to teach them to feel secure when alone. Finding a dog to suit your patterns of absence is important. If you are taking on a puppy, someone will need to be present all the time at first so that you can teach it to tolerate isolation in a slow, controlled way.

Possessive or happy to share

If you have children, you will need a dog that is relaxed around food and possessions, such as toys and chews. Owning a dog that hoards or protects food and possessions may not matter to you, although you will need to be careful when you have visitors or when your dog goes into kennels.

Willing to please or independent

If you like a dog to enjoy doing as you ask, choose one that is biddable by nature. Such dogs are usually easy to train and responsive. Some people prefer an independent dog who wants to please itself and is full

Below: If you want your dog to be well trained, choose one that is willing to please and playful so that training is easy and successful.

of character. These dogs prefer to do what they want and need plenty of incentives if they are to be happy doing things for you.

Above: Playful dogs are fun for active families and games with toys can be used as rewards for training exercises and good behaviour.

Fully trained or a work in progress

Some dogs will have had lots of training to respond to commands, such as 'sit', 'wait' and 'come here', while others have had hardly any at all. Puppies will need a lot of time and effort to train them fully. Even if a dog is trained to respond to commands, it will still need to learn your house rules, which may be different to those in a previous house. Puppies will need a lot of time to educate them to behave well. Some dogs will be fully housetrained, others will need help to learn.

Playful or not

Some dogs, particularly hound types, are less interested in playing with toys and rarely pick up anything in their mouths. This can be disappointing for some owners, and they would be better with a dog that enjoys playing. Other owners, who are not interested in playing, prefer a dog that is not constantly bringing toys or asking to play.

Good with children

Some dogs tolerate children in the family but are not keen on visiting children, some get overwhelmed by too much noise and activity, some are so small they get injured easily by young children and some are just right. Choose a dog that is good with children if you already have children, are planning a family or if children visit on a regular basis.

As well as a genetic propensity for tolerating and enjoying the company of children, a dog will also need to have plenty of happy social contact with them as it grows and matures. Making the time to go out to places where the puppy can have positive experiences with a whole range of different children will make all the difference to its future attitude towards them. If taking on a puppy, socialization with children of all ages is important.

Assessing whether an adult dog will be good with your children requires professional help so be prepared to ask experienced staff at the rescue home and listen carefully to what they say. You will need a dog that is sociable, unafraid, relaxed, friendly and calm. It is also best to find a dog whose response to sudden fright or unexpected noise is to move away and calmly assess the situation, rather than to respond with crazy excitement or aggression. Check out responses to toy play. Look for a dog that can play in a relaxed, enthusiastic way with plenty of self-control.

Good with other dogs

Dogs need to be socialized with others early in life if they are to get on well with them. Some breeds are less social with other dogs, particularly some of the terriers and those originally bred for fighting. If you have a lot of contact with other dogs, if you have another dog in the family or if you want to be able to take your dog for walks where other dogs go, choosing a sociable dog is highly recommended.

If you have a dog in the family already, make sure the dog you are taking on is compatible with this dog. Both dogs will need to enjoy each other's company so arrange more than one meeting before rehoming.

Below: There are many factors to be considered when bringing a new dog into a family with children. A tolerant and sociable dog will usually fit in well.

Left: Dogs that have grown up with a cat in the household are usually easier to introduce to a household with older cats later in life.

If you are taking on a puppy, make sure it is well socialized with lots of other friendly dogs and puppies when very young as this will help to make it tolerant and easy-going with other dogs in later life.

Good with other pets

Predatory behaviour is common in certain breeds. Although dogs can be good under supervision with small pets they were raised with, it may be easier to get a dog with weaker instincts if you have small pets too. Cats and dogs can live well together once the dog has accepted the cat as part of its family, but, again, it may be better to avoid terriers and dogs bred to chase and hunt, especially if you have a timid cat.

Good with strangers

Dogs need to be socialized well with lots of different people in early life if they are to get on well with strangers. Some dogs are more reactive and can be more aggressive as a result.

Protective dogs

Confident dogs with strong characters are better at being protective in an adverse situation and less likely to back down. However, the downside is that they are more likely to be aggressive if they need to make a point in other situations too. These dogs need very careful control and socialization.

Good watchdogs

Some breeds are more reactive and alert than others and are easily encouraged to bark at the slightest disturbance. This can be useful or can be a nuisance, depending on your circumstances. Most dogs bark but it is easier to discourage a dog that was bred to be more relaxed.

What do you want?

Consider all the above characteristics carefully, then, with the help of your family and anyone who will be involved with your dog, sit down and make a list of your 'ideal' dog. List any physical characteristics that are important to you as well, and include preferences on age and gender. Go down the list and mark which characteristics are essential and which are merely preferred. Armed with your list of requirements, you are in the perfect position to find the right dog for you.

LEGISLATION ISSUES

Some breeds of dog, usually those bred for fighting, are banned in some countries or regions. Others need to be on a public register, neutered and muzzled in public. Make sure you know the law and what the banned breeds look like, so you don't end up with one inadvertently.

Some countries require you to have a dog licence for your dog, or for your dog to wear a collar and tag, or to be microchipped and registered, so check government websites for this information. Most authorities require your dog to be on a lead near roads and under control around livestock. Some districts have lead laws in parks, so check with local councils or information signs in parks before letting your dog run free.

Almost all areas have laws requiring you to pick up after your dog has toileted so make sure you take bags out with you on walks.

Finding a dog

There are a number of places you can find adult dogs for sale or adoption. It is best to explore all the places that rehome dogs in your area. This is because the quality of the information about the dogs held there, and hence your ability to choose the right dog for you, will depend on the people responsible for looking after that dog. As with breeders, there are good and bad and it is best to look around.

Dos and don'ts

Be prepared to take your time looking for the right dog and to visit several places several times. If you have a young family, don't take the children on initial visits so you are not pressurized into taking the dog with the cutest face. If there is nothing suitable, look elsewhere. Do not feel that you have to take a particular dog because you feel sorry for it. There are thousands of dogs out there looking for homes and it is better that you find just the right dog than take one that will make both of you unhappy.

Rescue centres

With so many unwanted and abandoned dogs needing good homes, a rescue centre is an excellent place to start looking for a dog. It will often have a wide variety of dogs to choose from and give you the opportunity to provide a dog in need with a second chance in life. Rescue centres range from national networks of homes run by large charities to small concerns. Their quality and professionalism depend on their staff and it is best to ask friends and other animal professionals to recommend the best in your area. Rescue centres are expensive to run and if the dogs are well cared for, they will be vaccinated, health checked, properly fed and neutered. All this costs money, so expect to pay a reasonable donation to the centre.

Modern rescue centres should be light, airy places where dogs are well cared for and happy. However, some are not and you may be upset at the conditions the dogs live in, even if the rescue centre is doing its best. Be prepared to harden your heart and go armed with your list of essential and preferred characteristics. Try hard not to fall in love before you have made a sensible decision about whether or not that dog would suit your family.

Right: Dogs often behave differently in kennels compared to when they are at home so you may need the help of well-trained staff to help you choose a dog that is right for you.

Due to the pressures of life in kennels, a dog will not behave in the same way as it would at home. You will see a slightly distorted view of its behaviour and it is important to ask the staff that look after it what it is really like. Try to get opinions from several different staff and take the dog out to a quiet place to get to know it. If you can, play with it, stroke it, groom it and ask what it is like with other dogs, strangers and children. It is not easy to decide on a new dog in just one or two meetings, and if you are new to dog ownership, take a friend who has more experience with you to help. If the rescue centre will let you reserve your chosen dog, try to go back every day for a few days to visit it and get to know it better so that you are sure before you make the final decision.

Good practice

A good rescue centre will have a number of different ways to find out about the dogs in its care and will use this information to help new owners choose the right dog. It will also aim to reduce the dogs' stress and keep them social with both humans and other dogs to help them fit into new homes more easily.

A good centre will take care to ask lots of questions of those owners who are surrendering their dog. A lengthy interview helps reveal the true reasons behind surrender as well as gaining a good understanding of the dog's character and personality. For those dogs that come in as strays or are brought in by people that don't know them, the most experienced staff will assess them after a short settling-in period and continue to monitor them throughout their stay.

In a good rescue centre, experienced staff who know the dogs well will be on hand to help you get it right. This will involve lots of discussion about your requirements, and the needs of any dog you may be interested in. There should be a quiet area available where you and your family can get to know your new dog, as well as outside areas where your existing dog can get to meet any new dog you are considering. The rescue centre may make a visit to your home to check the dog will be happy there and to spot any potential problems in advance, or may check up on the dog later once it has had time to settle in. The centre may also provide behaviour advice should you have problems during the settling-in period.

Breed rescues

Breed rescues are organizations that rehome dogs of a particular breed. If you are interested in one breed but require an adult rather than a puppy, find out from the Kennel Club about your local breed rescue. Breed rescues rarely have kennels and the dogs are fostered by caring owners of the breed. This gives you a lot of information about that particular dog as the foster carers will know what it is like.

The disadvantage is that you may not have many dogs to chose from so be prepared to wait or travel further afield if they do not have a dog to meet your requirements. You may feel under a lot of pressure to take a dog, so be prepared to resist until you have had time to consider and weigh up all the pros and cons of taking on that particular dog.

Above: If only one or two dogs are available, try not to feel pressured into taking one home, but, instead, make the decision based on whether the dog is right for you.

Breeders

Breeders sometimes keep several puppies into adulthood to see which will be best for showing or working. If these dogs have lived all their life in kennels, they will not make good pets. Similarly, breeders sometimes decide to 'retire' their brood bitches into pet homes. These dogs may not have lived in a house, may not be accustomed to life with people and may not have met many other people or unfamiliar dogs. They make very poor pets and are nervous and difficult to rehabilitate. Be prepared for a long haul if you get such a dog but, if possible, avoid them altogether unless you know the dog was kept as a pet.

Sometimes caring breeders will have taken back a dog they have bred when the owner could no longer keep it. If the dog has been raised well by the previous owner and has a good temperament, it may make a very suitable pet. Visit and take time to get to know the dog, and be prepared to say no if you do not like what you see.

Friends

A good place to get a dog is through a friend who, for a good reason, can no longer keep their dog. If you already know the dog well and like it, there will be no surprises. Do not take on a dog as a favour to your friend. If the dog does not suit you, you may both be unhappy. Someone you know may know of someone who has a dog they want to give up. Again, go and visit but be prepared to say no politely and walk away.

Advertisements and the Internet

This is probably the worst way to find an adult dog. You may be lucky, but you may not. Question the owners at length before you go. If they do not have the answers, they may not be the original owner and it will be very difficult for you to decide just by looking at the dog if it is the right one for you. If they are a bit cagey about the answers, they may not be telling you the truth, so beware. If you have to travel

Below: Taking on a friend's dog can be a good option as long as you are not under pressure to do so and already know and like the dog.

to see the dog, your family will already have expectations and will have given the dog all sorts of fanciful qualities before you even get there. Saying no is difficult, especially if the dog does not have a very good home. If you must do this, spend some time with the dog once you are there so that you get to know it well, and perhaps even ask to take it for a walk. Go with the intention of going back later for a second visit so that you have time to consider, and do not be swayed by the owner saying that there is someone else coming to see the dog later so it may be gone.

KEY POINTS

- Be prepared to visit several places several times to find the right dog.

- Do not take a particular dog because you feel sorry for it.

- Expect to pay a reasonable donation to a rescue centre.

- Go armed with your list of essential and preferred characteristics.

- Take the dog out to a quiet place to get to know it.

- New owners need help to judge which dog is right for them.

- The rescue centre may make a visit to your home.

- Dogs that have lived all their lives in kennels will not make good pet dogs.

- If you already know the dog well and like it, there will be no surprises.

- Finding a dog via an advert is extremely risky.

Choosing a puppy breeder

There are many reasons why a breeder will breed puppies, and their motivation will have some bearing on the type of puppies they produce. Take your time when looking for a breeder to carefully assess their reasons for breeding and the quality of their dogs. You will also need to know how and where the puppies have been raised as their early experiences will shape their personalities in later life and their suitability as pets.

Why are puppies bred?

Most pedigree pet dogs are produced by breeders who want to further their breed and to win in the show ring. They sell excess puppies, keeping the best to show and breed from. Motivations vary, but dog shows reward breeders who can produce a dog that comes closest to the breed standard – a list of characteristics such as the position of the ears, the length of the tail and so on. The dog is judged on and awarded prizes for how it looks rather than how it behaves.

Some dogs are bred to work for their living and any excess puppies are sold as pets. Remember that a dog from working stock will have strong behavioural traits as well as more energy and stamina than most pet owners can cope with. Also, many farm or working gundogs are kept in kennels, and puppies raised outside a home environment will not make easy pets.

Some pet dogs are used for breeding because they have such a nice temperament that the owner wants to keep a puppy. Excess pups are sold and these can make very nice pets, providing all the health checks have been made.

Unscrupulous show breeders

The show system allows unscrupulous breeders to get away with paying no attention to health and temperament as long as they can get their dog to behave while being shown. Many show dogs live their lives in kennels and are handled only by skilled handlers. Consequently, adverse behavioural traits can be masked and unless the breeder takes care to monitor the progress of their progeny, they may not be aware, or care, that they are selling potentially difficult dogs to pet owners.

When seeing a litter of puppies, it is impossible to tell whether they have good natures or not, or potential health defects that will affect them later. Owners are usually much too attached to their dogs by the time their true nature has been revealed to take them back to the breeder.

Above: Motivations for breeding vary but the health and welfare of mother and puppies should always be top priority for any breeder.

Registration

Most pedigree puppies are registered at the Kennel Club and the papers will be given to you when you buy a puppy to show its parentage. Some unscrupulous breeders may try to give you false papers, so it is worth doing some research online to make sure you know what authentic Kennel Club papers look like. It is important to know that Kennel Club registration is not an indication of quality or a seal of approval. Anyone can register their litter with the Kennel Club.

Where to buy a puppy

It is worth taking the time to find a good breeder. Conscientious breeders take care when breeding their dogs and the puppies they produce are likely to be healthy and have good temperaments.

Find out more about individual breeders by looking on the internet, asking people who own and live with their dogs, and by attending dog shows. The big dog shows will be advertised by the Kennel Club, in the dog breed press and on the internet, or ask any large breeder for details. At shows you will be able to meet the breeders, as well as people who show their dog but also keep it as a pet. The more you talk to people, the more you will find out about who is producing puppies within the breed and which lines may be healthy and good-natured. It helps to have two or three breeders to visit so that you can choose the best puppy available and are not committed to a particular litter before you have seen several.

Fortunately, there are many responsible breeders who care very much about the temperament of the dogs they are breeding and what happens to them in future. They breed for temperament as well as physical conformity, taking care to choose good-natured parents. They stay in touch with owners of their puppies and help with problems and rehoming if necessary. Finding a good breeder is not easy but is essential if you want a healthy, well-adjusted dog.

Above: Puppies for sale in a pet shop, or in an outlet offering multiple breeds, are likely to have come from puppy farms and are best avoided.

Right: Dogs bred for show can make good parents providing temperament and health have been the most important considerations in the selection process.

As well as pedigree puppies, mongrel or crossbred puppies are often available from friends or rescue societies. Guessing what their adult size and inherited traits will be like is difficult, but they can make very good pets if you do not mind taking a chance.

Where not to buy a puppy
Avoid breeders who sell a number of different breeds, have many different puppies available and keep them outside in kennels. Puppies that are raised in kennels are more likely to have behaviour problems in later life. The 'professional' breeder may have lots of knowledge about their breeds, but with so many dogs to care for it is less likely they will make the same effort to raise and socialize each puppy as would a breeder who specializes in one breed and has one litter at a time.

Don't buy a puppy from an advert in the paper, from the internet or from a pet shop. All of these can be outlets for puppy farmers who keep dogs in small cages, breed from them continuously and often take the puppies away from the mother too early. The resulting puppies are often physically compromised, unhealthy and may show abnormal behaviour caused by stress in early life. It is not possible to tell whether a puppy comes from such a place just by its appearance, so it is better to avoid these outlets altogether.

Puppy farmers go to some lengths to disguise their trade. They may arrange to meet you in the car park of a pub or service station close to your home. Once there, it is very difficult to refuse when you see the puppy, even, or perhaps especially, if it is not well. Or they may deliver the puppies to a colleague's home so that you see the puppies there rather than on their premises. The mother will not be with them and the puppies have often travelled a long distance to get there and may have been taken away from their mother too soon.

Avoid outlets which keep many different breeds of puppy under the same roof. It is very likely that these puppies came from puppy farms and you may end up with problems as a result. It is also very easy to buy on impulse from such places without giving it proper consideration.

What is the breeder's primary motivation for producing the litter of puppies – to show, to work or to be pet dogs?

Does the registration document for the puppy you are considering contain accurate information about its parentage?

Do you know enough about breeders of your chosen breed to choose one that really cares about health and temperament?

Do you know anyone who has a healthy puppy from parents with good temperaments which is looking for a good home?

Has the puppy lived in a home rather than outside in a kennel?

Are you buying from a breeder who has just one litter and plenty of time to give necessary care and socialization?

Are you sure your puppy has not come from a puppy farm, making it prone to long-term ill health and behaviour problems?

Visiting a breeder

A visit to the breeder is your chance to find out if they are selling good puppies. Compile a list of questions before you go and be sure to prompt for details to help you make an accurate assessment of the breeder and his or her dogs. Be prepared to walk away if you do not like what you see or are dubious about what you hear.

Recognizing a good breeder

Good breeders do not breed often and do not breed to order so be prepared to wait – if you have chosen your breeder well, it will be worth it. Be prepared to ask questions and if you cannot get satisfactory answers, look elsewhere.

The signs of a good breeder are:

- The puppies look healthy and lively.

- The puppies approach you readily in a friendly manner and do not hang back or shy away when you try to make contact with them.

- Everything looks clean and smells fresh.

- The puppies have plenty of chews, toys and objects to play with and explore.

- The puppies will be kept in the house and have frequent access to areas where they will come into contact with the family and visitors.

- You can see the mother living in the house with the puppies.

- The mother is friendly and is happy to have you near her puppies.

Health and temperament of the puppies

It goes without saying that the puppies you see should be bouncing with health and vigour, with shiny coats and a zest for life. They should be clean with bright eyes, wet noses and no discharges. The breeder should be willing to talk about any inherited medical and behavioural conditions present in their lines, as well as any faults their own dog may have. They should only have bred from parents they know to have good temperaments. The rest of the family line should also have good temperaments as their genes will be contributing to your puppy.

Questions to ask	Considering the breeder's response
What inherited diseases and conditions are present in the breed?	You should already know the answers so you can check the breeder knows about them too.
Have both parents been tested for these diseases?	The answer should be yes.
Can you see the certificates?	The answer should be yes. Walk away if the breeder does not have them for any reason, no matter how plausible. Check the certificates carefully – you should already know what a good test result is.
Have the puppies been registered with the Kennel Club?	The answer should be yes and the breeder should be able to provide you with a registration document that details the puppy's family tree. Check this carefully to make sure it is authentic and for signs of close inbreeding (the same name appearing more than once) and be prepared to walk away if you do not like what you see.
What temperament does the mother have? How does she deal with stress and difficult conditions?	Let the breeder talk and keep prompting with questions so that the truth is revealed.
What does the breeder know about the temperament of the sire?	If the breeder does not know, ask for the contact details of the sire's owner and ask him or her direct.
How have the puppies been socialized?	Wait to see what the breeder says, but then ask extra questions to find out how much and how thoroughly this has been done.
How have the puppies been habituated to loud noises?	Only the best breeders will have thought of this. A breeder should be playing sounds, such as fireworks and thunder, to the puppies at low levels to acclimatize them to loud, sudden-onset noises in later life.
How have the puppies been prepared for easy house-training?	There should be a clear distinction between the bed area and the place to toilet. The puppies should have been encouraged to go outside frequently, especially after eating and on waking, to ensure they learn to toilet outside.
What will happen if something goes wrong or you are unable to take care of the puppy – will the breeder take it back?	Listen carefully to the answer. If the breeder truly care about the puppies, they will say yes. If they have bred previous litters, they may have stories about previous occasions when this has happened.

Meeting the mother and father

Gently insist on seeing the mother and be suspicious if your request is refused. If you are told she is out for a walk, wait until she returns or come back later to meet her.

The mother of the puppies should be friendly with visitors. Maternal hormones heighten any behaviour problems a bitch may have, including nervous aggression towards strangers. If the breeder says she is only like it when she has puppies, that may be true, but she still has an underlying problem. If you have to meet the mother in another room from the puppies, look elsewhere.

It is also a good idea to contact the stud dog owner and ask about his temperament. Better still, arrange to go and see him for yourself.

Where the puppies are kept

The best place for pet puppies to be raised is in a house as they will be less susceptible to behaviour problems in later life. There they can

Below: Puppies will socialize with each other and with their mother, but it also helps if they meet friendly, healthy dogs while still in the litter.

experience and get used to all the noises, smells and sights that accompany life in close proximity to humans.

Puppies make mess, and a litter of puppies makes a lot of mess, so do not expect to find them in the living room. However, they should not be so far away from the house that they are unlikely to spend any time there or are only taken in for occasional visits. If necessary, ask to see what the puppies are like in the house. If they slink about looking worried, walk away. A well-adjusted puppy will walk in confidently, investigating every corner.

Socialization of puppies

Puppies need to get used to people, other dogs and other animals early if they are to be friendly and unafraid later in life. A great deal of effort is needed to do this. Puppies should have met and played with men and women, toddlers, school-age children and teenagers before they go to their new homes. Take someone of the opposite sex with you to check their response to both men and women. Many puppies are raised by women and may never see a man until they go to new homes, with the result that they are anxious and worried by them. If the puppies are shy and keep away from you, it is likely they have not had sufficient contact with strangers. Look elsewhere for a breeder who takes more care.

Above: Access to a constantly changing variety of chews and toys while in the litter will help puppies to develop into curious and well-adjusted adults.

As well as getting used to people and other animals, it is important for young puppies to get used to sounds, smells and sights that they will see later in life. If this is done early, the puppy will be unafraid and well adjusted. This happens naturally if puppies are kept in a busy household, but special effort is needed if puppies spend a lot of time in a quiet pen. Check to see if breeders make an effort to get their puppies used to vacuum cleaners, washing machines, different surfaces, different smells and other sights and sounds that humans take for granted.

The dogs

The mongrel
Crossbreeds
Gundogs
Hounds
Pastoral
Terriers
Toys
Utility
Working

How to use this guide

The descriptions of the breeds given here are broad generalizations based on a range of opinions from people who know the breed well. There will be some dogs that don't fit the description, but, in general, these personality traits will be seen in most dogs of this breed. To make sure you know what you are getting when you buy a puppy, you need to thoroughly research the breed lines you are buying into and get to know individual dogs of that parentage to check they are what you want.

Attitude and behaviour

Whether the breed is good with children, other pets, strangers and unfamiliar dogs is, again, based on the knowledge of many individuals. Much will depend on its upbringing and socialization, so the information given here is for an average dog and owner.

Behaviour problems listed here are based on experience of dogs of this breed that have had issues. Not all dogs of this particular breed will have these behaviour problems, but some dogs of this breed will exhibit them or will have these tendencies.

Ideal owners

The description of the perfect owner is given so that you can match your own characteristics against them. If you do not match the description, consider how this will affect a dog of this breed if it came to live with you and your family and look again at the other breeds for one that is more suitable.

Some breeds will need strong-willed owners. This means they possess strong characters and, consequently, will need owners that are determined. All dog owners need to set boundaries for behaviour, teach their dogs how to behave well and how to respond to cues.

Dogs with strong characters will often prefer to behave in alternative ways even once they know what to do and so their owners will need to work hard to insist on good behaviour, especially during adolescence. No force or punishment is needed, but owners will need to be persistent and determined to keep control in order to maintain good behaviour.

Exercise needs

All breeds have been given a 'high', 'medium' or 'low' exercise score. High exercise is given to those dogs bred from generations of working dog. They have lots of energy, especially when young, and a lot of effort needs to be made to use up their desire to run and play. Low-energy breeds will still require exercise but will often be unable to tolerate too much because of physical issues, such as the compromised breathing of the English Bulldog, or are smaller with less of a need to go long distances.

Size at shoulder, weight, coat type, colour and lifespan

Name

Character

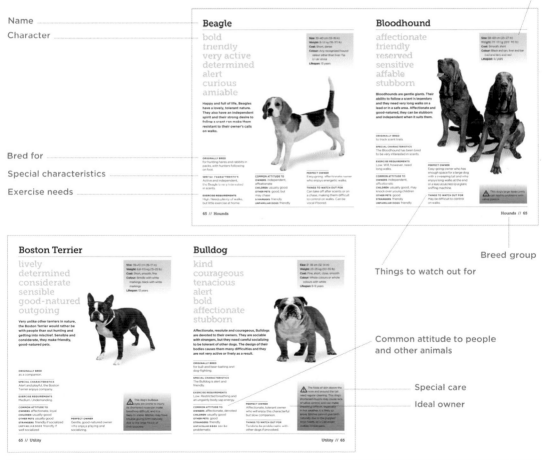

Bred for

Special characteristics

Exercise needs

Breed group

Things to watch out for

Common attitude to people and other animals

Special care

Ideal owner

The mongrel

unique
variable
from a large gene pool
from successful pet
parents

Size: Any
Weight: Any
Coat: Any
Colour: Any
Lifespan: 14–18 years

Mongrels are a complete mixture of genetic material and, consequently, come in a range of energy levels and temperaments. The puppies can grow into any shape or size, with any type or colour of coat, but they often resemble their parents.

ORIGINALLY BRED
themselves by choosing their own mates.

SPECIAL CHARACTERISTICS
Each dog is unique in look and character.

EXERCISE REQUIREMENTS
Every mongrel will be different.

COMMON ATTITUDE TO
OWNERS usually good
CHILDREN usually good
OTHER PETS unknown
STRANGERS usually good
UNFAMILIAR DOGS usually good

PERFECT OWNER
Families happy to own a dog that is unique and to take a chance on how it will turn out if buying a puppy.

THINGS TO WATCH OUT FOR
May grow too big for the house.

Where mongrels come from

Mongrels are a result of unplanned mating between dogs that are not purebred themselves, and that have chosen their own breeding partner. To be able to do this, they need to be let off once with another entire dog, or to have escaped once and found another entire dog. This is more likely to happen if they have not been neutered.

Historically, dogs had a lot more freedom when villages were smaller and fewer people populated the world. Before the arrival of cars, lorries and busy roads, dogs were often free to wander and find their own entertainment, coming home only when they wanted to be fed, needed warmth or shelter, or when they knew their owners would be at home to provide company.

These free-ranging dogs were often left entire rather than being neutered, as owners could rarely afford to get this done. Consequently, many mongrel puppies resulted from the unions of these dogs who were free to choose a mate from the many dogs they encountered daily. Overpopulation became a big problem, which caused welfare issues and overcrowding in rescue centres. As a result, many charities began neutering campaigns to encourage owners to have their pets neutered to reduce the number of puppies being produced.

At the same time, owners also began to keep dogs within the confines of their homes more. As more traffic appeared on roads, the risk of dogs being injured or killed while wandering became greater. A little later, local governments introduced control authorities in many areas, tasked to round up stray dogs and fine owners who came to collect their dogs. This meant that, in built-up areas particularly, there were far fewer dogs on the streets to produce litters of mongrel puppies. Consequently, in many areas, true mongrels have now become rarer and harder to find, although the most likely place to discover one is in a rescue centre.

Below: Mongrels are made up of a mixture of genes from many purebred dogs so each one is unique and will have its own individual character and physical appearance.

Mongrels and health

Mongrels have tremendous genetic variation and, consequently, will not breed true. This means the offspring of two mongrels will not necessarily have the physical appearance or traits and characteristics of their parents.

This genetic variation and large gene pool means that genes for inherited disorders are not concentrated within the mongrel population, so it is highly unlikely that both parents carry a defective gene that will manifest itself in an inherited condition in the puppies. Consequently, mongrels usually have health advantages over purebred dogs.

Several studies have looked at this health advantage and found that mongrels require less veterinary treatment, are less prone to many diseases than purebred dogs and are less likely to die from disease

Above: Mongrels tend to have no strong propensities for particular behaviours as this tends to occur in purebred dogs whose ancestors needed specific traits for working.

rather than old age. They also have a higher longevity, on average, than purebred dogs.

As a result, some pet insurance companies offer lower premiums for mongrels so it is worth shopping around for insurance if you are planning to own one.

Different types of mongrel

Mongrels generally fall into four basic categories: Collie-cross types, terrier-cross types, gundog-cross types, and 'others'. This is due to the high prevalence in the dog population of Collies, terriers and gundogs, producing mongrels that bear a high proportion of these genes.

If a mongrel resembles a Collie, terrier or gundog, you can expect it to have quite a few of the traits of these breeds, although they will be heavily diluted with other genes. The 'others' are individuals that do not resemble any breed in particular and, consequently, are a true mixture of genetic material.

Temperament and character

Mongrels can have any type of character and personality. Just like purebred dogs, they will be a product of their genetic make-up and the experiences they had as they were growing up. Since their genetic composition is so varied, they can have a wide variety of traits and propensities, and you are not likely to know which they have until they begin to develop their adult characters.

Due to the wide mix of genes in a mongrel, it is unlikely that it will have such strong traits as those found in purebreds. This makes mongrels more likely to be balanced individuals without powerful drives and behaviours, which tends to make them easier and more balanced pets.

In addition, mongrels are the progeny of successful pet dogs that people have wanted to keep in their homes. Consequently, it is likely that the puppies will inherit genes that make them more likely to become a successful pet. It is also likely that they will have had to get along with other dogs in the neighbourhood without fighting and, consequently, it is more likely they will be good with other dogs too.

WHERE TO FIND A MONGREL

It is not always easy to find a mongrel so be prepared for it to take time, depending on the area in which you live and the availability of puppies. To find mongrel puppies and adults, ask:

- Rescue centres – local and further afield.

- Friends if they know of anyone who has a suitable puppy or adult dog.

- Local veterinary practices as they may know of a litter that is due or an adult requiring a home.

- The local government office responsible for stray dog collection.

Crossbreeds

A crossbreed is a dog that has purebred parents of two different breeds. Puppies that result from such a mating carry a mixture of their parents' genes and, consequently, are likely to have a mixture of their physical characteristics and behaviour traits. They are usually named by combining the names of the parents' breeds, such as Labradoodle (a cross with a Labrador and a Poodle), Cockapoo (a cross with a Cocker Spaniel and a Poodle) and Jackador (a cross with a Jack Russell and a Labrador).

The genetics of crossbreeding

Genes control the physical characteristics of a dog, such as height, eye colour and coat type, as well as its personality traits. Every dog carries two copies of each gene, one from its mother and one from its father. When they produce a puppy, each parent gives one copy of each gene, chosen at random from its own two copies, to provide the two copies of each gene necessary in the puppy. Whether the gene from the mother or the gene from the father actually ends up determining the specific characteristic of the puppy depends on which gene is dominant.

Consequently, each puppy in a litter will have a variety of genes from its mother and its father and no two puppies in the litter will have exactly the same genetic make-up. This creates differences between the puppies with regard to appearance and character. For example, one may have the mother's coat type and the father's eye colour, another may have the father's coat type and the mother's eye colour. A puppy can even have the eye colour of its grandmother, for example, whose eye colour gene was present in its mother but not expressed because it was not dominant.

When two puppies from a cross are mated, the resulting puppies will also contain a mixture of genetic material. But if you select puppies of a particular physical appearance and breed from them generation after generation, they will, eventually, produce puppies that breed true as all of the genetic material they contain will be uniform.

When breeders talk about crossbreeds, they will often mention F1, F2 or F3. This refers to the generation in terms of distance from the original crossbreeds. So F1 (first filial) refers to the first generation of

Left: Every crossbreed is different but it will have a mixture of the various temperament and physical traits found in its parents.

puppies from two purebred dogs. F2 refers to the puppies that result from a mating of two F1 dogs, and F3 puppies are the result of the mating of two F2 puppies. Consequently, if the breeder is breeding for particular characteristics, the F3 are more likely to carry those characteristics than an F1 puppy and to breed true. This is really only of interest if you are looking for a particular type or are interested in breeding from your dog. The disadvantage of selective breeding in this way, as seen in purebred dogs, is a smaller gene pool and, as a result, more inherited defects.

A fashion for crossbreeds

Crosses between purebred dogs have been made periodically in history to try to take advantage of the good points of two different breeds. In the 1970s, a guide dog association in Australia began to breed Labradoodles to try to produce a non-shedding, hypoallergenic guide dog for allergy-suffering clients. Since then, there has been a steadily increasing demand for crossbred dogs, most noticeably Poodle crosses.

With the decline of mongrels, crossbreeds have become more popular, perhaps because owners want a dog that is more 'unique' than a purebred dog, or perhaps because they erroneously believe that they will be hypoallergenic and will not have the inherited diseases and conditions many purebred dogs suffer.

Left: Crossbreed puppies may grow up to resemble the father or the mother, or a little of both, depending on which genes are expressed.

Coat type and allergies

Poodles have non-shed coats and, consequently, can make easier pets for people with allergies than dogs that shed their hair. However, allergies can also be caused by contact with saliva and dander (shed skin cells), so there is no guarantee that someone with allergies can live with a Poodle crossbreed, whether or not it has a non-shed coat. While some dogs, particularly those with paler coat colours, may be better for allergic people than others, the idea of a 'hypoallergenic' dog is a myth. Adults and children who may be allergic to dogs need to spend as much time as they can with the type of dog they have chosen, preferably looking after one in their own home for a while, to see if they get a reaction before embarking on purchasing one for themselves.

Crossbreeds and health

Some owners purchase crossbreeds in an attempt to escape the inherited diseases and conditions now present in many purebreeds as a result of close inbreeding. While there may be a greater chance that a crossbred puppy will have inherited healthy genes, there are no guarantees that it will not inherit faulty genes instead. This is particularly the case if a genetic fault, such as hip dysplasia, is found in both of the parental breeds.

Consequently, it is still important to test for health defects in both purebred parents consistent with the diseases and conditions found In those breeds. If both the parents of your puppy are healthy and have good test results, it is likely that the puppy will be too. Relying on crossbreeding itself to produce healthy offspring is not enough.

Below: Crossbreeds are increasing in popularity as purebred dogs begin to become more closely inbred and, as a result, suffer more from inherited conditions.

Temperament and character

Due to the mixture of genes in a crossbred puppy, temperament and character traits can vary widely. However, the temperament traits will always be those of the parents and grandparents so if you are satisfied that the temperament of both breeds of dog would suit you and your family, you should be pleased with the character of a resulting puppy.

If you are getting an adult crossbred dog, you can test for various character traits that may be strong in the parental breeds. Enlist the help of rescue centre staff or an experienced person to make sure that you are getting the right dog for you and your family.

Where to find one

While crossbreeds remain in fashion, it will not be difficult to find a litter of crossbred puppies through adverts in newspapers or online. However, extreme care needs to be taken to make sure these puppies have been produced for the right reasons, not purely for profit, and that the breeder is knowledgeable (see pages 54–61).

Crossbreed litters are often produced by breeders with limited experience and so it is important to question them closely to see if they have adequate knowledge to have chosen the parents wisely, done all the necessary health testing and raised them well. If you do not trust yourself to visit and come away without a puppy, question the breeder carefully on the telephone before you visit. It helps to have two or three breeders to visit so that you can choose the best puppy available and are not committed to a particular litter before you have seen several.

Labradoodle

**intelligent
lively
keen to please
affectionate
playful
agile**

Size: 38–74 cm (15–29 in)
Weight: Up to 45 kg (99 lb)
Coat: Varies – wiry, fleecy or woolly
Colour: All solid colours
Lifespan: 14–16 years

Labradoodles have a mixture of Labrador and Poodle genetics. They come in different sizes depending on the size of the Poodle parent. They are energetic and make good workers for owners that like to be active.

ORIGINALLY BRED
in an attempt to produce a hypoallergenic guide dog.

SPECIAL CHARACTERISTICS
An energetic worker, willing to please.

EXERCISE REQUIREMENTS
High. Lively and agile in mind and body.

COMMON ATTITUDE TO
OWNERS usually affectionate
CHILDREN usually playful
OTHER PETS usually playful
STRANGERS usually friendly
UNFAMILIAR DOGS usually friendly

PERFECT OWNER
An active family with plenty of time to train and play. An owner who enjoys energetic walks as well as providing plenty of mental stimulation for this lively breed.

THINGS TO WATCH OUT FOR
Jumping up and boisterousness when young. Coat care can be time consuming.

Cockapoo

intelligent
active
extrovert
affectionate
agile

Size: 30–45 cm (12–18 in)
Weight: 9–15 kg (20–33 lb)
Coat: Varies – wiry, fleecy or woolly
Colour: Various
Lifespan: 14–16 years

Cockapoos have a mixture of Cocker Spaniel (American or English) and Poodle genetics. They are lively and affectionate, and need plenty to do if they are to be calm and content, especially when young.

ORIGINALLY BRED
As a pet in the 1960s.

SPECIAL CHARACTERISTICS
A joyful and clever companion.

EXERCISE REQUIREMENTS
High. Active and busy but content to rest at home.

COMMON ATTITUDE TO
OWNERS usually affectionate
CHILDREN usually playful
OTHER PETS usually playful
STRANGERS usually friendly
UNFAMILIAR DOGS usually friendly

PERFECT OWNER
Good dogs for busy families who enjoy a close bond with their dog and who have plenty of appetite for energetic walks and frequent play and training sessions.

THINGS TO WATCH OUT FOR
Separation issues unless care is taken to get them used to being alone.

Braque Italian (Bracco)

sensible
even-tempered
slightly stubborn
sensitive
gentle

Size: 55–67 cm (21½–26½ in)
Weight: 25–40 kg (55–88 lb)
Coat: Short, dense
Colour: White, white with orange, amber or chestnut markings. White may be speckled, roan with solid markings
Lifespan: 12–13 years

These dogs have the energy and enthusiasm to hunt all day and be ready to get up the next day and do it all again. Gentle and placid at home, they are tolerant, slightly stubborn but playful companions.

ORIGINALLY BRED
for tracking, pointing and retrieving on land and in water.

SPECIAL CHARACTERISTICS
A vigorous hunter, the Braque Italian is energetic and playful.

EXERCISE REQUIREMENTS
High. Quiet at home, but it needs plenty of long walks and free running.

COMMON ATTITUDE TO
OWNERS placid
CHILDREN usually tolerant
OTHER PETS may be problematic with smaller pets
STRANGERS usually friendly
UNFAMILIAR DOGS usually friendly

PERFECT OWNER
Active families who enjoy long, energetic walks, require a calm, gentle-natured pet at home and who do not desire fast responses to obedience requests.

THINGS TO WATCH OUT FOR
This dog's enthusiasm for hunting may lead to control problems on walks.

Brittany

energetic
responsive
busy
affectionate
enthusiastic

Enthusiastic, responsive Brittanys are energetic, reactive workaholics that are happiest when busy. Not a dog to leave behind at home while you work and party, these active dogs need both company and a job to do.

Size: 46–52 cm (18–20½ in)
Weight: 13–15 kg (28–33 lb)
Coat: Dense, fairly fine and slightly wavy
Colour: Orange and white, liver and white, black and white, tricolour, or roan of any of these colours
Lifespan: 13–15 years

ORIGINALLY BRED
for setting and flushing game, as well as pointing and retrieving.

SPECIAL CHARACTERISTICS
Playful, busy and active, the Brittany revels in exercise.

EXERCISE REQUIREMENTS
High. Busy in the house and energetic outside.

COMMON ATTITUDE TO
OWNERS willing to please
CHILDREN usually good-natured, playful
OTHER PETS good
STRANGERS usually friendly
UNFAMILIAR DOGS usually friendly

PERFECT OWNER
Active, busy owner who loves to play with a dog and include it in all aspects of life.

THINGS TO WATCH OUT FOR
Some lines of these dogs may be fearful and reactive with strangers.

Hungarian Vizsla

lively
responsive
obedient
sensitive
affectionate
biddable

Size: 53–64 cm (21–25 in)
Weight: 20–30 kg (44–66 lb)
Coat: Short, dense. Also less
   common wirehaired variety
Colour: Russet gold
Lifespan: 13–14 years

Sensitive, energetic Vizslas have plenty of energy and exuberance, especially when excited. They could send children or elderly people flying, but not on purpose. Given enough exercise, they can be calm and affectionate pets and respond eagerly to commands once they know what to do.

ORIGINALLY BRED
for pointing and retrieving
on land and water.

SPECIAL CHARACTERISTICS
This dog is playful, energetic
and good-tempered.

EXERCISE REQUIREMENTS
High. Full of energy, which
needs to be channelled.

**COMMON ATTITUDE TO
OWNERS** responsive, affectionate
CHILDREN good-natured,
may be too boisterous for
very young children
OTHER PETS care needed with
small animals
STRANGERS friendly
UNFAMILIAR DOGS friendly

PERFECT OWNER
Energetic families who are
active and busy, who want
a dog to play with, run with,
walk and train.

THINGS TO WATCH OUT FOR
If not given sufficient exercise
this dog may be boisterous and
may run away.

Italian Spinone

faithful
responsive
patient
affectionate
easy-going
biddable

The Spinone is a popular dog with families because of its easy-going, good nature. Exuberantly playful during the excitement of a walk, they are calm and gentle at home.

Size: 60–70 cm (23½–27½ in)
Weight: 29–39 kg (64–86 lb)
Coat: Tough, thick, slightly wiry
Colour: White, white with orange markings, solid white peppered orange, white with brown markings, white speckled with brown (brown roan), with or without large brown markings
Lifespan: 12–14 years

ORIGINALLY BRED
for retrieval of game and tracking.

SPECIAL CHARACTERISTICS
The Spinone is calm and playful, with a 'soft' mouth and is interested in scents.

EXERCISE REQUIREMENTS
High–Medium. Energetic outside, but content to rest at home.

COMMON ATTITUDE TO
OWNERS biddable, enjoys close bond
CHILDREN patient, good-natured
OTHER PETS good
STRANGERS friendly, can be cautious
UNFAMILIAR DOGS friendly

PERFECT OWNER
Families who enjoy long walks, like to play games with their dog and want a close companion.

THINGS TO WATCH OUT FOR
This breed may suffer from separation problems.

Kooikerhondje

sensitive
good-natured
alert

These attractive dogs are
both energetic and busy.
Cautious with strangers,
these loyal dogs like
to build strong bonds
with their owners.
They are sensitive and
industrious and like to
have something to do
to keep them occupied.

Size: 35–40 cm (14–16 in)
Weight: 9–11 kg (20–24 lb)
Coat: Medium–long, slightly waved
or straight
Colour: Clear orange-red-
coloured patches on white
Lifespan: 12–13 years

ORIGINALLY BRED
as a decoy to lure ducks and
for flushing and retrieval.

SPECIAL CHARACTERISTICS
The Kooikerhondje has
a lively, active mind that
needs stimulation.

EXERCISE REQUIREMENTS
High. Energetic, enjoys
being busy.

COMMON ATTITUDE TO
OWNERS friendly, loyal
CHILDREN good-natured if raised
with them
OTHER PETS good
STRANGERS initially cautious
but friendly
UNFAMILIAR DOGS initially
cautious but friendly

PERFECT OWNER
Active, gentle family or
owner who is happy to play
with this dog and want
a close companion.

⚠ This dog's feathers will
bring in mud and dirt
from outside.

Large Munsterlander

alert
energetic
keen worker
biddable
loyal
affectionate
trustworthy

Loyalty to their owners comes high on the Munsterlander's list of priorities, with exercise a close second. These strong-willed dogs are full of energy and will play games all day if they can. The Small Munsterlander is a different breed that looks similar, but is smaller and the coat is liver instead of black.

ORIGINALLY BRED
as a colour variation of the German Wirehaired Pointer for tracking, pointing and retrieving on land and in water.

SPECIAL CHARACTERISTICS
This dog is energetic and playful, and interested in scents.

EXERCISE REQUIREMENTS
High. Needs exercise both inside and outside the house.

COMMON ATTITUDE TO OWNERS biddable, loyal

CHILDREN usually tolerant, may be too boisterous for young children
OTHER PETS good
STRANGERS usually good if well socialized
UNFAMILIAR DOGS usually friendly

PERFECT OWNER
Experienced, active owner who can set clear guidelines for behaviour and provide plenty of activity, play and training.

This dog's feathers will bring in mud and dirt from outside.

THINGS TO WATCH OUT FOR
Some lines can be strong-willed and need a determined owner. Unless well socialized may see strangers as a threat.

Spanish Water Dog

faithful
obedient
good-tempered
brave
watchful

With its distinctive curly coat, this dog is loyal and likes to bond closely to its owners. It will naturally guard and is aloof or territorial with strangers. A hard-working, willing dog, it needs plenty of activity to be happy.

Size: 40–50 cm (16–19½ in)
Weight: 14–22 kg (31–48 lb)
Coat: Curled woolly texture, forming cords when long. Needs to be clipped
Colour: Solid black, brown or white of various shades; black and white or brown and white (particolour) but never tricoloured
Lifespan: 10–14 years

ORIGINALLY BRED
to work with fishermen and for herding and retrieving.

SPECIAL CHARACTERISTICS
Willing to please, the Spanish Water Dog is playful and energetic, and likes to swim.

EXERCISE REQUIREMENTS
High. Needs plenty of exercise.

COMMON ATTITUDE TO
OWNERS loyal and close-bonding
CHILDREN can be intolerant
OTHER PETS may be problematic with small pets
STRANGERS will naturally guard, territorial
UNFAMILIAR DOGS usually good

PERFECT OWNER
Experienced owner who wants an unusual breed and who can cope with the high energy level and the need to provide daily interest through play, socializing, training and activity.

THINGS TO WATCH OUT FOR
If not properly socialized, may display territorial aggression to strangers.

Weimaraner

**friendly
exuberant
protective
obedient
active
alert**

Size: 56–69 cm (22–27 in)
Weight: 32–39 kg (70–86 lb)
Coat: Short, smooth and sleek. (There is also a long-haired variety.)
Colour: Normally silver-grey, shades of mouse or roe-grey permissible. Whole coat gives an appearance of metallic sheen
Lifespan: 13 years

Weimaraners are exuberant and energetic. They thrive on action and enjoy curling up with their family after a long day's activity. Their good nature makes them excellent family dogs, but their enthusiasm can make them clumsy enough to knock over or squash things more delicate than themselves.

ORIGINALLY BRED
to track large game, then to hunt, point and retrieve.

SPECIAL CHARACTERISTICS
Active, exuberant and playful, the Weimaraner develops close bonds with its owner. It can be stubborn.

EXERCISE REQUIREMENTS
Very high. Needs plenty of exercise, particularly when young.

COMMON ATTITUDE TO OWNERS attentive, tactile **CHILDREN** usually good, may be too boisterous for small children

OTHER PETS good, but may chase or squash
STRANGERS good if well socialized, can be territorial
UNFAMILIAR DOGS friendly if well socialized

PERFECT OWNER
Energetic strong-willed owner who enjoys playing, training and being very active.

THINGS TO WATCH OUT FOR
Lack of exercise can result in boisterousness, running away or destructiveness. May be problematic with other dogs unless properly socialized. Can be prone to stress, high anxiety and separation issues.

⚠ The Weimaraner's sleek coat is thin and it can suffer from the cold if left outside.

Wirehaired Pointing Griffon

friendly
dependable
sensitive
energetic

Size: 56–61 cm (22–24 in)
Weight: 23–27 kg (50–60 lb)
Coat: Thick, medium length, wiry
Colour: Steel grey with brown markings
Lifespan: 12–15 years

Energetic Wirehaired Pointing Griffons are sensitive and hard-working. Responsive and close-bonding, they enjoy gentle, active families and have enough energy to play all day and be ready for action again the next morning.

ORIGINALLY BRED
for hunting and retrieving on land and water.

SPECIAL CHARACTERISTICS
This breed is playful and exuberant, and enjoys scenting and flushing out wildlife.

EXERCISE REQUIREMENTS
High. Needs plenty of opportunities to run.

COMMON ATTITUDE TO
OWNERS affectionate, responsive
CHILDREN usually good
OTHER PETS good, may chase
STRANGERS friendly
UNFAMILIAR DOGS friendly

PERFECT OWNER
Active families who enjoy energetic walks, playing and training and who want a close bond with their dog.

THINGS TO WATCH OUT FOR
Some submissive urination in females, especially if they are handled harshly.

Pointer

**gentle
obedient
sensitive
alert
kind**

Size: 61–69 cm (24–27 in)
Weight: 20–30 kg (44–66 lb)
Coat: Fine, short, hard
Colour: Lemon and white, orange
and white, liver and white or
black and white
Lifespan: 12–14 years

Long-legged and agile, the energetic Pointer needs plenty of exercise to stay calm at home where it will be affectionate and good-natured with its family. These dogs possess a great sense of smell and enjoy long, active, nose-to-the-ground walks.

ORIGINALLY BRED
to flush and point to game.

SPECIAL CHARACTERISTICS
Playful and active, the Pointer is particularly interested in scents.

EXERCISE REQUIREMENTS
High. Needs regular, long walks.

COMMON ATTITUDE TO
OWNERS affectionate, biddable
CHILDREN usually tolerant, gentle, but may be too boisterous for very young children
OTHER PETS good
STRANGERS friendly
UNFAMILIAR DOGS friendly

PERFECT OWNER
Kind, playful, sociable families who enjoy an active life with plenty of long, energetic walks and who can provide games and activities to keep this breed occupied.

German Shorthaired Pointer

gentle
affectionate
even-tempered
alert
biddable
loyal

Size: 53–64 cm (21–25 in)
Weight: 27–32 kg (60–70 lb)
Coat: Short, flat and slightly coarse to touch
Colour: Solid liver, liver and white spotted, liver and white spotted and ticked, liver and white ticked, solid black or black and white
Lifespan: 14–16 years

Enthusiastic German Shorthaired Pointers are full of life and vigour. Tolerant, responsive and easy-going by nature, they make excellent family pets providing they have an outlet for their abundant energy.

ORIGINALLY BRED
for flushing and pointing to game.

SPECIAL CHARACTERISTICS
Obedient and playful, this dog is very interested in scents.

EXERCISE REQUIREMENTS
High. Needs energetic walks.

COMMON ATTITUDE TO
OWNERS affectionate, biddable
CHILDREN usually good, may be too boisterous for young children
OTHER PETS good, may chase
STRANGERS friendly
UNFAMILIAR DOGS friendly

PERFECT OWNER
Active, sociable, affectionate families who enjoy energetic walks and games with their dog.

THINGS TO WATCH OUT FOR
Needs plenty of exercise or may become boisterous or destructive, or run away.

German Wirehaired Pointer

gentle
affectionate
even-tempered
alert
biddable
loyal

Size: 56–67 cm (22–26½ in)	
Weight: 20.5–34 kg (45–75 lb)	
Coat: Outer coat thick and harsh with a dense undercoat	
Colour: Liver and white, solid liver, black and white	
Lifespan: 10–12 years	

A little more strong-willed than the shorthaired version, the Wirehaired Pointer is energetic, affectionate and good-natured. These dogs have energy in abundance and they need homes where long walks and action are part of the package.

ORIGINALLY BRED
for flushing and pointing to game.

SPECIAL CHARACTERISTICS
Obedient and playful, the Wirehaired Pointer is interested in scents.

EXERCISE REQUIREMENTS
High. Needs long walks to burn off abundant energy.

COMMON ATTITUDE TO
OWNERS affectionate, biddable
CHILDREN usually good, may be too boisterous for young children
OTHER PETS good, may chase
STRANGERS friendly
UNFAMILIAR DOGS friendly

PERFECT OWNER
Active, sociable, affectionate families who enjoy energetic walks and games with their dog.

THINGS TO WATCH OUT FOR
Needs plenty of exercise or may become boisterous or destructive, or run away.

Chesapeake Bay Retriever

independent
affectionate
courageous
strong-willed
alert
responsive

Size: 53–66 cm (21–26 in)
Weight: 32–36 kg (70–80 lb)
Coat: Thick and reasonably short with harsh oily outer coat
Colour: Dead grass (straw to bracken), sedge (red gold) or any shade of brown
Lifespan: 12–13 years

Chesapeakes can be very protective of their owners' but need careful, experienced handling to ensure humans stay in control. These strong, active dogs have a coat that protects them from cold water so swimming is just one of the energetic activities they enjoy.

ORIGINALLY BRED
in the USA for retrieving waterfowl.

SPECIAL CHARACTERISTICS
Playful and active, this Retriever particularly enjoys swimming.

EXERCISE REQUIREMENTS
High. Full of energy that needs to be channelled.

COMMON ATTITUDE TO
OWNERS loyal, affectionate
CHILDREN good-natured if raised with them, can be intolerant
OTHER PETS good

STRANGERS usually good if well socialized, can be territorial
UNFAMILIAR DOGS usually good, can be territorial

PERFECT OWNER
Strong-willed, experienced, active owner who enjoys long, energetic walks, playing retrieve games and plenty of training.

THINGS TO WATCH OUT FOR
Can be strong-willed and needs a determined owner. May be problematic with strangers if not properly socialized.

Curly Coated Retriever

bold
friendly
self-confident
independent
aloof
enthusiastic
curious

Size: 64–69 cm (25–27 in)
Weight: 32–36 kg (70–80 lb)
Coat: Body coat a thick mass of
small tight, crisp curls lying
close to skin, short coat on face
Colour: Black or liver
Lifespan: 12–13 years

Independent, but affectionate and playful, these Retrievers are loyal to their families, but are not quite so keen on strangers. Their distinctive curly coats protect them from cold and rain so they will be always ready for long active walks whatever the weather.

ORIGINALLY BRED
for retrieving waterfowl.

SPECIAL CHARACTERISTICS
This Retriever is playful and active, and loves to swim.

EXERCISE REQUIREMENTS
High. Very active and needs regular, long walks.

COMMON ATTITUDE TO
OWNERS affectionate, tactile
CHILDREN usually good, may be too boisterous for young children
OTHER PETS good
STRANGERS reserved
UNFAMILIAR DOGS good

PERFECT OWNER
Active, confident owner who wants to play games and enjoy long, energetic walks.

THINGS TO WATCH OUT FOR
If not properly socialized, may be problematic with strangers.

Flat Coated Retriever

happy
kind
optimistic
friendly
active

Size: 56–61 cm (22–24 in)
Weight: 25–36 kg (55–80 lb)
Coat: Dense, fine, flat. Legs and tail well feathered
Colour: Black or liver only
Lifespan: 11–13 years

Flat Coated Retrievers are affectionate, lively and playful. Sociable, friendly and interested in everything, and responsive to requests, they make ideal family pets for active owners.

ORIGINALLY BRED
for retrieving game on land and in water.

SPECIAL CHARACTERISTICS
Active and playful, the Flat Coated Retriever loves to swim.

EXERCISE REQUIREMENTS
High. Full of energy outside, calmer in the house.

COMMON ATTITUDE TO
OWNERS affectionate, biddable
CHILDREN usually good
OTHER PETS good
STRANGERS friendly
UNFAMILIAR DOGS friendly

PERFECT OWNER
Active, affectionate, sociable families who enjoy energetic walks and playing games with their dog.

⚠️ These Retrievers will bring in mud and dirt from outside on its feathers.

✔️ Recommended for energetic, first-time owners, but it is important to find a dog from a healthy line.

Golden Retriever

**biddable
relaxed
kind
friendly
confident
responsive
sensible**

Size: 51–61 cm (20–24 in)
Weight: 27–36 kg (60–80 lb)
Coat: Flat or wavy with good
feathering
Colour: Any shade of gold or
cream
Lifespan: 12–13 years

A popular family dog for good reason, Golden Retrievers are good-natured, playful and kind. These dogs are people enthusiasts and are just as happy greeting people at the door with a shoe in their mouths as they are retrieving game in the fields.

ORIGINALLY BRED
for retrieving game on land and in water.

SPECIAL CHARACTERISTICS
The Golden Retriever is active and playful, and likes to swim.

EXERCISE REQUIREMENTS
High. Enjoys long walks and lots of games.

COMMON ATTITUDE TO
OWNERS affectionate, biddable
CHILDREN patient
OTHER PETS good

STRANGERS friendly
UNFAMILIAR DOGS friendly

PERFECT OWNER
Active, affectionate, sociable families who enjoy energetic walks and playing with their dog.

THINGS TO WATCH OUT FOR
Some lines may display problematic possession-guarding.

Labrador

kind
responsive
keen
biddable
enthusiastic
affable

Size: 55–57 cm (21½–22½ in)
Weight: 25–34 kg (55–75 lb)
Coat: Short, dense, without wave or feathering
Colour: Yellow, black or chocolate
Lifespan: 12–13 years

The friendly, good-natured Labrador is well known and well loved everywhere. Whether trained to provide assistance to disabled people or giving love and affection in a family home, this versatile dog is a playful, happy enthusiast.

ORIGINALLY BRED
to help fishermen bring in their nets, later for flushing and retrieving game.

SPECIAL CHARACTERISTICS
Active and playful, the Labrador loves to swim.

EXERCISE REQUIREMENTS
Very high. Needs regular long walks and play sessions.

COMMON ATTITUDE TO
OWNERS affectionate, biddable
CHILDREN patient
OTHER PETS good
STRANGERS friendly
UNFAMILIAR DOGS friendly

PERFECT OWNER
Affectionate, sociable, exuberant families who can provide enough energetic walks, plenty of play and active training routines.

THINGS TO WATCH OUT FOR
Often destructive chewers during adolescence. Lack of exercise may lead to boisterousness, reluctance to come back on walks and destructive behaviour.

Yellow and Black Labradors

Yellow Labradors tend to have a slightly softer temperament than the black ones and are more likely to be easy-going. Both can be bred for working or show purposes; it may be best to choose one from a show line rather than from working stock unless you are prepared for lots of exercise.

Chocolate Labrador

Chocolate Labradors tend to be more tolerant to pain and, consequently, often injure themselves more readily. They can be more exuberant and enthusiastic and are prone to running headlong into their owners, strangers or other dogs. This can cause problems with some people and other dogs who are unlikely to tolerate such impudence from others.

✔ Recommended for energetic, first-time owners. Its good nature makes the Labrador an ideal family pet.

Nova Scotia Duck-tolling Retriever

kind
confident
responsive
sensitive
easy to train
playful
active

Size: 45–51 cm (18–20 in)
Weight: 17–23 kg (37–50 lb)
Coat: Straight, double coat of medium/long length
Colour: All shades of red or orange with lighter featherings and underside of tail
Lifespan: 12–13 years

Nova Scotia Duck-tolling Retrievers were bred to lure ducks towards the hunts by leaping and playing by the water's edge and then to retrieve them once shot. Energetic and playful, they need plenty of activity to keep them well exercised.

ORIGINALLY BRED
to act as a decoy and to retrieve waterfowl.

SPECIAL CHARACTERISTICS
This Retriever has an active, playful and curious nature.

EXERCISE REQUIREMENTS
Very high. Enjoys plenty of exercise and play sessions.

COMMON ATTITUDE TO OWNERS affectionate, biddable
CHILDREN usually good
OTHER PETS good, may chase

STRANGERS reserved
UNFAMILIAR DOGS friendly

PERFECT OWNER
Active, affectionate families who enjoy energetic walks and can spend a great deal of time training and playing with this active breed.

⚠ This dog will bring in mud and dirt from outside on its feathers.

English Setter

graceful
able
outgoing
kind
very active
friendly
good-natured

Size: 61–69 cm (24–27 in)
Weight: 25–30 kg (55–66 lb)
Coat: Slightly wavy, not curly, long and silky
Colour: Black and white (blue belton), orange and white (orange belton), lemon and white (lemon belton), liver and white (liver belton) or tricolour
Lifespan: 12–13 years

English Setters are graceful and elegant in motion and like to run free to use up excess energy. Although affectionate and good-natured with their families, they are independent and are not always easy to train or responsive to requests.

ORIGINALLY BRED
for flushing and retrieving birds.

SPECIAL CHARACTERISTICS
This Setter is very active and exuberant.

EXERCISE REQUIREMENTS
High. Needs long walks on a regular basis.

COMMON ATTITUDE TO
OWNERS affectionate, easy-going
CHILDREN usually good, may knock over young children
OTHER PETS good
STRANGERS friendly
UNFAMILIAR DOGS friendly

PERFECT OWNER
Patient, affectionate, easy-going families with access to places where this dog can have plenty of freedom to run.

⚠ This dog will bring in mud and dirt from outside on its feathers.

Gordon Setter

relaxed
friendly
devoted
loyal
stubborn

Exuberant and lively, the Gordon Setter is affectionate and easy-going. These dogs love to run and need plenty of long, active walks. Their affectionate and devoted good nature makes up for their lack of responsiveness to requests.

ORIGINALLY BRED
for flushing birds.

SPECIAL CHARACTERISTICS
The exuberant Gordon Setter enjoys being very active.

EXERCISE REQUIREMENTS
High. Needs to be taken for long runs.

COMMON ATTITUDE TO
OWNERS affectionate, easy-going
CHILDREN usually good, may knock over young children
OTHER PETS good, may chase
STRANGERS friendly
UNFAMILIAR DOGS friendly

PERFECT OWNER
Patient, affectionate, easy-going, strong-willed families with access to places where this dog can have plenty of freedom to run.

THINGS TO WATCH OUT FOR
Can be strong-willed and needs a determined owner. Lack of exercise may lead to escapes and running away.

Size: 62–66 cm (24½–26 in)
Weight: 25.5–29.5 kg (56–65 lb)
Coat: Medium length; flat, with heavy feathering on legs and underside of body
Colour: Black, with markings of chestnut red
Lifespan: 12–14 years

⚠️ This dog will bring in mud and dirt from outside on its feathers.

Irish Setter

exuberant
tremendously active
affectionate
excitable

Size: 64–69 cm (25–27 in)
Weight: 27–32 kg (60–70 lb)
Coat: Fine, flat and of medium
length. Feathers on legs, feet,
belly and tail
Colour: Rich chestnut
Lifespan: 12–13 years

Irish Setters were born to run. They have a natural exuberance and energy as well as an easy-going, good nature that fits in well with active families. Independent but affectionate, this dog is not given to responding readily to requests.

ORIGINALLY BRED
for flushing and retrieving game.

SPECIAL CHARACTERISTICS
The Irish Setter is a very active, energetic and exuberant dog.

EXERCISE REQUIREMENTS
High. Needs long runs to burn off abundant energy.

COMMON ATTITUDE TO
OWNERS affectionate, easy-going
CHILDREN usually good, may knock over young children
OTHER PETS good, may chase
STRANGERS friendly
UNFAMILIAR DOGS friendly

PERFECT OWNER
Patient, affectionate, easy-going families with access to places where this dog can have plenty of freedom to run.

THINGS TO WATCH OUT FOR
Lack of exercise may lead to escapes, running away and hyperactivity.

⚠ This dog will bring in mud and dirt from outside on its feathers.

Irish Red and White Setter

biddable
good-natured
sensitive
affectionate

Size: 58–69 cm (23–27 in)
Weight: 27–32 kg (60–70 lb)
Coat: Fine, medium length with good feathering
Colour: Clearly particoloured, base colour pearl white, solid red patches
Lifespan: 12–13 years

The sensitive Irish Red and White Setter is reserved with strangers, but easy-going and affectionate to its family. Not known for being responsive to owners' requests, these dogs have a natural exuberance and energy that requires an outlet in the form of long walks and free running.

ORIGINALLY BRED
for flushing and retrieving game.

SPECIAL CHARACTERISTICS
This Setter is a very active and exuberant dog.

EXERCISE REQUIREMENTS
High. Full of energy and needs long runs.

COMMON ATTITUDE TO
OWNERS affectionate, easy-going
CHILDREN usually good, may knock over young children
OTHER PETS good, may chase
STRANGERS friendly or reserved
UNFAMILIAR DOGS friendly

PERFECT OWNER
Patient, gentle, affectionate, easy-going families with access to places where this dog can have plenty of freedom to run.

THINGS TO WATCH OUT FOR
Lack of exercise may lead to escapes, running away and hyperactivity. Can be shy with strangers unless well socialized.

⚠ This dog will bring in mud and dirt from outside on its feathers.

American Cocker Spaniel

happy
keen
affable
gentle
sometimes stubborn

Size: 34–39 cm (13½–15½ in)
Weight: 11–13 kg (24–28 lb)
Coat: Silky, medium length. Ears, chest, abdomen and legs well feathered
Colour: Black, buff, red, chocolate; black, red or chocolate with white
Lifespan: 12–14 years
Also known as Cocker Spaniel

American Cocker Spaniels are dogs for owners who like to groom, walk and play. They are happy little characters that can be unresponsive to requests at times, but they have a joyful, playful nature that easily wins people over.

ORIGINALLY BRED
for retrieving small game.

SPECIAL CHARACTERISTICS
This active and playful Spaniel is always busy.

EXERCISE REQUIREMENTS
High. Enjoys walks and plenty of play sessions.

COMMON ATTITUDE TO
OWNERS affectionate, loyal
CHILDREN usually good if well socialized
OTHER PETS good
STRANGERS friendly
UNFAMILIAR DOGS friendly

PERFECT OWNER
Active, affectionate families who enjoy energetic walks, playing and training and who have plenty of time and energy for coat care.

THINGS TO WATCH OUT FOR
Can be strong-willed and needs a determined owner. May display food- and possession-guarding. Dogs from some lines can be shy.

⚠ This Spaniel's coat will bring in mud and dirt from outside. Daily brushing and coat care are needed to keep it in good condition.

American Water Spaniel

active
alert
responsive
outgoing
enthusiastic
sensitive

Size: 36–46 cm (14–18 in)
Weight: 11–20 kg (24–44 lb)
Coat: Dense, curled
Colour: Liver, brown, dark chocolate
Lifespan: 12–14 years

American Water Spaniels are not very common, but they make enthusiastic, active pets. Finding an outlet for this dog's energy is essential, as is socializing it with other dogs and children.

ORIGINALLY BRED
for flushing and retrieving waterfowl.

SPECIAL CHARACTERISTICS
This active and playful Spaniel loves to swim.

EXERCISE REQUIREMENTS
High. Needs plenty of exercise to burn off abundant energy.

COMMON ATTITUDE TO
OWNERS affectionate, loyal
CHILDREN usually good when socialized with them
OTHER PETS good
STRANGERS friendly if well socialized
UNFAMILIAR DOGS can be problematic

PERFECT OWNER
Active, experienced families who enjoy energetic walks, playing and training, and who can provide plenty of early socialization with other dogs.

THINGS TO WATCH OUT FOR
Lack of exercise may lead to boisterousness, destructiveness and other behaviour problems. Has a tendency to jump up and is occasionally possessive over food and toys.

English Cocker Spaniel

**happy
affectionate
busy
exuberant
wilful**

Size: 38–41 cm (15–16 in)
Weight: 13–14.5 kg (28–32 lb)
Coat: Flat, silky, medium length. Well-feathered forelegs, body and hind legs
Colour: Black, liver or red; white with black, blue. liver or red markings, roaning or ticking
Lifespan: 12–14 years
Also known as Cocker Spaniel

As a puppy, the Cocker Spaniel is a cute bundle of fluff and many owners do not expect the wilful nature that appears later. Happy, exuberant and full of energy, they need plenty of exercise, together with strong-willed, active owners.

ORIGINALLY BRED
for flushing and retrieving small game.

SPECIAL CHARACTERISTICS
Energetic and playful, the Cocker Spaniel is interested in scents and independent when outside.

EXERCISE REQUIREMENTS
High. Needs energetic walks as well as play sessions.

COMMON ATTITUDE TO
OWNERS affectionate, loyal
CHILDREN usually tolerant if well socialized
OTHER PETS good if raised with them
STRANGERS friendly but reserved
UNFAMILIAR DOGS friendly

PERFECT OWNER
Active, strong-willed, sociable owner who enjoys energetic walks, playing and training.

THINGS TO WATCH OUT FOR
May be strong-willed with owners, especially in dogs of solid colours. May display possession-guarding.

⚠ The feathery coat will carry in mud and dirt from outside. The coat and long hairy ears require daily care to keep them in good healthy condition.

Clumber Spaniel

stoical
responsive
determined
reliable
kind
aloof
gentle
stubborn

Size: 48–51 cm (19–20 in)
Weight: 29–36 kg (64–80 lb)
Coat: Abundant, silky and straight. Legs and chest well feathered
Colour: Plain white body with lemon or orange markings
Lifespan: 12–13 years

Clumber Spaniels are calm and steady with enough stamina to keep going all day, every day. They are silent workers who are loving and affectionate to owners and friendly with visitors.

ORIGINALLY BRED
for tracking and retrieving game.

SPECIAL CHARACTERISTICS
This active Spaniel is interested in scents.

EXERCISE REQUIREMENTS
Medium. Plenty of stamina for long walks.

COMMON ATTITUDE TO
OWNERS affectionate, loyal
CHILDREN usually good
OTHER PETS good
STRANGERS friendly
UNFAMILIAR DOGS friendly

PERFECT OWNER
Steady, tolerant, social owner who enjoys long, quiet walks.

THINGS TO WATCH OUT FOR
Under-exercised Clumbers may be destructive.

Drooping lower eyelids are common in this breed and care is needed to prevent injury or infection.

Field Spaniel

docile
affectionate
enthusiastic
active
even-tempered
sensitive

Size: 43–46 cm (17–18 in)
Weight: 18–25 kg (40–55 lb)
Coat: Long, flat, glossy and silky in texture. Abundant feathering on chest, under body and behind legs
Colour: Black, liver or roan. Any one of these with tan markings
Lifespan: 12–13 years

Affectionate, happy and eager to please, Field Spaniels make entertaining, enthusiastic companions. They are easily trained and friendly and make ideal pets for active, playful families.

ORIGINALLY BRED
for retrieving game.

SPECIAL CHARACTERISTICS
The Field Spaniel is active, playful and enthusiastic.

EXERCISE REQUIREMENTS
High. Enjoys walks and games.

COMMON ATTITUDE TO
OWNERS affectionate, biddable
CHILDREN usually good
OTHER PETS good
STRANGERS friendly
UNFAMILIAR DOGS friendly

PERFECT OWNER
Active, affectionate, sociable families who enjoy energetic walks and playing games with their dog.

The silky coat requires daily grooming to keep it in good condition and the long hairy ears need special attention.

Recommended for energetic, first-time owners. It is important to find a healthy dog.

Irish Water Spaniel

affectionate
gentle
aloof
staunch
responsive
playful

Size: 51–58 cm (20–23 in)
Weight: 20–30 kg (44–66 lb)
Coat: Dense, tight, crisp ringlets
Colour: Rich, dark liver with
    purplish tint or bloom peculiar
    to the breed
Lifespan: 13 years

Playful and friendly, the Irish Water Spaniel makes a good pet for energetic families. Finding an outlet for their exuberant energy is important and swimming is high on the list of things they love to do.

ORIGINALLY BRED
for retrieving waterfowl.

SPECIAL CHARACTERISTICS
This Spaniel is active, interested in scents and loves to swim when given the opportunity.

EXERCISE REQUIREMENTS
High. Needs energetic walks and enjoys swimming.

COMMON ATTITUDE TO
OWNERS affectionate, responsive
CHILDREN usually good
OTHER PETS good
STRANGERS friendly
UNFAMILIAR DOGS friendly

PERFECT OWNER
Active, affectionate, sociable families who enjoy energetic walks and playing games with their dog.

Sussex Spaniel

kind
methodical
steady
determined

Sussex Spaniels are calm and steady workers with plenty of stamina to keep going all day. At home they are affectionate and friendly and are less exuberant and boisterous than many other gundogs.

Size: 38–41 cm (15–16 in)
Weight: 18–23 kg (40–50 lb)
Coat: Abundant and flat. Ears covered with soft, wavy hair. Forequarters and hindquarters moderately well feathered
Colour: Rich golden liver and hair shading to golden at tip
Lifespan: 11–12 years

ORIGINALLY BRED
for tracking and flushing game.

SPECIAL CHARACTERISTICS
Steady and active, this Spaniel is interested in scents.

EXERCISE REQUIREMENTS
Medium. Enjoys long walks as has plenty of stamina.

COMMON ATTITUDE TO
OWNERS affectionate, gentle
CHILDREN usually good
OTHER PETS good
STRANGERS friendly if well socialized
UNFAMILIAR DOGS friendly if well socialized

PERFECT OWNER
Steady, patient owner who enjoys long, quiet walks.

⚠ This dog's coat will bring in some mud and dirt from outside. Its long hairy ears need care. It has drooping lower eyelids that can result in eye infections.

English Springer Spaniel

active
enthusiastic
intense
friendly
happy
biddable

Size: 46–48 cm (18–19 in)
Weight: 16–20 kg (35–44 lb)
Coat: Close, straight, medium
length. Moderate feathering
on ears, forelegs, body and
hindquarters
Colour: Liver and white, black and
white, or either of these colours
with tan markings
Lifespan: 12–14 years

Vigorous, happy and enthusiastic, the English Springer Spaniel is renowned for its energetic, friendly approach to life. They like to be busy all day and make good pets for active, lively families.

ORIGINALLY BRED
for flushing (springing) and retrieving game.

SPECIAL CHARACTERISTICS
The English Springer Spaniel is energetic, playful and affectionate.

EXERCISE REQUIREMENTS
Very high. Has plenty of stamina for long walks.

COMMON ATTITUDE TO
OWNERS affectionate, active
CHILDREN usually good
OTHER PETS good
STRANGERS friendly
UNFAMILIAR DOGS friendly

PERFECT OWNER
Active, affectionate, sociable families who enjoy energetic walks and like to play and train every day.

⚠️ This dog's coat will bring in mud and dirt from outside and needs daily attention. Its long hairy ears also need care to keep them in good condition.

Welsh Springer Spaniel

strong
athletic
happy
very active
kind
responsive
determined

Size: 46-48 cm (18-19 in)
Weight: 16-20 kg (35-44 lb)
Coat: Straight or flat, silky texture, medium length. Forelegs and hind legs above hocks moderately feathered, ears and tail lightly feathered
Colour: Rich red and white only
Lifespan: 12-14 years

A little more wilful than the English, the Welsh Springer Spaniel has just as much energy and enthusiasm for life. Happy and active, they need plenty of play and long walks to prevent them being boisterous in the house.

ORIGINALLY BRED
for flushing (springing) and retrieving game

SPECIAL CHARACTERISTICS
This Spaniel has an active, playful and curious nature.

EXERCISE REQUIREMENTS
Very high. Enjoys long walks and plenty of play.

COMMON ATTITUDE TO OWNERS affectionate
CHILDREN friendly
OTHER PETS good
STRANGERS friendly
UNFAMILIAR DOGS friendly if well socialized

PERFECT OWNER
Active, experienced, strong-willed owner who enjoys long, energetic walks and who likes to play and train regularly.

THINGS TO WATCH OUT FOR
Can be strong-willed and needs a determined owner. Possessive aggression may be a problem and aggression towards other dogs may sometimes occur if lack of socialization.

⚠ This dog will bring in mud and dirt from outside on its feathers.

Afghan Hound

dignified
aloof
keen
graceful
elegant
sensitive

Size: 63–74 cm (25–29 in)
Weight: 23–27 kg (50–60 lb)
Coat: Very long and very fine
Colour: All colours acceptable
Lifespan: 12–14 years

Afghans look lovely when fully groomed, but it can take a long time every day to look after their coats. These elegant, independent dogs need regular energetic runs in a safe area.

ORIGINALLY BRED
for chasing large game such as deer and leopard by running ahead of hunters.

SPECIAL CHARACTERISTICS
This swift-moving dog has an independent character.

EXERCISE REQUIREMENTS
High. Needs energetic runs, although lazy at home.

COMMON ATTITUDE TO OWNERS affectionate, independent
CHILDREN usually tolerant, aloof
OTHER PETS may be problematic with small pets
STRANGERS indifferent, aloof
UNFAMILIAR DOGS playful

PERFECT OWNER
Patient owner who has time for the considerable coat maintenance, who wants a dog with an independent spirit and who can provide adequate space for several fast runs a day. For people who do not want a close bond with their dog.

THINGS TO WATCH OUT FOR
Prone to running away to chase other animals when off the lead.

⚠ Daily care of the coat is needed to keep it in good condition and de-tangling takes time.

Basenji

**quiet
independent
affectionate
aloof
alert
docile**

Size: 40–43 cm (16–17 in)
Weight: 9.5–11 kg (21–24 lb)
Coat: Short, sleek, very fine. Easily cleaned
Colour: Red and white, tan and white, black and white, brindle. White legs, blaze and white collar optional
Lifespan: 12 years

Developed as a hunting dog in the Congo, Basenjis do not bark, but instead make a yodelling sound when excited. Their coats are easy to keep clean, but they don't like to get wet, so avoid mud and puddles if you can. They are independent and have an aloof nature.

ORIGINALLY BRED
as a general-purpose hunting dog.

SPECIAL CHARACTERISTICS
This barkless breed is clean and curious.

EXERCISE REQUIREMENTS
Medium. Needs energetic walks.

COMMON ATTITUDE TO
OWNERS independent, spirited
CHILDREN usually good
OTHER PETS may be problematic with small pets
STRANGERS reserved, then friendly
UNFAMILIAR DOGS playful

PERFECT OWNER
Easy-going owner who requires an independent, sweet-natured, cat-like dog to take for energetic walks.

THINGS TO WATCH OUT FOR
May be difficult to control on walks as these dogs are independent thinkers and are likely to get sidetracked by smells and things to chase.

Basset Fauve de Bretagne

courageous
hardy
lively
friendly
amiable
tenacious

Size: 32–38 cm (12½–15 in)
Weight: 16–18 kg (35–40 lb)
Coat: Very harsh, dense and flat
Colour: Fawn, gold-wheaten or red-wheaten
Lifespan: 12–14 years

Easy-going and cheerful, the Basset Fauve de Bretagne thrives on exercise and needs plenty of long, active walks. This dog is affectionate and friendly, but independent, with a mind and opinion of its own.

ORIGINALLY BRED
for hunting rabbits and hares in a pack ahead of hunters on foot.

SPECIAL CHARACTERISTICS
An active, curious and very friendly hound.

EXERCISE REQUIREMENTS
Medium. Needs regular, long walks.

COMMON ATTITUDE TO
OWNERS affectionate, independent
CHILDREN usually good
OTHER PETS usually good, may chase
STRANGERS friendly
UNFAMILIAR DOGS playful

PERFECT OWNER
Easy-going, active, affectionate owner who enjoys long, energetic walks with this cheerful, independent little dog.

THINGS TO WATCH OUT FOR
A strong desire to hunt means these dog may be difficult to control on walks.

Basset Hound

placid
affectionate
stubborn
gentle

Size: 33–38 cm (13–15 in)
Weight: 18–27 kg (40–60 lb)
Coat: Smooth, short
Colour: Generally black, white and tan (tricolour), lemon and white (bicolour)
Lifespan: 12 years

Basset Hounds are placid and calm and friendly to all, but can be stubbornly independent when asked to do something. Affectionate and placid, they are very interested in scents when outside, which can make walks difficult.

ORIGINALLY BRED
for hunting rabbits and hares.

SPECIAL CHARACTERISTICS
An independent character, the Bassett is particularly interested in scents.

EXERCISE REQUIREMENTS
Medium. Needs steady exercise.

COMMON ATTITUDE TO
OWNERS affectionate, independent
CHILDREN usually good
OTHER PETS good
STRANGERS friendly
UNFAMILIAR DOGS friendly

PERFECT OWNER
Patient, easy-going owner who will enjoy the independent character of these friendly but solemn hounds.

Breeders have exaggerated the ear length of this dog so special care is needed to ensure they are kept clean and free from damage.

⚠️ This dog has drooping lower eyelids that can result in eye infections. Ears and low-slung body will carry dirt into the house. Heavy jowls cause lack of saliva control.

Beagle

bold
friendly
very active
determined
alert
curious
amiable

Size: 33–40 cm (13–16 in)
Weight: 8–14 kg (18–31 lb)
Coat: Short, dense
Colour: Any recognized hound colour other than liver. Tip of tail white
Lifespan: 13 years

Happy and full of life, Beagles have a lovely, tolerant nature. They also have an independent spirit and their strong desire to follow a scent can make them resistant to their owners' calls on walks.

ORIGINALLY BRED
for hunting hares and rabbits in packs, with hunters following on foot.

SPECIAL CHARACTERISTICS
Active and independent, the Beagle is very interested in scents.

EXERCISE REQUIREMENTS
High. Needs plenty of long and energetic walks.

COMMON ATTITUDE TO
OWNERS independent, affectionate
CHILDREN usually good
OTHER PETS good, but may chase
STRANGERS friendly
UNFAMILIAR DOGS friendly

PERFECT OWNER
Easy-going, affectionate owner who enjoys energetic walks.

THINGS TO WATCH OUT FOR
Can take off after scents or on a chase, making them difficult to control on walks. Can be boisterous and vocal if bored.

Bloodhound

affectionate
friendly
reserved
sensitive
affable
stubborn

Size: 58–69 cm (23–27 in)	
Weight: 36–50 kg (80–110 lb)	
Coat: Smooth, short	
Colour: Black and tan, liver and tan (red and tan) or red	
Lifespan: 10 years	

Bloodhounds are gentle giants. Their ability to follow a scent is legendary and they need very long walks on a lead or in a safe area. Affectionate and good-natured, they can be stubborn and independent when it suits them.

ORIGINALLY BRED
to track scent trails.

SPECIAL CHARACTERISTICS
The Bloodhound has been bred to be very interested in scents.

EXERCISE REQUIREMENTS
Low. Will, however, need long walks.

COMMON ATTITUDE TO
OWNERS independent, affectionate
CHILDREN usually good, may knock over young children
OTHER PETS good
STRANGERS friendly
UNFAMILIAR DOGS friendly

PERFECT OWNER
Easy-going owner who has enough space for a large dog with a sweeping tail and who enjoys long walks at the end of a lead attached to a giant sniffing machine.

THINGS TO WATCH OUT FOR
May be difficult to control on walks because they are unlikely to respond once they are following a scent trail.

⚠ This dog's large loose jowls can lead to problems with saliva control.

Black and Tan Coonhound

**very active
alert
mellow
gentle
watchful
curious
affectionate**

Size: 58–69 cm (23–27 in)
Weight: 23–34 kg (50–75 lb)
Coat: Smooth, short, glossy
Colour: Black and tan
Lifespan: 11–12 years

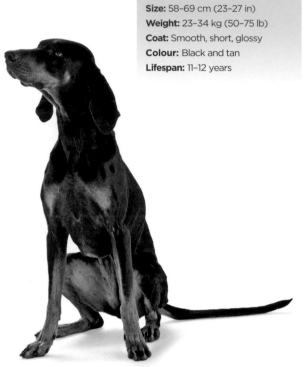

Gentle, good-natured, affectionate Black and Tan Coonhounds are easy-going in the house. Outside they are independent, scent-orientated hunters and need long lead walks or a safe area where they can run free.

ORIGINALLY BRED
to 'tree' raccoons or opossum until the hunter could catch up on foot.

SPECIAL CHARACTERISTICS
This hound is very interested in scents and hunting.

EXERCISE REQUIREMENTS
High. Needs plenty of long walks, but little exercise at home.

COMMON ATTITUDE TO
OWNERS independent, affectionate
CHILDREN usually good
OTHER PETS may be problematic with small pets

STRANGERS accepting
UNFAMILIAR DOGS friendly

PERFECT OWNER
Easy-going owner who wants a large, independent dog to take for long walks.

THINGS TO WATCH OUT FOR
May be difficult to control on walks because they are unlikely to respond once they are following a scent trail.

Extra long ears frame this dog's face and need special care.

Borzoi

sensitive
alert
aloof
gentle
amenable

Aloof, sensitive and elegant, the Borzoi is a gentle aristocrat. Independent and not very responsive to owners' wishes, outside they can transform Into graceful running machines when allowed off-lead in safe areas, and enjoy chasing things they shouldn't.

Size: 68–74 cm (27–29 in)
Weight: 35–48 kg (77–105 lb)
Coat: Silky, flat, wavy or rather curly, long on body
Colour: Any
Lifespan: 11–13 years

ORIGINALLY BRED
by the Russian aristocracy to course wolves in pairs.

SPECIAL CHARACTERISTICS
This elegant hound likes to chase.

EXERCISE REQUIREMENTS
Low. Needs brisk walks.

COMMON ATTITUDE TO
OWNERS affectionate, independent
CHILDREN will tolerate
OTHER PETS good, may chase
STRANGERS indifferent
UNFAMILIAR DOGS friendly

PERFECT OWNER
Gentle, easy-going owner who will enjoy taking this elegant, independent dog for brisk walks.

THINGS TO WATCH OUT FOR
May decide to chase instead of responding to owner's call.

Borzois have a long distinctive Roman nose and narrow head.

Dachshund

Dachshunds are gentle and sweet-natured. They like to be with people and their small size makes them easy to exercise. They can also be wilful and independent, preferring to do their own thing rather than comply with requests.

Size: 20–25 cm (8–10 in)
Weight: 6.5–11.5 kg (14–25 lb)
Coat: Soft and straight long hair
Colour: Any, except white
Lifespan: 14–16 years

Long Haired

good-tempered
gentle
courageous
docile
outgoing
versatile

ORIGINALLY BRED
to dig out badgers and foxes from their earths.

SPECIAL CHARACTERISTICS
Independent and inquisitive, the Dachshund likes to dig.

EXERCISE REQUIREMENTS
Low. Accepts exercise readily, but is not over-demanding.

COMMON ATTITUDE TO
OWNERS independent, affectionate
CHILDREN usually good
OTHER PETS may be problematic with small pets
STRANGERS friendly
UNFAMILIAR DOGS friendly

PERFECT OWNER
Easy-going owner who will enjoy this independent, tough little dog and who is prepared to groom its long hair daily.

⚠ This dog's long hair will bring in mud and dirt from outside. Daily grooming is needed to keep the coat in good condition.

Dachshund

Smooth Haired

gentle
courageous
docile
outgoing
versatile
good-tempered

Size: 20–25 cm (8–10 in)
Weight: 6.5–11.5 kg (14–25 lb)
Coat: Dense, short, smooth
Colour: Any, except white
Lifespan: 14–16 years

ORIGINALLY BRED
to dig out badgers and foxes
from their earths.

SPECIAL CHARACTERISTICS
Independent and inquisitive,
the Dachshund likes to dig.

EXERCISE REQUIREMENTS
Low. Accepts exercise readily,
but is not over-demanding.

COMMON ATTITUDE TO
OWNERS independent,
affectionate
CHILDREN usually good
OTHER PETS may be problematic
with small pets
STRANGERS friendly
UNFAMILIAR DOGS friendly

PERFECT OWNER
Easy-going owner who will
enjoy this independent, tough
little dog.

Dachshund

Wire Haired

good-tempered
gentle
courageous
docile
outgoing
versatile

Size: 20–25 cm (8–10 in)
Weight: 6.5–11.5 kg (14–25 lb)
Coat: Short, straight, harsh with dense undercoat
Colour: Any, except white
Lifespan: 14–16 years

ORIGINALLY BRED
to dig out badgers and foxes from their earths.

SPECIAL CHARACTERISTICS
Independent and inquisitive, the Dachshund likes to dig.

EXERCISE REQUIREMENTS
Low. Accepts exercise readily, but is not over-demanding.

COMMON ATTITUDE TO
OWNERS independent, affectionate
CHILDREN usually good
OTHER PETS may be problematic with small pets
STRANGERS friendly
UNFAMILIAR DOGS friendly

PERFECT OWNER
Easy-going owner who will enjoy this independent, tough little dog.

⚠ This dog's beard and whiskers will require frequent washing to keep them sweet-smelling.

Dachshund

Miniature Long Haired

gentle
courageous
docile
outgoing
versatile
good-tempered

Size: 13–16 cm (5–6 in)
Weight: 4–5 kg (9–11 lb)
Coat: Soft and straight long hair
Colour: Any, except white
Lifespan: 14 16 years

ORIGINALLY BRED
to dig out rabbits from
their earths.

SPECIAL CHARACTERISTICS
Independent and inquisitive,
the Dachshund likes to dig.

EXERCISE REQUIREMENTS
Low. Accepts exercise readily,
but is not over-demanding.

COMMON ATTITUDE TO
OWNERS independent,
affectionate
CHILDREN usually good, may be
injured by boisterous children
OTHER PETS may be problematic
with small pets

STRANGERS friendly
UNFAMILIAR DOGS friendly, may
be injured by boisterous dogs

PERFECT OWNER
Easy-going owner who will enjoy
this independent, tough little
dog and who is prepared for the
daily grooming required.

⚠ This dog's long hair
will bring in mud and
dirt from outside, so daily
grooming is needed to keep
it in good condition.

Dachshund

Miniature Smooth Haired

gentle
courageous
docile
outgoing
versatile
good-tempered

Size: 13–16 cm (5–6 in)
Weight: 4–5 kg (9–11 lb)
Coat: Dense, short, smooth
Colour: Any, except white
Lifespan: 14–16 years

ORIGINALLY BRED
to dig out rabbits from
their earths.

SPECIAL CHARACTERISTICS
Independent and inquisitive,
the Dachshund likes to dig.

EXERCISE REQUIREMENTS
Low. Accepts exercise readily,
but is not over-demanding.

COMMON ATTITUDE TO
OWNERS independent,
affectionate
CHILDREN usually good, may be
injured by boisterous children
OTHER PETS may be problematic
with small pets
STRANGERS friendly
UNFAMILIAR DOGS friendly, may
be injured by boisterous dogs

PERFECT OWNER
Easy-going owner who will
enjoy this independent, tough
little dog.

Dachshund

Miniature Wire Haired

gentle
courageous
docile
outgoing
versatile
good-tempered

Size: 13–16 cm (5–6 in)
Weight: 4–5 kg (9–11 lb)
Coat: Short, straight, harsh with dense undercoat
Colour: Any, except white
Lifespan: 14–16 years

ORIGINALLY BRED
to dig out rabbits from their earths.

SPECIAL CHARACTERISTICS
Independent and inquisitive, the Dachshund likes to dig.

EXERCISE REQUIREMENTS
Low. Accepts exercise readily, but is not over-demanding.

COMMON ATTITUDE TO
OWNERS independent, affectionate
CHILDREN usually good, may be injured by boisterous children
OTHER PETS may be problematic with small pets
STRANGERS friendly
UNFAMILIAR DOGS friendly, may be injured by boisterous dogs

PERFECT OWNER
Easy-going owner who will enjoy this independent, tough little dog.

⚠ This dog's beard and whiskers will require frequent washing to keep them sweet-smelling.

Deerhound

gentle
calm
friendly
good-tempered
easy-going
independent

Size: 71–76 cm (28–30 in)
Weight: 36.5–45.5 kg (80–100 lb)
Coat: Shaggy, but not overcoated
Colour: Dark blue-grey, darker and lighter greys; brindles and yellows, sandy-red or red fawns with black points
Lifespan: 10–11 years
Also known as Scottish Deerhound

Deerhounds enjoy long runs and are fast and elegant in motion. Independent and deaf to commands once on a chase, these sensitive, gentle dogs are calm and quiet in the house.

ORIGINALLY BRED
for hunting deer in forests.

SPECIAL CHARACTERISTICS
The inquisitive Deerhound likes to run fast for short periods.

EXERCISE REQUIREMENTS
Low. Needs regular fast runs, but is quiet at home.

COMMON ATTITUDE TO
OWNERS independent, affectionate
CHILDREN usually good, will tolerate
OTHER PETS may be problematic with small pets
STRANGERS reserved but friendly
UNFAMILIAR DOGS friendly

PERFECT OWNER
Gentle owner who will enjoy this independent, calm, graceful dog.

THINGS TO WATCH OUT FOR
May be difficult to control on walks.

Elkhound

active
vocal
bold
independent
outgoing

Size: 49–52 cm (19–20½ in)
Weight: 20–23 kg (44–50 lb)
Coat: Thick, short to medium length
Colour: Various shades of grey
Lifespan: 12–13 years

Unlike many hounds, Elkhounds are vocal and strong-willed. They are independent, active hunters and own a coat that could protect them from the worst of weathers, but which can be problematic in a warm house and requires daily care.

ORIGINALLY BRED
to hunt elk, lynx, wolves and small game.

SPECIAL CHARACTERISTICS
The Elkhound is playful, active and inquisitive.

EXERCISE REQUIREMENTS
High. Very active and needs plenty of exercise.

COMMON ATTITUDE TO
OWNERS independent, loyal
CHILDREN usually good
OTHER PETS may be problematic with small pets
STRANGERS reserved, need to be well socialized
UNFAMILIAR DOGS can be difficult with dogs they live with

PERFECT OWNER
Active, easy-going owner with tolerant neighbours who likes the Elkhound's independent, extrovert nature and who can provide plenty of exercise and grooming.

THINGS TO WATCH OUT FOR
May bark excessively. Lack of exercise may lead to digging or escaping.

The Elkhound's bushy tail is tightly curled over the back.

⚠ This dog sheds loose hair in the house and will need daily grooming.

Finnish Spitz

alert
lively
friendly
independent
eager
courageous
strong-willed

Size: 39–50 cm (15½–19½ in)
Weight: 14–16 kg (31–35 lb)
Coat: Thick, short to medium length
Colour: Reddish-brown or gold
Lifespan: 13 years
In the 'Non-sporting' class in the USA

Clean and cat-like, the Finnish Spitz is an eager, energetic, independent companion for vigorous walks. Active and curious, they are alert and very vocal and make good watchdogs.

ORIGINALLY BRED
for flushing birds, squirrels and martens into trees, then barking continually while waiting for the hunter.

SPECIAL CHARACTERISTICS
The Finnish Spitz is active and curious, with a tendency to bark.

EXERCISE REQUIREMENTS
High. Needs energetic walks.

COMMON ATTITUDE TO
OWNERS independent, wilful
CHILDREN usually good

OTHER PETS may be problematic with small pets
STRANGERS reserved, good watchdog
UNFAMILIAR DOGS friendly

PERFECT OWNER
Active, easy-going owner who has tolerant neighbours and who will enjoy vigorous walks with an energetic, independent pet.

THINGS TO WATCH OUT FOR
May bark excessively. Owners need to discourage this during puppyhood.

⚠️ The thick coat will need daily grooming to keep it in good condition, but these dogs like to keep themselves clean.

Foxhound (English)

stamina
endurance
strong desire to hunt
friendly

Size: 53–69 cm (21–27 in)
Weight: 25–34 kg (55–75 lb)
Coat: Short and dense
Colour: Any combination of black, white and tan
Lifespan: 11 years

Bred to hunt in packs, Foxhounds are happiest with constant company. Large and eager, they investigate everything and anything, often at the expense of household furnishings. Their energy and stamina is more than the average pet owner needs and wants and exercising these active, independent hunters can be difficult. American Foxhounds are taller and lighter-boned than English Foxhounds.

ORIGINALLY BRED
to hunt foxes in a pack with huntsmen on horseback.

SPECIAL CHARACTERISTICS
Active and very inquisitive, the Foxhound is also interested in scents.

EXERCISE REQUIREMENTS
High. Needs a great deal of exercise to burn off energy.

COMMON ATTITUDE TO
OWNERS independent, affectionate
CHILDREN usually good
OTHER PETS due to a high prey drive and chase instincts, may cause harm to small pets.
STRANGERS friendly
UNFAMILIAR DOGS friendly

PERFECT OWNER
Owner with facilities and land to keep a working pack, or very tolerant, non-house-proud, active, energetic pet owner with access to safe places to exercise.

THINGS TO WATCH OUT FOR
Tends to run off on walks, escape from the garden or yard and may be destructive if bored or under-exercised. May be problematic if left alone at home.

Grand Bleu de Gascogne

gentle
active
kind
methodical
determined
confident

Size: 60–70 cm (23½–27½ in)
Weight: 32–35 kg (70–77 lb)
Coat: Smooth, short
Colour: Black marked on a white base, but covered entirely with black mottling, which gives a blue appearance
Lifespan: 12–14 years

Grand Bleu de Gascognes are large and powerful, but gentle and friendly. With enough stamina to keep running all day, long walks in safe areas are essential. At home, these independent hounds are calm, affectionate and placid.

ORIGINALLY BRED
to trail wolves, wild boar and deer for hunters.

SPECIAL CHARACTERISTICS
This active dog is very interested in scents.

EXERCISE REQUIREMENTS
High. Needs plenty of exercise outdoors, calm at home.

COMMON ATTITUDE TO
OWNERS independent, affectionate
CHILDREN usually good
OTHER PETS good, may chase
STRANGERS friendly, can be reserved
UNFAMILIAR DOGS friendly

PERFECT OWNER
Active, easy-going owner who enjoys long walks with a large dog that is interested in scent trails.

THINGS TO WATCH OUT FOR
May be difficult to control on walks because they are unlikely to respond once they are following a scent trail.

Greyhound

even-tempered affectionate calm gentle

Size: 69–76 cm (27–30 in)
Weight: 27–32 kg (60–70 lb)
Coat: Fine and close
Colour: Black, white, red, blue, tawn, fallow, brindle, or any of these colours broken with white
Lifespan: 11–12 years

The fastest animal on earth apart from the cheetah, Greyhounds run in short bursts of breakneck speed. At home, these gentle, affectionate pets are happy to lie around all day, but prefer the sofa to the floor, where they can be more comfortable.

ORIGINALLY BRED
for coursing hares.

SPECIAL CHARACTERISTICS
The Greyhound loves to chase, and is fast enough to catch most animals.

EXERCISE REQUIREMENTS
Medium. Needs off-lead running.

COMMON ATTITUDE TO
OWNERS independent, affectionate
CHILDREN usually good, usually tolerant
OTHER PETS may be problematic with small pets, may chase and injure cats unless raised with them
STRANGERS friendly
UNFAMILIAR DOGS friendly, may chase small dog

PERFECT OWNER
Gentle, easy-going owner who enjoys frequent short, energetic walks and who lives near to safe, open areas where these elegant dogs can run free.

THINGS TO WATCH OUT FOR
May be difficult to control on walks. Most Greyhounds will chase if given the chance and may cause harm to small animals if they catch them.

⚠️ This dog has a fine coat and may feel the cold. It prefers soft bedding.

Basset Griffon Vendeen (Petit & Grand)

happy
extrovert
bold
independent
willing to please

Size: Petit: 33–38 cm (13–15 in)
Grand: 38–42 cm (15–16½ in)
Weight: Petit: 14–18 kg (31–40 lb)
Grand: 18–20 kg (40–44 lb)
Coat: Rough, long, harsh with thick undercoat
Colour: White with any combination of lemon, orange, tricolour or grizzle markings
Lifespan: 12 years

The good-natured, extrovert Basset Griffon Vendeen is friendly and willing to please. Walks can quickly turn into a hunt unless exercise is restricted to lead-walking or safe areas.

ORIGINALLY BRED
to flush out rabbits and hares.

SPECIAL CHARACTERISTICS
Very active, this hound has a special interest in scents.

EXERCISE REQUIREMENTS
High. Enjoys long walks.

COMMON ATTITUDE TO
OWNERS affectionate, independent streak
CHILDREN usually good
OTHER PETS good
STRANGERS friendly
UNFAMILIAR DOGS friendly

PERFECT OWNER
Active, easy-going owner who enjoys plenty of energetic walks.

THINGS TO WATCH OUT FOR
May be difficult to control on walks because they are unlikely to respond once they are scenting or chasing. Barking may be a problem. Lack of exercise may result in digging and other behaviour problems.

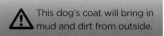
⚠ This dog's coat will bring in mud and dirt from outside.

Hamiltonstövare

gentle
even-tempered
happy
exuberant
extrovert
strong-willed

Size: 46–60 cm (18–23½ in)
Weight: 23–27 kg (50–60 lb)
Coat: Smooth, short
Colour: Black and brown with white markings
Lifespan: 12–13 years

Bred from Foxhounds and Harriers, the Hamiltonstövare was originally called the Swedish Foxhound. Easy-going and friendly at home, these dogs quickly turn into determined hunters outside that will efficiently follow a scent or chase prey to the exclusion of all else.

ORIGINALLY BRED
for hunting hares and foxes, finding and flushing game.

SPECIAL CHARACTERISTICS
Active and interested in scents, the Hamiltonstövare also has a strong desire to hunt.

EXERCISE REQUIREMENTS
High. Active and energetic outside, lazy indoors.

COMMON ATTITUDE TO OWNERS independent, affectionate

CHILDREN usually good, usually tolerant
OTHER PETS may be problematic with small pets
STRANGERS friendly
UNFAMILIAR DOGS friendly

PERFECT OWNER
Easy-going owner who is able to provide plenty of exercise for this active, energetic dog.

THINGS TO WATCH OUT FOR
A strong desire to hunt may make it difficult to find safe places to exercise this dog. Lack of exercise may lead to destructiveness and other behaviour problems.

Harrier

active independent gregarious

Size:	46–56 cm (18–22 in)
Weight:	22–27 kg (48–60 lb)
Coat:	Smooth, short
Colour:	Any
Lifespan:	10–12 years

Bred to hunt in a pack, Harriers love company and are affectionate and friendly. They have tremendous energy and a strong desire to hunt and for this reason are less than ideal pets unless owners have the facilities to exercise them safely.

ORIGINALLY BRED
to hunt hares in a pack with hunters on foot.

SPECIAL CHARACTERISTICS
The active Harrier has a strong desire to hunt and is interested in scents.

EXERCISE REQUIREMENTS
High. Needs plenty of space to run off abundant energy.

COMMON ATTITUDE TO
OWNERS independent, affectionate
CHILDREN usually good
OTHER PETS may be problematic with small pets
STRANGERS friendly
UNFAMILIAR DOGS friendly

PERFECT OWNER
Owner who has facilities and enough land to keep a working pack, or experienced, easy-going owner who will run or bike with the Harrier every day and will appreciate this dog's independent nature.

THINGS TO WATCH OUT FOR
May be difficult to control on walks because it is unlikely to respond once it is scenting or chasing. Lack of exercise may lead to destructiveness and other behaviour problems. May be problematic if left alone at home.

Ibizan Hound

reserved dignified independent alert affectionate

Size: 56–74 cm (22–29 in)
Weight: 19–25 kg (42–55 lb)
Coat: Smooth, close, dense. Can also be wiry or long
Colour: White, chestnut or lion solid colour, or any combination of these
Lifespan: 12 years

Sensitive, gentle and loyal, Ibizan Hounds make elegant, independent pets. They are built for speed so large and safe exercise areas are essential for these alert, enthusiastic chasers.

ORIGINALLY BRED
to course rabbits and hares.

SPECIAL CHARACTERISTICS
This hound likes to run fast, jump and chase.

EXERCISE REQUIREMENTS
High. Needs to run outside, but lazy at home.

COMMON ATTITUDE TO
OWNERS independent, affectionate
CHILDREN usually good, usually tolerant
OTHER PETS may be problematic with small pets unless raised with them
STRANGERS reserved
UNFAMILIAR DOGS friendly

PERFECT OWNER
Easy-going owner who can offer frequent walks to a safe place for off-lead running and who will enjoy this dog's gentle, independent spirit.

THINGS TO WATCH OUT FOR
May be difficult to control on walks .

Irish Wolfhound

gentle kind friendly calm patient

Size: 71–80 cm (28–31½ in)
Weight: 41–55 kg (90–120 lb)
Coat: Rough and harsh
Colour: Grey, brindle, red, black, pure white, fawn, wheaten and steel grey
Lifespan: 8–10 years

These gentle giants are calm, affectionate and friendly. Once bred by royalty to hunt wolves, they are fast runners outside and need fast runs in a safe area. At home they are relaxed and independent.

ORIGINALLY BRED
to hunt wolves in packs.

SPECIAL CHARACTERISTICS
The Irish Wolfhound likes to run fast for short periods and to chase.

EXERCISE REQUIREMENTS
Medium. Content to be lazy when at home.

COMMON ATTITUDE TO
OWNERS independent, affectionate
CHILDREN usually good, may knock over young children
OTHER PETS may be problematic with small pets
STRANGERS friendly
UNFAMILIAR DOGS friendly

PERFECT OWNER
Strong, easy-going, affectionate owner who has enough space to accommodate this giant and who can provide a safe area for daily off-lead running.

THINGS TO WATCH OUT FOR
May be difficult to control on walks if they see something to chase.

Lurcher

gentle affectionate even-tempered

Size: 51–61 cm (20–24 in)
Weight: 12.5–14.5 kg (27½–32 lb)
Coat: Wiry or smooth
Colour: Any
Lifespan: 14 years

Bred originally for hare coursing, Lurchers have a combination of the speed of the Greyhound and the reactivity of the Collie. They are gentle, affectionate and independent at home, but quickly move in for the chase when out on a walk.

ORIGINALLY BRED
for coursing hares.

SPECIAL CHARACTERISTICS
Fast enough to catch most animals, the Lurcher loves to chase.

EXERCISE REQUIREMENTS
Medium. Needs off-lead running.

COMMON ATTITUDE TO
OWNERS independent, affectionate
CHILDREN usually good, usually tolerant
OTHER PETS may be problematic with small pets, may chase and injure cats unless raised with them
STRANGERS friendly
UNFAMILIAR DOGS friendly, may chase small dogs

PERFECT OWNER
Gentle, easy-going owner who enjoys frequent energetic walks and who lives near to safe, open areas where these elegant dogs can run free.

THINGS TO WATCH OUT FOR
May be difficult to control on walks. Most Lurchers will chase if given the chance and may cause harm to small animals if they catch them.

Norwegian Lundehund

agile
alert
energetic
lively
responsive

Size: 32–38 cm (12½–15 in)
Weight: 6–7 kg (13–15½ lb)
Coat: Dense, rough outer coat with soft undercoat
Colour: Reddish-brown to fallow with black tips to hairs preferred, black or grey, all with white markings. White with dark markings
Lifespan: 12 years

Bred to collect puffins from cliff nests, these unusual dogs have extra toes to help give a better grip on the rocks. They are also more agile than most with a very flexible neck, and are lively, affectionate and playful.

ORIGINALLY BRED
in northen Norway to collect puffins from nests on cliffs.

SPECIAL CHARACTERISTICS
This playful dog has at least six toes on each foot with big pads and double dewclaws to give it better grip.

EXERCISE REQUIREMENTS
Medium. Enjoys playing.

COMMON ATTITUDE TO
OWNERS affectionate
CHILDREN usually good, playful
OTHER PETS good
STRANGERS friendly
UNFAMILIAR DOGS friendly

PERFECT OWNER
Active, easy-going affectionate owner who likes to play with their dog.

THINGS TO WATCH OUT FOR
May be difficult to housetrain.

Otterhound

cheerful
affectionate
even-tempered
independent
amiable

Size: 61–69 cm (24–27 in)
Weight: 30–55 kg (66–120 lb)
Coat: Long, dense, rough, harsh
Colour: Any hound colour
Lifespan: 12 years

These happy, shaggy dogs
are good swimmers and have
a coat that keeps out the cold.
Otterhounds are good-natured
and amiable, but following scents
and hunting are high on the list of
things they like to do best.

ORIGINALLY BRED
to hunt otters.

SPECIAL CHARACTERISTICS
Active and interested in scents,
the Otterhound is happy to
completely submerge in water.

EXERCISE REQUIREMENTS
High. Enjoys running and
swimming.

COMMON ATTITUDE TO
OWNERS independent,
affectionate
CHILDREN usually good, usually
tolerant
OTHER PETS may be problematic
with small pets
STRANGERS friendly
UNFAMILIAR DOGS friendly

PERFECT OWNER
Active, easy-going, affectionate
owner who is able to provide
safe places for this dog to run
and swim.

THINGS TO WATCH OUT FOR
May be difficult to control
on walks because they are
unlikely to respond once they
are scenting or chasing.

Pharaoh Hound

alert
aloof
friendly
affectionate

Size: 53–63 cm (21–25 in)
Weight: 20–25 kg (44–55 lb)
Coat: Short and glossy
Colour: Tan or rich tan
Lifespan: 12–14 years

Sensitive and gentle, the Pharaoh Hound has origins that can be traced back to the Ancient Egyptians. Their hunting and chasing instincts are still strong so care is needed on walks. Aloof and independent, they will be affectionate and friendly but on their own terms.

ORIGINALLY BRED
for hunting using sight, sound and smell.

SPECIAL CHARACTERISTICS
This dog has a curious nature. It is a keen, energetic hunter, and will blush when excited.

EXERCISE REQUIREMENTS
Very high. Needs to run and chase.

COMMON ATTITUDE TO OWNERS independent, affectionate
CHILDREN usually good
OTHER PETS may be problematic with small pets
STRANGERS reserved but friendly
UNFAMILIAR DOGS friendly

PERFECT OWNER
Active easy-going owner who has time and access to safe places to exercise this energetic, independent dog daily.

THINGS TO WATCH OUT FOR
May be difficult to control on walks because they are unlikely to respond once they are scenting or chasing. Some dogs bark excessively.

Plott Hound

affectionate
independent
easy-going
energetic

Size: 51–61 cm (20–24 in)
Weight: 20–25 kg (44–55 lb)
Coat: Short and glossy
Colour: Brindle or blue
Lifespan: 12–13 years
In 'Miscellaneous' class in the USA

Plott Hounds are strong, vigorous hunters. Affectionate, friendly and easy-going at home, they are very active and need plenty of free-running exercise in safe areas to keep them happy.

ORIGINALLY BRED
to 'tree' bears and raccoons until the hunters arrived.

SPECIAL CHARACTERISTICS
This very active hound is interested in scents and hunting.

EXERCISE REQUIREMENTS
High. Loves to run freely, quieter at home.

COMMON ATTITUDE TO
OWNERS independent, affectionate
CHILDREN usually good
OTHER PETS may be problematic with small pets
STRANGERS friendly
UNFAMILIAR DOGS friendly

PERFECT OWNER
Active, easy-going owner who enjoys energetic walks in areas where this independent hunter can run loose safely.

THINGS TO WATCH OUT FOR
May be difficult to control on walks because they are unlikely to respond once they are scenting or chasing. Can be noisy.

Rhodesian Ridgeback

dignified
aloof
strong-willed
loyal
confident

Size: 61–69 cm (24–27 in)
Weight: 30–39 kg (66–86 lb)
Coat: Short and dense
Colour: Light wheaten to red wheaten
Lifespan: 12 years

Rhodesian Ridgebacks are strong and courageous and like to chase. They have a discerning, independent character and are prone to ignoring owners' requests unless they see a reason for compliance.

ORIGINALLY BRED
in Africa to track lions and hold them at bay while hunters arrived.

SPECIAL CHARACTERISTICS
The Rhodesian Ridgeback is a powerful dog that likes to chase. It has a distinctive ridge of hair on its back that gives it its name.

EXERCISE REQUIREMENTS
High. Lazy at home.

COMMON ATTITUDE TO OWNERS independent, affectionate
CHILDREN usually good
OTHER PETS may be problematic with small pets, will chase cats unless raised with them
STRANGERS discerning, intuitive
UNFAMILIAR DOGS good if well socialized

PERFECT OWNER
Experienced, strong-willed, active owner who has safe places to walk this independent, powerful hunter.

THINGS TO WATCH OUT FOR
May take off hunting on walks. They have a strong and independent nature and need plenty of socialization and training when young.

Saluki

dignified
sensitive
gentle
independent

Size: 58–71 cm (23–28 in)
Weight: 14–25 kg (31–55 lb)
Coat: Smooth, soft silky texture
Colour: Any other than brindle
Lifespan: 12 years

Elegant, gentle, sensitive Salukis are aloof and independent by nature. They are very fast runners and care is needed to exercise them in places where they can use up their energy, but where they cannot chase other animals.

ORIGINALLY BRED
to hunt gazelle.

SPECIAL CHARACTERISTICS
The Saluki is a fast runner and loves to chase.

EXERCISE REQUIREMENTS
High. Enjoys long runs, but quiet at home.

COMMON ATTITUDE TO
OWNERS independent, not tactile
CHILDREN will tolerate, but may dislike young children
OTHER PETS may be problematic with small pets
STRANGERS reserved
UNFAMILIAR DOGS reserved but friendly

PERFECT OWNER
Active, easy-going owner who can find safe places for this active breed to run free and who will enjoy their independent, aloof nature.

THINGS TO WATCH OUT FOR
Will chase anything that looks like prey.

Segugio Italiano

gentle
affectionate
even-tempered

Size: 48–59 cm (19–23 in)
Weight: 18–28 kg (40–62 lb)
Coat: Smooth, thick, shiny. Coarse haired: harsh, dense, wiry
Colour: Black and tan, any shade from deep red to wheaten
Lifespan: 12–13 years

A popular hunting dog in Italy, the Segugio Italiano is friendly and easy-going with people. Independent but affectionate, these dogs need long, active walks to use up their high energy reserves.

ORIGINALLY BRED
to hunt large game by sight and scent.

SPECIAL CHARACTERISTICS
This active dog is very interested in scents.

EXERCISE REQUIREMENTS
High. Enjoys long walks.

COMMON ATTITUDE TO
OWNERS independent, affectionate
CHILDREN usually good
OTHER PETS can be problematic with small pets
STRANGERS friendly
UNFAMILIAR DOGS friendly

PERFECT OWNER
Active, easy-going owner who has access to safe areas to exercise this energetic, independent hunter.

THINGS TO WATCH OUT FOR
May be difficult to control on walks because they are unlikely to respond once they are scenting or chasing.

Sloughi

**quiet
alert
dignified
haughty
aloof
sensitive
loyal**

Size: 61–72 cm (24–28 in)
Weight: 20–27 kg (44–60 lb)
Coat: Fine and short
Colour: Light sand to red sand
Lifespan: 12 years

Fast-moving Sloughis have strong hunting instincts and are built to run at speed after prey. Aloof and sometimes shy, they prefer their owners to strangers. Quiet at home, they need long, vigorous, energetic walks to keep them well exercised.

ORIGINALLY BRED
for hunting desert animals such as gazelles.

SPECIAL CHARACTERISTICS
The Sloughi has strong hunting instincts and a timid, sensitive nature.

EXERCISE REQUIREMENTS
High. Content to be lazy at home.

COMMON ATTITUDE TO OWNERS independent, affectionate

CHILDREN can be difficult as these sensitive, shy dogs can be easily worried by boisterous children
OTHER PETS may be problematic with small pets
STRANGERS reserved, territorial
UNFAMILIAR DOGS tolerates

PERFECT OWNER
Experienced, gentle owner who leads a quiet life and has access to places to exercise this energetic hunter.

THINGS TO WATCH OUT FOR
May be difficult to control on walks and may be territorial or nervous towards people. May prey on small pets.

Whippet

gentle
affectionate
even disposition

Size: 44–51 cm (17½–20 in)
Weight: 12.5–13.5 kg (27½–30 lb)
Coat: Fine, short
Colour: Any
Lifespan: 13–14 years

Sweet-natured and affectionate with owners, Whippets can sometimes be shy and timid with strangers. Nicknamed 'the poor man's racehorse', they are perfectly built for speed so they need safe exercise areas.

ORIGINALLY BRED
to chase and kill rabbits.

SPECIAL CHARACTERISTICS
The Whippet is a fast runner, especially interested in hunting.

EXERCISE REQUIREMENTS
Medium. Needs to run free, but lazy at home.

COMMON ATTITUDE TO
OWNERS independent, affectionate
CHILDREN usually good
OTHER PETS problematic with small pets
STRANGERS reserved, then friendly
UNFAMILIAR DOGS friendly

PERFECT OWNER
Gentle, easy-going active owner who has safe places to allow free running of this small, independent hunter.

THINGS TO WATCH OUT FOR
May be difficult to control on walks because they are unlikely to respond once they are scenting or chasing.

⚠ This dog has a fine coat and may feel the cold. It prefers soft bedding.

Anatolian Shepherd Dog

**strong-willed
bold
independent
proud
confident**

Size: 71–81 cm (28–32 in)
Weight: 41–64 kg (90–140 lb)
Coat: short and dense with thick undercoat
Colour: Cream to fawn, with black mask and ears
Lifespan: 10–11 years
In 'Working' class in the USA

Bred to guard, Anatolian Shepherd Dogs are a force to be reckoned with. Strongly built, they have a strong nature and are bold and independent, requiring a great deal of socialization to ensure they are pleasant to visitors and other dogs.

ORIGINALLY BRED
to guard sheep from wolves and bears.

SPECIAL CHARACTERISTICS
This dog is naturally suspicious.

EXERCISE REQUIREMENTS
Low. Needs plenty of mental stimulation.

COMMON ATTITUDE TO
OWNERS loyal, affectionate
CHILDREN will naturally guard them
OTHER PETS accepted
STRANGERS suspicious, territorial
UNFAMILIAR DOGS playful

PERFECT OWNER
Experienced, strong-willed, physically strong owner with a secure garden or yard who is willing to give this powerful dog a job to do to keep its lively mind occupied.

THINGS TO WATCH OUT FOR
May be fearful and problematic with strangers and unfamiliar dogs. Can be strong-willed and needs a determined owner.

Australian Cattle Dog

loyal
protective
amenable
biddable
alert
courageous

Size: 43–51 cm (17–20 in)
Weight: 16–20 kg (35–44 lb)
Coat: Smooth, straight, hard topcoat with short dense undercoat
Colour: Blue, red speckle
Lifespan: 12 years

Reactive and responsive, but robust and courageous, Australian Cattle Dogs are strong-willed and tough. They are very active dogs and need a job to pour their energies into.

ORIGINALLY BRED
for cattle herding.

SPECIAL CHARACTERISTICS
This playful dog has great strength of character. It is particularly suspicious of strangers.

EXERCISE REQUIREMENTS
Very high. Needs a great deal of stimulation and play.

COMMON ATTITUDE TO OWNERS affectionate, loyal
CHILDREN usually tolerant, but not of their friends unless well socialized.

OTHER PETS usually good if well socialized
STRANGERS suspicious, territorial
UNFAMILIAR DOGS can be problematic unless well socialized

PERFECT OWNER
Experienced, strong-willed, considerate owner who has enough time and energy to give this powerful dog a job to do and an outlet for its strong drives through play and training.

THINGS TO WATCH OUT FOR
May be problematic with strangers and other animals unless properly socialized. Can be strong-willed and needs a determined owner. May nip at heels in play.

Australian Shepherd

responsive
loyal
attentive
enthusiastic
reserved
biddable

Size: 46–58 cm (18–23 in)
Weight: 16–32 kg (35–70 lb)
Coat: Medium wavy with undercoat
Colour: Blue merle, black, red merle, red, all with or without tan points
Lifespan: 12–13 years

Virtually unknown in Australia, the Australian Shepherd was developed exclusively in the USA, being useful on farms and ranches. The resulting dog has strong herding and guarding instincts and a high energy level.

ORIGINALLY BRED
to herd sheep.

SPECIAL CHARACTERISTICS
This dog has strong herding and guarding instincts.

EXERCISE REQUIREMENTS
High. Full of energy.

COMMON ATTITUDE TO
OWNERS loyal, affectionate
CHILDREN protective
OTHER PETS good, may chase
STRANGERS reserved, territorial
UNFAMILIAR DOGS tolerant

PERFECT OWNER
Experienced, strong-willed, considerate owner who has enough time and energy to give this active dog a job and an outlet for its strong drives through play and training.

THINGS TO WATCH OUT FOR
Some dogs may display chasing problems. May be problematic with strangers if they are inadequately socialized.

Bearded Collie

alert
lively
exuberant
confident
active

Size: 51–56 cm (20–22 in)
Weight: 18–27 kg (40–60 lb)
Coat: Outer coat flat, harsh, strong and shaggy with soft, furry undercoat
Colour: Slate-grey, reddish-fawn, black, blue, all shades of grey, brown and sandy with or without white markings
Lifespan: 12–13 years

Bearded Collies are lively, exuberant and full of energy, but can be exercised easily as they are playful by nature. Close-bonding and responsive, they need daily care to keep their coats in good condition.

ORIGINALLY BRED
to herd sheep.

SPECIAL CHARACTERISTICS
This Collie is lively and playful, and enjoys chasing.

EXERCISE REQUIREMENTS
High. Needs to run and play.

COMMON ATTITUDE TO
OWNERS affectionate, biddable
CHILDREN usually good
OTHER PETS good, will chase
STRANGERS friendly, can be reserved
UNFAMILIAR DOGS friendly

PERFECT OWNER
Gentle, active owner who has enough time and energy to play with, exercise and train this exuberant, energetic, playful dog.

THINGS TO WATCH OUT FOR
May display chase problems if not directed on to toys. May be possessive over toys. Sound sensitive and prone to developing noise phobias.

⚠ This dog's coat needs daily attention to keep it in good condition, and its hair should be tied up out of its eyes so that it can see clearly.

Belgian Shepherd Dog

Belgian Shepherd Dogs come in four different coat varieties. They have a reactive, retiring nature and, as a result, can be timid and easily frightened. They are energetic, active dogs that need an outlet for their strong desire to chase, and are responsive and like to form close attachments to their owners.

Size: 56–66 cm (22–26 in)
Weight: 27.5–28.5 kg (61–63 lb)
Coat: Short with woolly undercoat
Colour: All shades of red, fawn, grey with black overlay. Black mask on face
Lifespan: 12–13 years

Malinois

wary
active
alert
resourceful
biddable
protective

ORIGINALLY BRED
to herd livestock.

SPECIAL CHARACTERISTICS
This active and playful dog likes to chase.

EXERCISE REQUIREMENTS
High. Needs both physical exercise and mental stimulation.

COMMON ATTITUDE TO
OWNERS loyal, affectionate
CHILDREN usually good if well socialized
OTHER PETS good, may chase
STRANGERS wary, territorial
UNFAMILIAR DOGS good if well socialized

PERFECT OWNER
Experienced, considerate owner who will take care with this shy breed and provide plenty of exercise, games and training to use up its boundless mental and physical energy.

THINGS TO WATCH OUT FOR
May be problematic with strangers. Chasing instincts may cause a problem.

Belgian Shepherd Dog

Groenendael

wary
active
alert
resourceful
biddable
protective

Size: 56–66 cm (22–26 in)
Weight: 27.5–28.5 kg (61–63 lb)
Coat: Outer coat long, straight and abundant with very dense undercoat
Colour: Black
Lifespan: 12–13 years

ORIGINALLY BRED
to herd livestock.

SPECIAL CHARACTERISTICS
This active and playful dog likes to chase.

EXERCISE REQUIREMENTS
High. Needs both physical exercise and mental stimulation.

COMMON ATTITUDE TO
OWNERS loyal, affectionate
CHILDREN usually good if well socialized
OTHER PETS good, may chase
STRANGERS wary, territorial
UNFAMILIAR DOGS good if well socialized

PERFECT OWNER
Experienced, considerate owner who will take care with this shy breed and provide plenty of exercise, games and training to use up its boundless mental and physical energy.

THINGS TO WATCH OUT FOR
May be problematic with strangers. Chasing instincts may cause a problem.

Belgian Shepherd Dog

Laekenois

wary
active
alert
resourceful
biddable
protective

Size: 56–66 cm (22–26 in)
Weight: 27.5–28.5 kg (61–63 lb)
Coat: Harsh, wiry, dry and not curly
Colour: Reddish-fawn with black shading
Lifespan: 12–13 years

ORIGINALLY BRED
to herd livestock.

SPECIAL CHARACTERISTICS
This active and playful dog likes to chase.

EXERCISE REQUIREMENTS
High. Needs both physical exercise and mental stimulation.

COMMON ATTITUDE TO
OWNERS loyal, affectionate
CHILDREN usually good if well socialized
OTHER PETS good, may chase
STRANGERS wary, territorial
UNFAMILIAR DOGS good if well socialized

PERFECT OWNER
Experienced, considerate owner who will take care with this shy breed and provide plenty of exercise, games and training to use up its boundless mental and physical energy.

THINGS TO WATCH OUT FOR
May be problematic with strangers, although less likely than in the other Belgian Shepherds. Chasing instincts may cause problems.

Belgian Shepherd Dog

Tervueren

wary
active
alert
resourceful
biddable
protective

Size: 56–66 cm (22–26 in)
Weight: 27.5–28.5 kg (61–63 lb)
Coat: Outer coat long, straight and abundant with very dense undercoat. Hair especially long and abundant, ruff-like around neck, particularly in males. Fringe of long hair down back of forelegs, on hindquarters and tail
Colour: All shades of red, fawn, grey with black overlay. Black mask on face. Tail should have a darker or black tip
Lifespan: 12–13 years

ORIGINALLY BRED
to herd livestock.

SPECIAL CHARACTERISTICS
This active and playful dog likes to chase.

EXERCISE REQUIREMENTS
High. Needs both physical exercise and mental stimulation.

COMMON ATTITUDE TO
OWNERS loyal, affectionate
CHILDREN usually good if well socialized
OTHER PETS good, may chase
STRANGERS wary, territorial
UNFAMILIAR DOGS good if well socialized

PERFECT OWNER
Experienced, considerate owner who will take care with this shy breed and provide plenty of exercise, games and training to use up its boundless mental and physical energy.

THINGS TO WATCH OUT FOR
May be problematic with strangers. Chasing instincts may cause a problem.

Bergamasco

vigilant
strongly protective
cautious
patient

Relatively rare, Bergamascos are an ancient, hardy breed that originated in the Iranian mountains where they were bred to tend and guard sheep. Resilient and vigorous, Bergamascos are independent and protective.

Size: 54–62 cm (21–24½ in)
Weight: 26–38 kg (57–84 lb)
Coat: Abundant and long with short, dense undercoat. Tends to form into strands or loose mats. Greasy to the touch
Colour: Black, various shades of grey
Lifespan: 12 years

ORIGINALLY BRED
to guard flocks of sheep from wolves.

SPECIAL CHARACTERISTICS
This dog has a strong desire to guard.

EXERCISE REQUIREMENTS
Low. Needs mental stimulation.

COMMON ATTITUDE TO
OWNERS loyal, affectionate
CHILDREN usually good, but may not be with visiting children
OTHER PETS good if raised with them
STRANGERS suspicious, territorial

UNFAMILIAR DOGS can be problematic

PERFECT OWNER
Experienced, strong-willed owner with a secure garden or yard who is willing to find activities to keep its lively mind occupied.

THINGS TO WATCH OUT FOR
This dog may display aggression towards strangers.

⚠️ Pet dogs may be more comfortable and less smelly if shaved, especially if living indoors. Hair needs to be pulled back or shaved around the eyes so they can see clearly.

Border Collie

tenacious
keen
biddable
alert
responsive
sensitive

Size: 46–54 cm (18–21 in)
Weight: 14–22 kg (31–48 lb)
Coat: Medium length, abundant, smooth with soft, dense undercoat
Colour: Variety of colours permissible. White should never predominate
Lifespan: 12–14 years

Quick, alert and reactive, Border Collies are well known around the world. They have a strong desire to chase from an early age, which needs to be channelled into acceptable outlets such as games with toys. They form close bonds with owners and have abundant energy and stamina.

ORIGINALLY BRED
to herd sheep.

SPECIAL CHARACTERISTICS
The Border Collie has plenty of stamina and likes to chase.

EXERCISE REQUIREMENTS
Very high. Needs exercise and plenty of games.

COMMON ATTITUDE TO
OWNERS devoted, affectionate
CHILDREN usually good, may chase/nip in play
OTHER PETS good, may chase
STRANGERS good if well socialized
UNFAMILIAR DOGS good if well socialized

PERFECT OWNER
Energetic, loving families who have enough time to find this dog a job to do and enough energy to exercise, train and channel this dog's strong chase drives into games and play.

THINGS TO WATCH OUT FOR
May display chase problems and aggression to strangers if not well socialized. Some dogs may have noise phobias.

⚠ This dog's coat will bring in mud and dirt from outside.

Briard

**versatile
bold
calm
courageous
biddable**

Size: 58–69 cm (23–27 in)
Weight: 33.5–34.5 kg (74–76 lb)
Coat: Long, slightly wavy and dry with a fine dense undercoat
Colour: Black, fawn, slate grey
Lifespan: 12 years

Strong-natured Briards were bred to be sheep herders and guarders so they are active and like to chase. They need plenty of socialization to prevent their suspicious nature getting the better of them, but are calm and courteous if raised well.

ORIGINALLY BRED
for herding and guarding livestock.

SPECIAL CHARACTERISTICS
The Briard is an active and protective dog.

EXERCISE REQUIREMENTS
Medium. Needs plenty of games.

COMMON ATTITUDE TO
OWNERS affectionate, protective
CHILDREN usually good if raised with them
OTHER PETS good if raised with them
STRANGERS friendly if well socialized
UNFAMILIAR DOGS friendly if well socialized, can be bossy

PERFECT OWNER
Experienced, strong-willed, active owner who can provide this responsive dog with a job to do as well as plenty of games, activity and socialization.

THINGS TO WATCH OUT FOR
May be problematic with strangers and other dogs if not well socialized.

⚠ The long hair over this dog's eyes needs to be cut or tied back so it can see clearly.

Collie (Rough)

sensitive
aloof
affectionate
gentle

Size: 51–61 cm (20–24 in)
Weight: 18–30 kg (40–66 lb)
Coat: Outer coat long, profuse, straight and harsh to touch, with soft, furry undercoat
Colour: Sable and white, tricolour, blue merle with white collar, full or part, white shirt, legs and feet, white tail tip
Lifespan: 12–13 years

Sensitive and aloof, the Rough Collie is well known thanks to the 'Lassie' films. Gentle, affectionate and responsive to owners, this heavily coated breed is quite difficult to socialize well and tends to be reserved with strangers and concerned about anything new.

ORIGINALLY BRED
to herd sheep.

SPECIAL CHARACTERISTICS
This playful Collie likes to chase.

EXERCISE REQUIREMENTS
Low.

COMMON ATTITUDE TO
OWNERS loyal, affectionate
CHILDREN will tolerate
OTHER PETS good
STRANGERS reserved
UNFAMILIAR DOGS reserved
or indifferent

PERFECT OWNER
Gentle, sensitive owner who will enjoy the daily grooming sessions and the close bond.

THINGS TO WATCH OUT FOR
May be wary of strangers and some dogs may have noise phobias.

⚠ Daily coat care is required to ensure this dog remains tangle-free. Its profuse coat can lead to overheating in summer, when special care must be taken to keep it cool.

Collie (Smooth)

sensitive
aloof
affectionate
gentle

Size: 51-61 cm (20-24 in)
Weight: 18-30 kg (40-66 lb)
Coat: Short, flat topcoat of harsh texture, with very dense undercoat
Colour: Sable and white, tricolour, blue merle with white collar, full or part, white shirt, legs and feet, white tail tip
Lifespan: 12-13 years

Sensitive and aloof, Smooth Collies are gentle, affectionate and responsive to owners. This breed can be difficult to socialize well and tends to be reserved with strangers and concerned about anything new.

ORIGINALLY BRED
to herd sheep.

SPECIAL CHARACTERISTICS
This Collie is playful and likes to chase.

EXERCISE REQUIREMENTS
Low.

COMMON ATTITUDE TO
OWNERS loyal, affectionate
CHILDREN will tolerate
OTHER PETS good
STRANGERS shy
UNFAMILIAR DOGS reserved or indifferent

PERFECT OWNER
Gentle, sensitive owner who will enjoy the close bond with this shy breed.

THINGS TO WATCH OUT FOR
May be snappy with strangers and suffer from noise phobias.

Estrela Mountain Dog

active
loyal
affectionate
alert
strong-willed
stubborn

Size: 62–72 cm (24½–28 in)
Weight: 30–50 kg (66–110 lb)
Coat: Long coat: Thick, moderately harsh outer coat, with very dense, paler undercoat. Short coat: Short, thick, moderately harsh and straight, with shorter dense undercoat
Colour: Fawn, brindle, wolf with black muzzle or mask
Lifespan: 10–12 years

Powerful and sturdy, Estrela Mountain Dogs are loyal and alert with a strong guarding instinct. They are independent and can be stubborn, too, and need strong-willed, experienced owners.

ORIGINALLY BRED
to guard flocks of sheep from wolves.

SPECIAL CHARACTERISTICS
This strong-willed dog has a powerful guarding instinct.

EXERCISE REQUIREMENTS
Low.

COMMON ATTITUDE TO
OWNERS loyal, affectionate
CHILDREN protective and will naturally guard them
OTHER PETS accepted
STRANGERS suspicious, territorial
UNFAMILIAR DOGS not generally tolerant of others

PERFECT OWNER
Experienced, strong-willed, physically strong owner with a secure garden or yard who is willing to give this powerful dog a job to do to keep its lively mind occupied.

THINGS TO WATCH OUT FOR
Tendency to be problematic with strangers and unfamiliar dogs. Can be strong-willed and needs a determined owner.

Finnish Lapphund

responsive
brave
calm
faithful
cooperative

Size: 41–52 cm (16–20½ in)
Weight: 20–21 kg (44–46 lb)
Coat: Profuse, long, coarse outer coat with soft, thick undercoat
Colour: All colours are allowed, but the main colour must dominate
Lifespan: 11–12 years

The thickly coated Finnish Lapphund was bred for life in cold countries and can get uncomfortably hot in summer. Playful, with a desire to chase, they are loyal and cooperative with owners.

ORIGINALLY BRED
to herd reindeer.

SPECIAL CHARACTERISTICS
This playful dog has a strong desire to chase.

EXERCISE REQUIREMENTS
Medium. Loves to play.

COMMON ATTITUDE TO
OWNERS loyal, affectionate
CHILDREN usually good
OTHER PETS good, may chase
STRANGERS good if well socialized
UNFAMILIAR DOGS good if well socialized

PERFECT OWNER
Easy-going owner who has the time to train and play with a dog that loves to chase.

THINGS TO WATCH OUT FOR
May chase things it should not.

⚠ This dog requires regular grooming to keep its thick coat free from mats.

German Shepherd Dog (Alsatian)

attentive
alert
steady
loyal
self-assured
sensitive
responsive

Size: 58–63 cm (23–25 in)
Weight: 34–43 kg (75–95 lb)
Coat: Straight, hard outer coat of medium to long length with thick undercoat
Colour: Black or black saddle with tan or gold to light grey markings. All black, all grey, with lighter or brown markings
Lifespan: 12–13 years

The ubiquitous German Shepherd Dog is a versatile breed, chosen to be police dogs, guide dogs and guard dogs around the world. Loyal and protective, these dogs are alert, reactive and have abundant energy, but need early socialization to prevent them being wary of strangers and other dogs.

ORIGINALLY BRED
to herd sheep.

SPECIAL CHARACTERISTICS
This active and powerful dog has a strong desire to chase.

EXERCISE REQUIREMENTS
High. Needs long walks and enjoys playing games.

COMMON ATTITUDE TO
OWNERS loyal, affectionate
CHILDREN usually good, may chase in play

OTHER PETS good, may chase
STRANGERS wary unless well socialized, territorial
UNFAMILIAR DOGS good if well socialized

PERFECT OWNER
Experienced, considerate owner who has plenty of energy for long walks, training and chase games, and who will enjoy the close bond.

THINGS TO WATCH OUT FOR
May be problematic with strangers and other dogs. This is particularly a problem with white-coated German Shepherds. May chase things it should not.

⚠ Considerable brushing is needed to remove dead hair. An owner should be prepared for loose hair around the house.

Hungarian Kuvasz

bold
courageous
protective
devoted
gentle
patient

Size: 66–75 cm (26–29½ in)
Weight: 30–52 kg (66–115 lb)
Coat: Thick, slight wavy, coarse, medium-length topcoat, fine woolly undercoat
Colour: Pure white. Skin highly pigmented with patches of slate grey
Lifespan: 11–13 years
In the 'Working' class in the USA

Well built and powerful, the Kuvasz has a strong, protective nature. They are loyal and devoted to their owners and need plenty of socialization to keep them tolerant of strangers and other dogs.

ORIGINALLY BRED
to guard livestock.

SPECIAL CHARACTERISTICS
The Kuvasz has a strong guarding instinct.

EXERCISE REQUIREMENTS
Medium. Needs a fair amount of exercise.

COMMON ATTITUDE TO
OWNERS loyal, affectionate
CHILDREN will naturally guard them
OTHER PETS good if raised with them
STRANGERS suspicious, territorial
UNFAMILIAR DOGS can be problematic

PERFECT OWNER
Experienced, strong-willed, physically strong owner with a secure garden or yard who is willing to give this powerful dog a job to do to keep its lively mind occupied.

THINGS TO WATCH OUT FOR
May be problematic with strangers and unfamiliar dogs. Can be strong-willed and needs a determined owner.

⚠ Daily grooming is required to keep the thick coat in good condition. An owner should be prepared for loose hair in the house.

Hungarian Puli

lively
wary of strangers
responsive

Size: 37–44 cm (14½–17½ in)
Weight: 10–15 kg (22–33 lb)
Coat: Corded coat, which may grow down to the ground
Colour: Black, rusty black, white and various shades of grey and apricot
Lifespan: 12–13 years

Lively and responsive, the Hungarian Puli is a natural guard. Although its distinctive corded coat may protect it from extremes of weather in its native land, a pet dog may be more comfortable and less smelly if clipped.

ORIGINALLY BRED
to herd sheep.

SPECIAL CHARACTERISTICS
This dog has a protective nature and likes to chase.

EXERCISE REQUIREMENTS
High. Enjoys playing.

COMMON ATTITUDE TO
OWNERS loyal, affectionate
CHILDREN protective and will naturally guard them as part of its family
OTHER PETS may chase
STRANGERS suspicious, territorial
UNFAMILIAR DOGS can be problematic

PERFECT OWNER
Experienced, sensible owner who has the time and energy for training and playing.

THINGS TO WATCH OUT FOR
May bark excessively. Lack of activity may lead to problems and some dogs may be problematic with strangers.

⚠️ The corded coat needs assistance to form dreadlocks as otherwise it will mat.

The corded coat helps to protect against extreme weather conditions when working.

Komondor

protective
wary of strangers
courageous
devoted

Size: 60–80 cm (23½–31½ in)
Weight: 36–61 kg (80–135 lb)
Coat: Corded coat, which may grow down to the ground
Colour: White
Lifespan: 12 years
In the 'Working' class in the USA

Alert and protective, Komondors make loyal, independent guard dogs. Although its distinctive corded coat may protect it from extremes of weather in its native land, a pet dog may be more comfortable and less smelly if clipped.

ORIGINALLY BRED
for guarding flocks of sheep from wolves.

SPECIAL CHARACTERISTICS
The Komondor is a protective dog.

EXERCISE REQUIREMENTS
Medium.

COMMON ATTITUDE TO
OWNERS loyal, affectionate
CHILDREN will naturally guard them
OTHER PETS good if raised with them
STRANGERS wary, territorial
UNFAMILIAR DOGS can be problematic

PERFECT OWNER
Experienced, sensible owner who has time and energy for training and coat care.

THINGS TO WATCH OUT FOR
Tends to be problematic with strangers and other dogs.

⚠️ The corded coat needs assistance to form dreadlocks as otherwise it will mat.

Lancashire Heeler

courageous
happy
alert
playful
affectionate

Size: 26–30 cm (10–12 in)
Weight: 3–6 kg (6½–13 lb)
Coat: Short, thick, hard topcoat with fine undercoat
Colour: Black or liver with rich tan markings
Lifespan: 12–13 years

Lancashire Heelers have strong herding instincts and may try to round up errant children or dogs with a well-aimed nip at the heels. Alert and playful, they are constantly busy with abundant energy.

ORIGINALLY BRED
to herd cattle and catch rats and rabbits.

SPECIAL CHARACTERISTICS
This playful dog likes to chase and nip.

EXERCISE REQUIREMENTS
High. Tends to be busy indoors as well as out.

COMMON ATTITUDE TO
OWNERS loyal, affectionate
CHILDREN usually good if raised with them, may nip in play
OTHER PETS may be problematic with small pets
STRANGERS wary but friendly if well socialized
UNFAMILIAR DOGS good if well socialized

PERFECT OWNER
Active, sensible owner who can provide an outlet for this dog's boundless energy and desire to play and be busy.

THINGS TO WATCH OUT FOR
Nipping heels in play. May be problematic with strangers if not well socialized.

Maremma Sheepdog

strong-willed aloof independent courageous

Strong, powerful Maremmas are naturally protective and need plenty of socialization to ensure they are tolerant of strangers and other dogs. They have an independent, aloof nature and a thick coat that will shed hair in a warm house.

Size: 60–73 cm (23½–28½ in)
Weight: 30–45 kg (66–99 lb)
Coat: Long, plentiful and rather harsh with thick, close undercoat
Colour: All white
Lifespan: 10–12 years

ORIGINALLY BRED
to guard sheep from wolves.

SPECIAL CHARACTERISTICS
The Maremma has a very protective nature.

EXERCISE REQUIREMENTS
Medium. Not very energetic, but muscular so needs good walks.

COMMON ATTITUDE TO
OWNERS loyal, affectionate
CHILDREN will naturally guard them
OTHER PETS good if raised with them
STRANGERS wary, territorial
UNFAMILIAR DOGS can be problematic

PERFECT OWNER
Experienced, strong-willed, physically strong owner with a secure garden or yard who can give this powerful dog a job to do to keep its lively mind occupied.

THINGS TO WATCH OUT FOR
Tends to be problematic with strangers and unfamiliar dogs. Can be strong-willed and needs a determined owner.

⚠ Daily grooming is required to keep hair in good condition.

Norwegian Buhund

alert
courageous
energetic
independent
playful
curious

Size: 41–45 cm (16–18 in)
Weight: 24–26 kg (53–57 lb)
Coat: Outer coat smooth, harsh, with soft, woolly undercoat
Colour: Wheaten, black, red (red not too dark), wolf-sable
Lifespan: 12–15 years

Once a farm dog, the Buhund has a strong chasing instinct and abundant energy. Curious and playful, they enjoy barking and need to live an active, busy life to prevent boredom.

ORIGINALLY BRED
to herd sheep and cattle and guard farms.

SPECIAL CHARACTERISTICS
This active and playful dog has a protective nature, and likes to chase.

EXERCISE REQUIREMENTS
High. Thoroughly enjoys being exercised.

COMMON ATTITUDE TO
OWNERS loyal, responsive
CHILDREN usually good
OTHER PETS good, may chase
STRANGERS will bark but friendly
UNFAMILIAR DOGS good

PERFECT OWNER
Active, sensible owner who enjoys exercising, playing and training.

THINGS TO WATCH OUT FOR
May bark excessively and chase things it should not.

Old English Sheepdog

biddable
bold
faithful
affectionate

Size: 56–61 cm (22–24 in)
Weight: 29.5–30.5 kg (65–67 lb)
Coat: Profuse, of good harsh texture, with thick undercoat
Colour: Any shade of grey, grizzle or blue. Body and hindquarters of solid colour with or without white socks
Lifespan: 12–13 years

Lively, playful Old English Sheepdogs have a massive coat. Prolonged daily grooming is needed if they are to remain tangle-free and pet dogs may be more comfortable and more manageable if they are clipped, especially in summer.

ORIGINALLY BRED
to herd sheep.

SPECIAL CHARACTERISTICS
The Old English Sheepdog likes to chase.

EXERCISE REQUIREMENTS
Medium. Joins in with enthusiasm.

COMMON ATTITUDE TO
OWNERS loyal, affectionate
CHILDREN usually good, may be clumsy with young children
OTHER PETS good, may chase
STRANGERS usually friendly
UNFAMILIAR DOGS good if well socialized

PERFECT OWNER
Active, confident owner who has plenty of time for exercise, play, training and coat care.

THINGS TO WATCH OUT FOR
Dogs from some lines may display possessive aggression over toys or food.

⚠ This dog's coat requires prolonged daily grooming to keep it in good condition. The hair above its eyes needs to be tied back so that the dog can see clearly.

Polish Lowland Sheepdog

lively
watchful
bright
clever
perceptive
alert
composed

Size: 42–50 cm (16½–19½ in)
Weight: 14–16 kg (31–35 lb)
Coat: Long, dense, shaggy, thick coat of harsh texture with soft undercoat
Colour: All colours acceptable
Lifespan: 13–14 years

Lively and agile, Polish Lowland Sheepdogs need a job to do to keep them happy. They are responsive and affectionate with owners, but can be wary of strangers so early socialization is important.

ORIGINALLY BRED
for herding livestock.

SPECIAL CHARACTERISTICS
This dog is curious by nature and likes to chase.

EXERCISE REQUIREMENTS
Medium–High. Enjoys play and exercise.

COMMON ATTITUDE TO OWNERS affectionate, responsive
CHILDREN usually good if socialized with them
OTHER PETS good, may chase
STRANGERS suspicious, territorial

UNFAMILIAR DOGS good if well socialized

PERFECT OWNER
Active, strong-willed owner who has plenty of energy to exercise, train and play with this active dog.

THINGS TO WATCH OUT FOR
Tends to be problematic with strangers. May be problematic if under-exercised.

⚠ The long hair above this dog's eyes needs to be cut or tied back so that it can see clearly.

166 // Pastoral

Pyrenean Mountain Dog

alert
confident
patient
steady
courageous

Size: 65–81 cm (25½–32 in)
Weight: 45–60 kg (99–132 lb)
Coat: Profuse undercoat of very fine hairs; outer coat longer, coarser-textured. Long, very dense woollier hair on rear of thighs giving pantaloon effect
Colour: White or white with patches of badger, wolf-grey or pale yellow. Black nose and eye rims
Lifespan: 9–11 years
In the 'Working' class in the USA

Being bred for generations as a pet dog has toned down the natural guarding instincts of the Pyrenean Mountain Dog, but they still have a tendency to protect their own, making continual socialization with strangers and other dogs essential. Powerful, loyal and independent, they require daily coat care to keep them looking their best.

ORIGINALLY BRED
to guard flocks of sheep.

SPECIAL CHARACTERISTICS
This dog is naturally protective.

EXERCISE REQUIREMENTS
Low. Tends to be calm in the house.

COMMON ATTITUDE TO
OWNERS loyal, independent
CHILDREN will naturally guard them
OTHER PETS good if raised with them
STRANGERS suspicious, territorial
UNFAMILIAR DOGS dogs can be problematic

PERFECT OWNER
Experienced, strong-willed, active owner who has enough space for this large, independent dog and the energy to look after its coat and keep it occupied and exercised.

THINGS TO WATCH OUT FOR
Some lines may be fearful and reactive with strangers and other dogs.

⚠️ Daily coat care is needed, and this breed tends to shed loose hair in the house.

Pyrenean Sheepdog

alert
lively
wary of strangers

Size: 38–48 cm (15–19 in)
Weight: 8–15 kg (18–33 lb)
Coat: Long or semi-long
Colour: Various shades of fawn, light to dark grey, blue merle, slate blue or brindle, black or black and white
Lifespan: 12–13 years

Active, lively and responsive, the Pyrenean Sheepdog has strong chase instincts and likes to work. Sensitive and wary, they require early socialization to ensure they are agreeable with strangers and other dogs.

ORIGINALLY BRED
to guard and herd sheep.

SPECIAL CHARACTERISTICS
This sheepdog is a fast runner, and likes to chase.

EXERCISE REQUIREMENTS
High. Needs plenty of exercise and games.

COMMON ATTITUDE TO
OWNERS affectionate, responsive
CHILDREN usually good if raised with them
OTHER PETS may chase
STRANGERS wary, territorial
UNFAMILIAR DOGS okay if well socialized

PERFECT OWNER
Active, experienced owner who will socialize this dog well and provide it with plenty of games and activity.

THINGS TO WATCH OUT FOR
May be problematic with strangers. May display chase problems.

Samoyed

alert
affectionate
good-natured
independent

Bred to live in cold climates and herd reindeer, Samoyeds have thick coats that need a great deal of brushing and that can cause them to overheat in summer. Good-natured and affectionate, they are also independent and not necessarily responsive to requests.

Size: 46–56 cm (18–22 in)
Weight: 23–30 kg (50–66 lb)
Coat: Thick, close, soft and short undercoat, with harsh hair growing through
Colour: Pure white, white and biscuit, cream; outer coat silver-tipped
Lifespan: 12 years
In the 'Working' class in the USA

ORIGINALLY BRED
to herd and guard reindeer.

SPECIAL CHARACTERISTICS
This lively dog likes to chase.

EXERCISE REQUIREMENTS
Medium. Enjoys exercise but likes to have human company.

COMMON ATTITUDE TO
OWNERS affectionate, independent
CHILDREN usually good
OTHER PETS good
STRANGERS friendly
UNFAMILIAR DOGS friendly

PERFECT OWNER
Sociable, easy-going families who will enjoy this dog's independent, engaging character.

⚠ Daily prolonged grooming is needed to keep the heavy coat in good shape. The thick coat makes this dog prone to overheating in summer. Loose hair will be shed in the house.

Shetland Sheepdog

alert
gentle
active
affectionate
responsive
reserved

Size: 36–37 cm (14–14½ in)
Weight: 6–7 kg (13–15½ lb)
Coat: Long, harsh-textured, straight topcoat, with soft, short undercoat. Mane and frill very abundant, forelegs well feathered
Colour: Sable, tricolour, blue merle, black and white, black and tan
Lifespan: 13–14 years

Reserved and prone to shyness, Shetland Sheepdogs are gentle, affectionate and close-bonding to owners. They are also sensitive and timid. Their coats will need daily attention to keep them tangle-free.

ORIGINALLY BRED
to herd sheep.

SPECIAL CHARACTERISTICS
This sheepdog is gentle, reserved and sensitive.

EXERCISE REQUIREMENTS
Medium. Will take exercise if offered.

COMMON ATTITUDE TO
OWNERS affectionate, responsive
CHILDREN can be timid with boisterous children
OTHER PETS good, may chase
STRANGERS reserved, timid
UNFAMILIAR DOGS reserved

PERFECT OWNER
Active, gentle owner who will appreciate this dog's sensitivities and devotion, and enjoy the constant grooming needed to keep its coat in good shape.

THINGS TO WATCH OUT FOR
May bark if lonely or excited. May suffer from noise phobias.

⚠️ The profuse coat needs regular grooming to keep it tangle-free.

Swedish Lapphund

**patient
kind
friendly
devoted
lively
alert
independent**

Size: 40–51 cm (16–20 in)
Weight: 19.5–20.5 kg (43–45 lb)
Coat: Thick, medium length, longer on brisket, thighs and tail, forming a ruff round neck, with dense and finely curled undercoat
Colour: Bear-brown, black, brown
Lifespan: 12–13 years

Bred to herd and guard reindeer, Swedish Lapphunds have thick coats that would have protected them from cold climates, but which can prove too hot in summer. Lively and independent, these dogs are active, curious and prone to barking.

ORIGINALLY BRED
to herd and guard reindeer.

SPECIAL CHARACTERISTICS
This active dog has a curious, energetic nature.

EXERCISE REQUIREMENTS
High. Enjoys exercise.

COMMON ATTITUDE TO
OWNERS affectionate, responsive
CHILDREN usually good
OTHER PETS good
STRANGERS friendly, will bark
UNFAMILIAR DOGS friendly

PERFECT OWNER
Active, playful owner who will enjoy the independent, rather stubborn nature of this energetic dog.

THINGS TO WATCH OUT FOR
Barking, especially when left alone.

⚠ Daily grooming is needed to keep the thick coat in good condition.

Swedish Vallhund

watchful
alert
energetic
friendly
eager to please
courageous

Size: 31–35 cm (12–14 in)
Weight: 11.5–16 kg (25–35 lb)
Coat: Medium-length, harsh topcoat with abundant, soft, woolly undercoat
Colour: Steel grey, greyish-brown, greyish-yellow, reddish-yellow, reddish-brown
Lifespan: 12–14 years

Swedish Vallhunds are strong, playful and vigorous. Bred to herd cattle, they have a tendency to nip at heels when excited and need active, playful owners to channel their energy into more acceptable games.

ORIGINALLY BRED
to herd and guard cattle and for vermin control on farms.

SPECIAL CHARACTERISTICS
The Swedish Vallhund is playful and energetic.

EXERCISE REQUIREMENTS
High. Needs to have its abundant energy channelled.

COMMON ATTITUDE TO OWNERS affectionate, independent
CHILDREN usually good, may nip heels in play
OTHER PETS can be problematic
STRANGERS good if well socialized

UNFAMILIAR DOGS can be problematic

PERFECT OWNER
Active, experienced owner who has plenty of free time for training, play and exercise.

THINGS TO WATCH OUT FOR
Likely to nip heels in play or to see off strangers.

Welsh Corgi (Cardigan)

alert
active
steady
confident

Size: 27–30 cm (10½–12 in)
Weight: 11–17 kg (24–37 lb)
Coat: Medium length, straight, of hard texture, with good undercoat
Colour: Any, with or without white markings
Lifespan: 12–14 years

Cardigan Corgis have a full tail and are slightly more easy-going than Pembroke Corgis. They can be reserved with strangers, courageous and determined, and they are playful and independent with owners.

ORIGINALLY BRED
to drive cattle.

SPECIAL CHARACTERISTICS
This is a courageous and determined dog.

EXERCISE REQUIREMENTS
Medium.

COMMON ATTITUDE TO OWNERS affectionate, independent
CHILDREN usually good, but may nip ankles in play
OTHER PETS good, may chase
STRANGERS reserved
UNFAMILIAR DOGS good if well socialized

PERFECT OWNER
Experienced, easy-going owner who can provide exercise, play and training to ensure that nipping ankles does not become this dog's job.

THINGS TO WATCH OUT FOR
Likely to nip heels in play or to see off strangers.

Welsh Corgi (Pembroke)

bold
outgoing
alert
active
steady
confident

Pembrokes are born without a tail and have a character that is wilful, determined and reckless. Reserved with strangers, they make good watchdogs, but can be snappy when defending property unless they have been properly socialized.

ORIGINALLY BRED
to drive cattle.

SPECIAL CHARACTERISTICS
This corgi is by nature courageous and determined.

EXERCISE REQUIREMENTS
Medium.

COMMON ATTITUDE TO
OWNERS affectionate, independent
CHILDREN usually good, may nip ankles in play
OTHER PETS problematic with small pets
STRANGERS reserved
UNFAMILIAR DOGS good if well socialized

PERFECT OWNER
Experienced, strong-willed owner who can provide exercise, play and training to ensure that nipping ankles does not become this dog's job.

THINGS TO WATCH OUT FOR
Likely to nip heels in play or to see off strangers.

Airedale Terrier

outgoing confident friendly courageous tenacious

Size: 56–61 cm (22–24 in)
Weight: 20–23 kg (44–50 lb)
Coat: Hard, dense and wiry, with shorter, softer undercoat
Colour: Tan with black saddle; top of the neck and top surface of tail also black
Lifespan: 10–13 years

Airedales are feisty, easily aroused and courageous. With owners they are affectionate but independent and early training and socialization are important to ensure these large terriers are well behaved with other dogs.

ORIGINALLY BRED
to hunt and kill badgers and otters.

SPECIAL CHARACTERISTICS
The Airedale is feisty and easily aroused.

EXERCISE REQUIREMENTS
High. This is the largest of the terriers and needs plenty of exercise.

COMMON ATTITUDE TO OWNERS affectionate, independent
CHILDREN usually good if raised with them
OTHER PETS due to a high prey drive and chase instincts, may cause harm to small pets; may injure cats unless raised with them

STRANGERS friendly if well socialized
UNFAMILIAR DOGS can be problematic

PERFECT OWNER
Experienced, strong-willed, active owner who has plenty of time for playing with and exercising this independent, powerful character.

THINGS TO WATCH OUT FOR
There may be control problems unless owners are able to win cooperation.

⚠ Regular grooming and clipping is needed to keep the coat in good order.

American Staffordshire Terrier

loyal
obedient
tenacious
independent
affectionate

Size: 43–48 cm (17–19 in)
Weight: 18–23 kg (40–50 lb)
Coat: Short, sleek
Colour: Any
Lifespan: 12 years

Taller and heavier than its English ancestor, the American Staffordshire Terrier is tenacious. Easily aroused, they have tremendous jaw strength and continued socialization is needed to ensure they remain well behaved with other dogs.

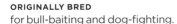

ORIGINALLY BRED
for bull-baiting and dog-fighting.

SPECIAL CHARACTERISTICS
This terrier has tremendous jaw strength and the ability to hold on when biting, and is easily aroused.

EXERCISE REQUIREMENTS
High. Very active and enjoys exercise.

COMMON ATTITUDE TO
OWNERS affectionate, loving
CHILDREN usually good if raised with them, play biting can be problematic when young
OTHER PETS due to a high prey drive and chase instincts, may cause harm to small pets; may injure cats unless raised with them
STRANGERS usually friendly
UNFAMILIAR DOGS tendency to be problematic. Adequate early socialization needed

PERFECT OWNER
Experienced, strong-willed active owner who has time and knowledge to teach this dog to be nice to other dogs when it is a puppy and who can provide a great deal of affection, exercise and play when older.

THINGS TO WATCH OUT FOR
May become agitated with other dogs quickly.

Australian Terrier

alert
active
loyal
friendly
extrovert
obedient
courageous

Australian Terriers are high-energy workers. Easily aroused by quick movement, these dogs are alert, courageous hunters and need plenty to do and a great deal of exercise to keep them happy.

Size: 24.5–25.5 cm (9½–10 in)
Weight: 5–6.5 kg (11–14 lb)
Coat: Harsh, straight, dense topcoat, with short, soft-textured undercoat
Colour: Blue, sandy or red
Lifespan: 14 years

ORIGINALLY BRED
to hunt and kill rats.

SPECIAL CHARACTERISTICS
This terrier is fast, alert and excited by quick movement, and easily aroused.

EXERCISE REQUIREMENTS
High. Needs plenty of exercise to burn off abundant energy.

COMMON ATTITUDE TO
OWNERS affectionate, biddable
CHILDREN usually good if raised with them
OTHER PETS due to a high prey drive and chase instincts, may cause harm to small pets; may injure cats unless raised with them
STRANGERS good
UNFAMILIAR DOGS can be problematic

PERFECT OWNER
Experienced owner who can provide an outlet for this dog's high energy levels through games, play and exercise.

THINGS TO WATCH OUT FOR
May be problematic with other dogs unless well socialized.

Bedlington Terrier

spirited
calm
confident
affectionate
dignified
courageous

Size: 38–43 cm (15–17 in)
Weight: 8–10 kg (18–22 lb)
Coat: Thick and linty
Colour: Blue, liver or sandy with or without tan
Lifespan: 14–15 years

Graceful and lamb-like, Bedlington Terriers are calm and sweet-natured with owners, and spirited and playful when given the chance. They are reserved with strangers and need plenty of socialization to help them feel at ease.

ORIGINALLY BRED
to hunt and kill rats and badgers.

SPECIAL CHARACTERISTICS
This feisty and tenacious terrier is easily aroused.

EXERCISE REQUIREMENTS
High. Enjoys exercise outside, but calm at home.

COMMON ATTITUDE TO
OWNERS affectionate, biddable
CHILDREN usually good if raised with them
OTHER PETS due to a high prey drive and chase instincts, may cause harm to small pets; may injure cats unless raised with them

STRANGERS reserved
UNFAMILIAR DOGS good if well socialized

PERFECT OWNER
Active, calm owner who can provide plenty of stimulation through exercise and play for this dog 'in sheep's clothing'.

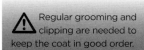
Regular grooming and clipping are needed to keep the coat in good order.

Border Terrier

active
sensible
kind
affectionate
devoted

Size: 25–28 cm (10–11 in)
Weight: 5–7 kg (11–15½ lb)
Coat: Harsh and dense, with close undercoat
Colour: Red, wheaten, grizzle and tan or blue and tan
Lifespan: 13–14 years

Sweet-natured and affectionate, Border Terriers can be happy lying beside the fire or going out all day on long walks. Alert and playful, they are usually friendly and easy-going with strangers and other dogs and are also good watchdogs, without excessive barking.

ORIGINALLY BRED
to hunt and kill rats and to dig foxes from lairs.

SPECIAL CHARACTERISTICS
This terrier is alert, easily aroused and playful.

EXERCISE REQUIREMENTS
Medium. Enjoys exercise but will not demand it.

COMMON ATTITUDE TO
OWNERS affectionate, loyal
CHILDREN usually good
OTHER PETS can be problematic with small pets
STRANGERS good
UNFAMILIAR DOGS good if well socialized

PERFECT OWNER
Easy-going families without small pets who will enjoy exercising and playing with this sweet-natured little dog.

✓ Recommended for first-time owners who do not keep small pets. The coat requires hand-stripping every 6 months.

Bull Terrier (English)

courageous
tenacious
obstinate

Size: 53–56 cm (21–22 in)
Weight: 24–28 kg (53–62 lb)
Coat: Short, flat, glossy
Colour: White, black, brindle, red, fawn and tricolour
Lifespan: 11–13 years

Exuberant and powerful, English Bull Terriers are courageous and have strong jaws. With their high pain threshold, they play roughly and careful training and socialization are needed to prevent this becoming a problem. They are usually friendly with people, but early socialization is needed to ensure they remain tolerant of other dogs.

ORIGINALLY BRED
for dog-fighting.

SPECIAL CHARACTERISTICS
Tenacious and courageous, English Bull Terriers have a strong bite.

EXERCISE REQUIREMENTS
Medium. Expect explosive bursts of energy.

COMMON ATTITUDE TO
OWNERS affectionate, devoted
CHILDREN usually good if raised with them
OTHER PETS due to a high prey drive and chase instincts, may cause harm to small pets; may injure cats unless raised with them

STRANGERS good if well socialized
UNFAMILIAR DOGS can be problematic. Adequate early socialization is required

PERFECT OWNER
Experienced owner who has time and energy to play with, train and exercise this dog safely.

THINGS TO WATCH OUT FOR
Tendency to be problematic with other dogs unless well socialized. Dogs from some lines may display tail-chasing and other repetitive movement disorders. Lack of exercise may lead to destructiveness.

⚠ White dogs will need protection in high ultraviolet conditions to avoid sunburn on exposed pink areas of skin.

Bull Terrier (Miniature)

courageous
tenacious
playful
obsessive
obstinate

Size: 25–35 cm (10–14 in)
Weight: 11–15 kg (24–33 lb)
Coat: Short, flat, glossy
Colour: White, black, brindle, red, fawn and tricolour
Lifespan: 11–13 years

Miniature versions of the English Bull Terrier, these dogs also have exuberance and the same determination. With their high pain threshold, they play roughly and careful training and socialization are needed to prevent this becoming a problem. They are usually friendly with people, but early socialization is needed to ensure they remain tolerant of other dogs.

ORIGINALLY BRED
for dog-fighting, hunting and killing rats

SPECIAL CHARACTERISTICS
This dog is tenacious and courageous, with a strong bite.

EXERCISE REQUIREMENTS
Medium. Expect explosive bursts of energy.

COMMON ATTITUDE TO
OWNERS affectionate, devoted, independent
CHILDREN usually good if raised with them

OTHER PETS due to a high prey drive and chase instincts, may cause harm to small pets; may injure cats unless raised with them
STRANGERS good if well socialized
UNFAMILIAR DOGS can be problematic. Adequate early socialization is required

PERFECT OWNER
Experienced, active owner who has time and energy to play with, train and exercise this determined dog.

⚠ White dogs will need protection in high ultraviolet conditions to avoid sunburn on exposed pink areas of skin.

THINGS TO WATCH OUT FOR
Tendency to be problematic with other dogs unless well socialized. Dogs from some lines may display tail-chasing and other repetitive movement disorders. Lack of exercise may lead to destructive problems.

Cairn Terrier

courageous
tenacious
sensible
confident
feisty
stubborn

Size: 28–31 cm (11–12 in)
Weight: 6–7.5 kg (13–16½ lb)
Coat: Abundant, harsh outer coat with short, soft undercoat
Colour: Cream, wheaten, red, grey or nearly black
Lifespan: 14–15 years

Intense and inquisitive, Cairn Terriers are confident, feisty and playful. They are usually friendly to all, but quick to defend themselves if they feel threatened. Busy and active in the house, they will always be curious about what their owners are doing.

ORIGINALLY BRED
to hunt and kill foxes, otters and weasels in rock piles (cairns) on Scottish farms.

SPECIAL CHARACTERISTICS
This terrier is alert and curious.

EXERCISE REQUIREMENTS
Medium. Busy at home and outside.

COMMON ATTITUDE TO
OWNERS affectionate, devoted
CHILDREN usually good if raised with them
OTHER PETS due to a high prey drive and chase instincts, may cause harm to small pets; may injure cats unless raised with them
STRANGERS good
UNFAMILIAR DOGS good if socialized

PERFECT OWNER
Patient, fun-loving owner with tolerant neighbours who has time to play and exercise this active dog.

THINGS TO WATCH OUT FOR
Tendency to bark excessively. Lack of exercise may lead to digging. May display possessiveness over toys and food.

Cesky Terrier

hardy
tough
feisty
persistent
stubborn
inquisitive

Size: 28–35.5 cm (11–14 in)
Weight: 7–8 kg (15½–18 lb)
Coat: Wavy with silky sheen
Colour: Grey-blue or light brown
Lifespan: 12–14 years

Curious, inquisitive Cesky Terriers are devoted to their owners, but reserved with strangers and make good watchdogs. Feisty and courageous, they need plenty of early socialization to ensure they are tolerant of strangers and other dogs.

ORIGINALLY BRED
to dig out and kill rats and foxes.

SPECIAL CHARACTERISTICS
This terrier is easily aroused.

EXERCISE REQUIREMENTS
Medium. Enjoys exercising with owner.

COMMON ATTITUDE TO
OWNERS affectionate, devoted
CHILDREN usually good if raised with them
OTHER PETS due to a high prey drive and chase instincts, may cause harm to small pets; may injure cats unless raised with them

STRANGERS reserved
UNFAMILIAR DOGS good if well socialized

PERFECT OWNER
Active, gentle owner who has time to socialize this dog well as a puppy and provide plenty of play and exercise when older.

THINGS TO WATCH OUT FOR
May be snappy with strangers if under-socialized. Lack of exercise may lead to digging and destructiveness.

⚠️ Regular grooming and clipping are needed to keep the coat in good order.

Dandie Dinmont Terrier

tenacious
stubborn
independent
sensitive
affectionate
calm
easy-going

Size: 20–28 cm (8–11 in)
Weight: 8–11 kg (18–24 lb)
Coat: Hard topcoat with soft linty undercoat
Colour: Pepper or mustard
Lifespan: 15–16 years

Independent and sometimes a bit stubborn, Dandie Dinmont Terriers are loyal and affectionate to their owners, but reserved with strangers. Courageous and easily aroused, they require plenty of socialization when young.

ORIGINALLY BRED
to dig out and kill foxes, weasels, badgers and rats.

SPECIAL CHARACTERISTICS
This dog is courageous and easily aroused.

EXERCISE REQUIREMENTS
Low. Enjoys playing.

COMMON ATTITUDE TO OWNERS affectionate, loyal
CHILDREN usually good if raised with them

OTHER PETS due to a high prey drive and chase instincts, may cause harm to small pets; may injure cats unless raised with them
STRANGERS reserved
UNFAMILIAR DOGS friendly if well socialized

PERFECT OWNER
Experienced, strong-willed affectionate owner who can provide plenty of play and attention to focus this wilful, protective dog.

THINGS TO WATCH OUT FOR
May be problematic with strangers if not well socialized. Can be strong-willed and needs a determined owner.

Fox Terrier

Fox terriers are quick, alert, curious and active. They are good watchdogs and need plenty to do to stop them from getting into mischief. Affectionate, but independent with owners, these extrovert dogs are usually friendly with strangers, but careful socialization is needed to ensure they are tolerant of other dogs. Care is needed with small pets as their desire to hunt and kill small prey is strong.

Size: 38.5–39.5 cm (15–15½ in)
Weight: 7–8 kg (15½–18 lb)
Coat: Straight, smooth, hard
Colour: White should predominate; all white, white with tan, black and tan or black markings
Lifespan: 13–14 years

Smooth

alert
quick
keen
friendly
extrovert
curious

ORIGINALLY BRED
to hunt foxes and hunt and kill rabbits and rats.

SPECIAL CHARACTERISTICS
The Fox Terrier is alert and easily aroused.

EXERCISE REQUIREMENTS
High. Busy at home, active on walks.

COMMON ATTITUDE TO OWNERS affectionate, independent
CHILDREN usually good if raised with them

OTHER PETS due to a high prey drive and chase instincts, may cause harm to small pets; may injure cats unless raised with them
STRANGERS friendly if well socialized, territorial
UNFAMILIAR DOGS can be problematic unless well socialized

PERFECT OWNER
Active, experienced, strong-willed, playful owner who will enjoy the energy of this active, curious dog.

THINGS TO WATCH OUT FOR
Tends to bark excessively and may be problematic with other animals. May escape or dig if under-exercised.

Fox Terrier

Wire

alert
quick
keen
friendly
extrovert
obstinate
curious

Size: 38.5–39.5 cm (15–15½ in)
Weight: 7–8 kg (15½–18 lb)
Coat: Dense, very wiry texture
Colour: White should predominate; all white, white with tan, black and tan or black markings
Lifespan: 13–14 years

The Wire Fox Terrier is the rough-haired version of the Smooth Fox Terrier and has a similar personality and characteristics.

ORIGINALLY BRED
to hunt foxes and hunt and kill rabbits and rats.

SPECIAL CHARACTERISTICS
Alert and easily aroused.

EXERCISE REQUIREMENTS
High. Busy at home, active on walks.

COMMON ATTITUDE TO OWNERS affectionate, independent
CHILDREN usually good if raised with them

OTHER PETS due to a high prey drive and chase instincts, may cause harm to small pets; may injure cats unless raised with them
STRANGERS friendly if well socialized, territorial
UNFAMILIAR DOGS can be problematic unless well socialized

PERFECT OWNER
Active, experienced, strong-willed, playful owner who will enjoy the energy of this active, curious dog.

THINGS TO WATCH OUT FOR
Tends to bark excessively and may be problematic with other animals. May escape or dig if under-exercised.

Glen of Imaal Terrier

active
spirited
courageous
quiet
independent

Size: 35–36 cm (14 in)
Weight: 15.5–16.5 kg (34–36 lb)
Coat: Medium length, harsh texture with soft undercoat
Colour: Blue, brindle and wheaten (all shades)
Lifespan: 13–14 years
In the 'Miscellaneous' class in the USA

Courageous and tenacious, Glen of Imaal Terriers are unlikely to back down if challenged. Affectionate, loyal and independent with owners, they are easily aroused and need plenty of socialization to keep them tolerant of other dogs.

ORIGINALLY BRED
to hunt and kill foxes and badgers.

SPECIAL CHARACTERISTICS
Alert and easily aroused.

EXERCISE REQUIREMENTS
High. Enjoys exercise.

COMMON ATTITUDE TO
OWNERS affectionate, loyal
CHILDREN usually good if raised with them
OTHER PETS due to a high prey drive and chase instincts, may cause harm to small pets; may injure cats unless raised with them
STRANGERS good if well socialized

UNFAMILIAR DOGS can be problematic

PERFECT OWNER
Experienced, active owner who can provide plenty of safe exercise and play for this active, feisty, independent little dog.

THINGS TO WATCH OUT FOR
Tendency to be problematic with other dogs.

Irish Terrier

inquisitive
affectionate
courageous
good-tempered
devoted

Size: 46–48 cm (18–19 in)
Weight: 11–12 kg (24–26 lb)
Coat: Harsh and wiry
Colour: Red, red and wheaten or yellow and red
Lifespan: 13 years

Similar in appearance to Airedales but smaller, Irish Terriers are good-natured with their owners and, usually, strangers. Feisty and easily aroused, they can be reactive and problematic around other dogs and need plenty of early socialization to remain tolerant.

ORIGINALLY BRED
to hunt and kill rats and rabbits.

SPECIAL CHARACTERISTICS
The Irish Terrier is fast and curious.

EXERCISE REQUIREMENTS
High. Needs plenty of exercise in a safe environment.

COMMON ATTITUDE TO
OWNERS affectionate, loyal
CHILDREN usually good if raised with them
OTHER PETS due to a high prey drive and chase instincts, may cause harm to small pets; may injure cats unless raised with them
STRANGERS territorial

UNFAMILIAR DOGS needs adequate, early and continued socialization, otherwise can be problematic

PERFECT OWNER
Experienced, strong-willed active owner who has the time and knowledge to adequately socialize this dog as a puppy and provide games and safe exercise when it is older.

THINGS TO WATCH OUT FOR
Tends to be problematic with other dogs and strangers.

⚠️ This dog's coat will bring in mud and dirt from outside.

Jack Russell Terrier

**active
resilient
courageous
tenacious
independent
feisty
exuberant**

Size: 23–26 cm (9–10 in)
Weight: 4–7 kg (9–15½ lb)
Coat: Smooth-haired and rough-haired varieties known
Colour: Any
Lifespan: 12–18 years

Jack Russell Terriers are popular and well known. They are active, inquisitive and extrovert, as well as being easily aroused and unlikely to back down if challenged. They need careful socialization with children, adults and other dogs when young.

ORIGINALLY BRED
to hunt and kill rats and mice.

SPECIAL CHARACTERISTICS
Jack Russells are alert and easily aroused.

EXERCISE REQUIREMENTS
High. Needs plenty of exercise.

COMMON ATTITUDE TO
OWNERS affectionate, loyal
CHILDREN usually good if raised with them
OTHER PETS due to a high prey drive and chase instincts, may cause harm to small pets; may injure cats unless raised with them
STRANGERS good if well socialized
UNFAMILIAR DOGS can be problematic unless well socialized

PERFECT OWNER
Experienced, active owner who has the knowledge and time to socialize this dog well when a puppy and provide plenty of activity, exercise and play when an adult.

THINGS TO WATCH OUT FOR
May be problematic with strangers and other dogs, tendency to be 'snappy'.

Kerry Blue Terrier

alert
determined
tenacious
courageous
playful
active

Size: 46–48 cm (18–19 in)
Weight: 15–17 kg (33–37 lb)
Coat: Non-shedding soft, wavy topcoat with no undercoat
Colour: Any shade of blue with or without black points
Lifespan: 14 years

Active, alert and curious, Kerry Blue Terriers are devoted and playful with their owners and people they know. Reserved with strangers, they make good watchdogs and need early and continued socialization, especially with other dogs.

ORIGINALLY BRED
to hunt and kill rats and rabbits.

SPECIAL CHARACTERISTICS
This terrier is alert and easily aroused.

EXERCISE REQUIREMENTS
High. Playful and full of energy.

COMMON ATTITUDE TO
OWNERS affectionate, devoted
CHILDREN usually good, protective
OTHER PETS due to a high prey drive and chase instincts, may cause harm to small pets; may injure cats unless raised with them

STRANGERS reserved, territorial
UNFAMILIAR DOGS likely to be problematic. Early and continued socialization needed

PERFECT OWNER
Experienced, active owner who can provide a safe outlet for this dog's high energy levels.

THINGS TO WATCH OUT FOR
Problematic with other dogs unless well socialized.

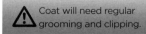
Coat will need regular grooming and clipping.

Lakeland Terrier

keen
quick
friendly
confident
courageous
tenacious
independent

Size: 33–37 cm (13–14½ in)
Weight: 7–8 kg (15½–18 lb)
Coat: Dense, harsh and weather-resistant with good undercoat
Colour: Black and tan, blue and tan, red, wheaten, red grizzle, liver, blue or black
Lifespan: 13–14 years

Lakeland Terriers are alert, active and keen. They like to be busy and will find their own things to do if bored. More easy-going with other dogs than many other terriers, Lakelands are friendly with strangers and other dogs if they have been properly socialized.

ORIGINALLY BRED
to hunt and kill rats, mice and rabbits.

SPECIAL CHARACTERISTICS
This terrier is alert and easily aroused.

EXERCISE REQUIREMENTS
High. Busy and loves plenty of exercise.

COMMON ATTITUDE TO
OWNERS affectionate, loyal
CHILDREN usually good if raised with them
OTHER PETS due to a high prey drive and chase instincts, may cause harm to small pets; may injure cats unless raised with them
STRANGERS friendly if well socialized

UNFAMILIAR DOGS good if well socialized

PERFECT OWNER
Active, playful owner who likes to include this dog in plenty of exercise and activity.

THINGS TO WATCH OUT FOR
Tends to be problematic with other dogs unless well socialized.

Manchester Terrier

keen
alert
discerning
determined
devoted

Size: 38–41 cm (15–16 in)
Weight: 5–10 kg (11–22 lb)
Coat: Close, smooth and glossy
Colour: Jet black and rich mahogany tan
Lifespan: 13–14 years

Manchester Terriers appear very delicate, but are robust and determined underneath. Active and curious, they have not lost their desire to hunt. They are wary and aloof with strangers, but affectionate and devoted to their owners.

ORIGINALLY BRED
to hunt and kill rats and rabbits.

SPECIAL CHARACTERISTICS
The Manchester Terrier is alert and easily aroused.

EXERCISE REQUIREMENTS
Medium. Active and likes to be entertained.

COMMON ATTITUDE TO
OWNERS affectionate, devoted
CHILDREN usually good if raised with them
OTHER PETS due to a high prey drive and chase instincts, may cause harm to small pets; may injure cats
STRANGERS wary, aloof

UNFAMILIAR DOGS good if well socialized

PERFECT OWNER
Gentle, playful, experienced owner who can provide enough activity to keep this active dog entertained and who will enjoy its independent nature.

THINGS TO WATCH OUT FOR
Tends to bark excessively. Lack of exercise may lead to escapes.

Manchester Terriers, unlike the smaller English Toy Terrier, have ears that fold over and hang down.

Norfolk Terrier

alert
good-natured
tenacious
courageous
independent
lively

Norfolk Terriers are similar to Norwich Terriers, but have folded ears, giving them a softer appearance. They are feisty little hunters, good watchdogs, responsive and loyal to their owners and usually friendly with strangers and other dogs, although proper socialization is essential.

Size: 24–25 cm (9½–10 in)
Weight: 5–5.5 kg (11–12 lb)
Coat: Hard, wiry, medium length, straight
Colour: All shades of red, wheaten, black and tan or grizzle
Lifespan: 14 years

ORIGINALLY BRED
to hunt and kill rats.

SPECIAL CHARACTERISTICS
This terrier is alert and easily aroused.

EXERCISE REQUIREMENTS
Medium. Enjoys rough-and-tumble play.

COMMON ATTITUDE TO OWNERS affectionate, loyal
CHILDREN usually good if raised with them

OTHER PETS due to a high prey drive and chase instincts, may cause harm to small pets; may chase cats unless raised with them
STRANGERS friendly
UNFAMILIAR DOGS friendly if well socialized

PERFECT OWNER
Active, easy-going owner who will provide plenty of play and exercise for this exuberant, independent little dog.

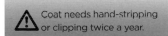

Coat needs hand-stripping or clipping twice a year.

Norwich Terrier

**alert
good-natured
tenacious
courageous
independent
lively**

Size: 24–25 cm (9½–10 in)
Weight: 5–5.5 kg (11–12 lb)
Coat: Hard, wiry, medium length, straight
Colour: All shades of red, wheaten, black and tan or grizzle
Lifespan: 14 years

Norwich Terriers are similar to Norfolk Terriers, but have pricked ears. They are feisty little hunters, good watchdogs, responsive and loyal to their owners and usually friendly with strangers and other dogs, although proper socialization is essential.

ORIGINALLY BRED
to hunt and kill rats.

SPECIAL CHARACTERISTICS
The Norwich Terrier is alert and easily aroused.

EXERCISE REQUIREMENTS
Medium. Enjoys play.

COMMON ATTITUDE TO
OWNERS affectionate, loyal
CHILDREN usually good if raised with them
OTHER PETS due to a high prey drive and chase instincts, may cause harm to small pets; may chase cats unless raised with them

STRANGERS friendly
UNFAMILIAR DOGS friendly if well socialized

PERFECT OWNER
Active, easy-going owner who will provide plenty of play and exercise for this exuberant, independent little dog.

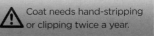
Coat needs hand-stripping or clipping twice a year.

Parson Russell Terrier

bold
friendly
tenacious
courageous
spirited

Size: 33–36 cm (13–14 in)
Weight: 5–8 kg (11–18 lb)
Coat: Naturally harsh and dense, whether rough or smooth
Colour: Entirely white or predominantly white with tan, lemon or black markings
Lifespan: 13–14 years

The show cousin of the Jack Russell Terrier, Parson Russell Terriers are lively, active and curious. They are easily aroused extroverts, unlikely to back down if challenged and need careful socialization with children, adults and other dogs when young.

ORIGINALLY BRED
to follow the hunt and dig out foxes from their lairs.

SPECIAL CHARACTERISTICS
This dog is feisty and easily aroused.

EXERCISE REQUIREMENTS
High. Needs plenty of exercise to burn off its abundant energy.

COMMON ATTITUDE TO
OWNERS affectionate, loyal
CHILDREN usually good if raised with them
OTHER PETS due to a high prey drive and chase instincts, may cause harm to small pets; may injure cats unless raised with them

STRANGERS good if well socialized
UNFAMILIAR DOGS good if well socialized

PERFECT OWNER
Active, tolerant, playful owner who can provide energetic walks and enough playful activity to use up this lively dog's mental and physical energy.

THINGS TO WATCH OUT FOR
Tends to bark excessively. May be 'snappy' if inadequately socialized, especially with other dogs.

Scottish Terrier

dignified
sensible
independent
reserved
courageous
stubborn

Size: 25–28 cm (10–11 in)
Weight: 8.5–10.5 kg (19–23 lb)
Coat: Harsh, dense and wiry topcoat, with short, dense and soft undercoat
Colour: Black, wheaten or brindle of any shade
Lifespan: 13–14 years

Wilful and independent, the Scottish Terrier is courageous and unlikely to back down if challenged. Loyal to their owners, Scotties need plenty of early socialization with people and other dogs.

ORIGINALLY BRED
to hunt and kill small mammals.

SPECIAL CHARACTERISTICS
Feisty and easily aroused.

EXERCISE REQUIREMENTS
Medium. Needs exercise to burn off energy.

COMMON ATTITUDE TO
OWNERS affectionate, loyal
CHILDREN usually tolerant if raised with them
OTHER PETS due to a high prey drive and chase instincts, may cause harm to small pets; may injure cats unless raised with them

STRANGERS reserved, territorial
UNFAMILIAR DOGS can be problematic

PERFECT OWNER
Experienced, strong-willed, determined owner who can match this dog's personality and who is willing to provide plenty of safe activity to use up its energy.

THINGS TO WATCH OUT FOR
Can be strong-willed and needs a determined owner. Tends to be problematic with strangers and other dogs if inadequately socialized.

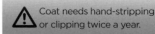
⚠ Coat needs hand-stripping or clipping twice a year.

Sealyham Terrier

alert
courageous
friendly
tenacious
stubborn
independent

Wilful and independent, Sealyhams have plenty of self-assurance. They are loyal and affectionate watchdogs, have retained a strong hunting instinct and need plenty of activity to keep them occupied.

Size: 25–31 cm (10–12 in)
Weight: 8–9 kg (18–20 lb)
Coat: Long, hard and wiry topcoat with thick undercoat
Colour: All white or white with lemon, brown, blue or badger pied markings on head and ears
Lifespan: 14 years

ORIGINALLY BRED
to hunt and kill badgers and otters.

SPECIAL CHARACTERISTICS
The Sealyham is feisty and easily aroused.

EXERCISE REQUIREMENTS
Medium. Needs exercise to burn off energy.

COMMON ATTITUDE TO OWNERS affectionate, loyal
CHILDREN usually good if raised with them

OTHER PETS due to a high prey drive and chase instincts, may cause harm to small pets; may injure cats unless raised with them
STRANGERS reserved, territorial
UNFAMILIAR DOGS can be problematic

PERFECT OWNER
Experienced, strong-willed, active owner able to enjoy this independent character and provide plenty of activity and play to use up its energy.

THINGS TO WATCH OUT FOR
Can be strong-willed and needs a determined owner. Tends to be problematic with strangers and other dogs if inadequately socialized.

Skye Terrier

dignified
tenacious
bold
confident
independent

Size: 25–26 cm (10 in)
Weight: 8.5–10.5 kg (19–23 lb)
Coat: Long, hard outer coat, with short, soft, woolly undercoat
Colour: Black, dark or light grey, fawn or cream, all with black points
Lifespan: 13 years

Skye Terriers have a coat that needs care and attention to keep it free of tangles. They are reserved and territorial with strangers, but affectionate and loyal to owners. They have retained a strong desire to hunt and need careful socialization to ensure they are tolerant with strangers and other dogs.

ORIGINALLY BRED
to hunt and kill otter, badger and weasel.

SPECIAL CHARACTERISTICS
This terrier is alert and easily aroused.

EXERCISE REQUIREMENTS
Medium.

COMMON ATTITUDE TO
OWNERS affectionate, loyal
CHILDREN usually good if raised with them
OTHER PETS due to a high prey drive and chase instincts, may cause harm to small pets; may injure cats unless raised with them

STRANGERS reserved, territorial
UNFAMILIAR DOGS can be problematic

PERFECT OWNER
Experienced, strong-willed, active owner able to enjoy this independent character and provide plenty of socialization when young and activity when older.

THINGS TO WATCH OUT FOR
Tendency to be problematic with strangers. Can be strong-willed and needs a determined owner.

⚠ Daily coat care is needed to prevent tangling. Hair should be cut or tied up out of the eyes so this dog can see clearly.

Soft Coated Wheaten Terrier

good-tempered spirited confident affectionate independent

Size: 46–49 cm (18–19 in)
Weight: 16–20.5 kg (35–45 lb)
Coat: Soft and silky
Colour: A good clear wheaten
Lifespan: 13–14 years

High-spirited Soft Coated Wheaten Terriers are good-tempered, but can be wilful and independent. They are active and playful with owners and have coats that will need careful cleaning after long, boisterous walks.

ORIGINALLY BRED
for droving, herding and hunting.

SPECIAL CHARACTERISTICS
This terrier is active, playful and versatile.

EXERCISE REQUIREMENTS
High. Enjoys plenty of exercise.

COMMON ATTITUDE TO
OWNERS affectionate, loyal
CHILDREN usually good if raised with them
OTHER PETS due to a high prey drive and chase instincts, may cause harm to small pets; may injure cats unless raised with them
STRANGERS good if well socialized
UNFAMILIAR DOGS can be problematic

PERFECT OWNER
Experienced, strong-willed owner who can provide this exuberant dog with a job to do, plenty of exercise, play and training.

THINGS TO WATCH OUT FOR
Can be strong-willed and needs a determined owner. Tends to be problematic with other dogs.

⚠ This dog's coat will bring in mud and dirt from outside and will need careful cleaning.

Staffordshire Bull Terrier

courageous
tenacious
affectionate
bold

Size: 36–41 cm (14–16 in)
Weight: 11–17 kg (24–37 lb)
Coat: Smooth, short and close
Colour: Red, fawn, white, black or blue, or any one of these colours with white; any shade of brindle or any shade of brindle with white
Lifespan: 11–12 years

Staffordshire Bull Terriers are very loyal and tolerant with family members. They are resilient and physically robust. They are spirited and tenacious. They need kind handling and good socialization when young, particularly with other dogs.

ORIGINALLY BRED
for dog-fighting.

SPECIAL CHARACTERISTICS
The Staffordshire Bull Terrier is resilient and physically robust. It has the ability to hold on when biting; it is also easily aroused.

EXERCISE REQUIREMENTS
High. Will walk a long way if required.

COMMON ATTITUDE TO
OWNERS affectionate, loving
CHILDREN very good if raised with them, play biting can be problematic when young

OTHER PETS due to a high prey drive and chase instincts, may cause harm to small pets
STRANGERS usually friendly
UNFAMILIAR DOGS tendency to be problematic. Adequate early socialization needed

PERFECT OWNER
Experienced, strong-willed, active owner who has the time and knowledge to teach this dog to be nice to other dogs and who can provide plenty of affection, exercise and play.

THINGS TO WATCH OUT FOR
May be problematic with other dogs unless adequate and appropriate early socialization is given.

Welsh Terrier

sociable
curious
playful
tenacious

Welsh Terriers are active, curious and busy, always looking for something to do. Courageous and independent, they have not lost their hunting spirit and are unlikely to back down if challenged.

Size: 36–39 cm (14–15½ in)
Weight: 9–9.5 kg (20–21 lb)
Coat: Wiry, hard, very close and abundant
Colour: Black and tan for preference, or black grizzle and tan
Lifespan: 14 years

ORIGINALLY BRED
to hunt and kill rats and other small animals.

SPECIAL CHARACTERISTICS
Alert and easily aroused.

EXERCISE REQUIREMENTS
Medium. Enjoys exercise and games.

COMMON ATTITUDE TO
OWNERS affectionate, loyal
CHILDREN usually good if raised with them
OTHER PETS due to a high prey drive and chase instincts, may cause harm to small pets; may injure cats unless raised with them
STRANGERS can be wary, territorial
UNFAMILIAR DOGS can be problematic

PERFECT OWNER
Experienced, confident owner who has the time and energy to play with, train and exercise a dog with an exuberant, independent character.

THINGS TO WATCH OUT FOR
Tends to be problematic with other dogs.

⚠ This dog's coat needs regular stripping or clipping to keep it in good condition.

West Highland White Terrier

confident
alert
courageous
independent
friendly

Size: 25–28 cm (10–11 in)
Weight: 7–10 kg (15½–22 lb)
Coat: Harsh topcoat with short, soft undercoat
Colour: White
Lifespan: 14 years

Active and high-spirited, West Highland White Terriers are popular pets. Feisty and easily aroused, they can also be wilful and independent. Westies are excellent watchdogs, but the desire to bark should be calmed early to prevent them becoming too noisy.

ORIGINALLY BRED
to hunt and kill rats.

SPECIAL CHARACTERISTICS
The Westie is alert and easily aroused.

EXERCISE REQUIREMENTS
High. Enjoys exercise and play.

COMMON ATTITUDE TO
OWNERS affectionate, loyal
CHILDREN usually good if raised with them
OTHER PETS due to a high prey drive and chase instincts, may cause harm to small pets; may injure cats unless raised with them

STRANGERS friendly if well socialized
UNFAMILIAR DOGS friendly if well socialized

PERFECT OWNER
Strong-willed, active owner who will enjoy this dog's excitable, independent spirit and who can provide plenty of play, exercise and training.

THINGS TO WATCH OUT FOR
Dogs from some lines can be strong-willed and need a determined owner (especially male dogs). Tends to bark excessively.

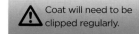
⚠ Coat will need to be clipped regularly.

Affenpinscher

busy
pushy
affectionate
curious
alert
fast

Size: 24-28 cm (9½-11 in)
Weight: 3-4 kg (6½-9 lb)
Coat: Hard, wiry, medium length
Colour: Black, black and tan, red, brindle and tan
Lifespan: 14 years

Monkeyish in looks and behaviour, Affenpinschers are wilful, stubborn and independent. They are lively and inquisitive, and have strong hunting instincts. They are reserved with strangers and make good little watchdogs.

ORIGINALLY BRED
to catch rats and mice, later to be ladies' companions.

SPECIAL CHARACTERISTICS
The Affenpinscher is alert, reactive and playful.

EXERCISE REQUIREMENTS
Medium. Busy in the house and outside.

COMMON ATTITUDE TO OWNERS affectionate, independent
CHILDREN puppies and adults may be injured by boisterous children
OTHER PETS may be problematic with small pets

STRANGERS reserved, good watchdog
UNFAMILIAR DOGS good if well socialized

PERFECT OWNER
Confident owner who will enjoy the independent, wilful nature of this lively little dog and who can provide plenty of exercise and play.

THINGS TO WATCH OUT FOR
May be difficult to housetrain. Can be strong-willed and needs a determined owner. May bark excessively.

⚠ This dog's shortened nose can make breathing difficult and it is likely to snore.

The Affenpinscher's shortened face and bushy eyebrows give it a monkeyish appearance.

Australian Silky Terrier

energetic
determined
courageous
alert
friendly
responsive

Size: 22–23 cm (8½–9 in)
Weight: 4–5 kg (9–11 lb)
Coat: Long, fine and glossy, silky
Colour: Blue and tan, grey-blue and tan
Lifespan: 14–16 years
Also known as Silky Terrier

Energetic, alert and lively, Australian Silky Terriers make excellent watchdogs and care is needed to prevent their barking becoming excessive. They are friendly and playful.

ORIGINALLY BRED
to be a watchdog and to kill rats and mice.

SPECIAL CHARACTERISTICS
This dog is alert, reactive and playful.

EXERCISE REQUIREMENTS
Medium. Busy both at home and outside.

COMMON ATTITUDE TO
OWNERS affectionate, independent
CHILDREN usually good, puppies are very small and may be injured by young children
OTHER PETS due to a high prey drive and chase instincts, may cause harm to small pets; may injure cats unless raised with them

STRANGERS friendly
UNFAMILIAR DOGS good if well socialized

PERFECT OWNER
Active, confident owner who will enjoy this dog's independent spirit and will be able to provide exercise, play and activities to keep this busy dog occupied.

THINGS TO WATCH OUT FOR
May bark excessively. Can easily get frustrated or excited.

⚠ The silky coat needs careful daily brushing to prevent mats from forming. There is no undercoat so the dog may be cold in winter.

Bichon Frise

happy
lively
vivacious
affectionate

Size: 23–28 cm (9–11 in)
Weight: 3–6 kg (6½–13 lb)
Coat: Fine, silky with soft corkscrew curls
Colour: White
Lifespan: 14 years
In the 'Non-sporting' class in the USA

Although their coats need daily care, Bichon Frise are good-natured dogs that make excellent pets. Lively and vivacious, they are friendly with everyone and they make easy, delightful companions.

ORIGINALLY BRED
to be a companion.

SPECIAL CHARACTERISTICS
This is a friendly dog that enjoys human company.

EXERCISE REQUIREMENTS
Low–Medium. Enjoys playing family games.

COMMON ATTITUDE TO
OWNERS affectionate, devoted
CHILDREN usually good
OTHER PETS good
STRANGERS friendly
UNFAMILIAR DOGS friendly

PERFECT OWNER
Sociable, affectionate owner who will enjoy the daily coat-care ritual.

THINGS TO WATCH OUT FOR
May be hard to housetrain.

✔ Recommended for first-time owners who like to groom their dogs on a daily basis.

⚠ This dog's coat will bring in mud and dirt from outside and needs daily care and occasional clipping to keep it in good condition.

Bolognese

devoted affectionate to owners serious docile reserved with strangers

Size: 25.5–30.5 cm (10–12 in)
Weight: 3–4 kg (6½–9 lb)
Coat: Long, flocked without curl covering entire head and body
Colour: White. Lips, eyelids, nose and nails black
Lifespan: 14 years

Similar to the Bichon Frise but more serious, shy and reserved with strangers. Bologneses like to form strong bonds with their owners, with whom they are affectionate and devoted.

ORIGINALLY BRED
to be a companion.

SPECIAL CHARACTERISTICS
This gentle dog enjoys company.

EXERCISE REQUIREMENTS
Low. Enjoys free exercise.

COMMON ATTITUDE TO
OWNERS affectionate, devoted
CHILDREN usually good
OTHER PETS good
STRANGERS reserved, shy
UNFAMILIAR DOGS friendly if well socialized

PERFECT OWNER
Gentle, affectionate, quiet-living owner.

THINGS TO WATCH OUT FOR
May suffer from separation problems. May be hard to housetrain.

Cavalier King Charles Spaniel

sporting
lively
gentle
affectionate
friendly

Size: 31–33 cm (12–13 in)
Weight: 5–8 kg (11–18 lb)
Coat: Long, silky, with plenty of feathering
Colour: Black and tan, ruby, Blenheim (chestnut markings on white ground), tricolour
Lifespan: 9–11 years

Happy and playful, Cavalier King Charles Spaniels make ideal companions. They are plagued with inherited health problems so finding a healthy strain is important. Devoted and affectionate with owners, they are friendly with all and make excellent pets for families with children.

ORIGINALLY BRED
to be a companion.

SPECIAL CHARACTERISTICS
This Spaniel is affectionate, sweet-natured and playful.

EXERCISE REQUIREMENTS
Medium. Enjoys and needs regular exercise.

COMMON ATTITUDE TO OWNERS affectionate, devoted
CHILDREN playful, good-natured

OTHER PETS good
STRANGERS friendly
UNFAMILIAR DOGS friendly

PERFECT OWNER
Affectionate, gentle families who will enjoy this lively, playful dog.

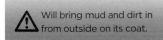
Will bring mud and dirt in from outside on its coat.

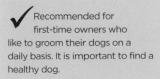
Recommended for first-time owners who like to groom their dogs on a daily basis. It is important to find a healthy dog.

Chihuahua (Long haired, Smooth Coated)

**alert
spirited
bold
friendly
affectionate**

Size: 15–23 cm (6–9 in)
Weight: 1–3 kg (2–6½ lb)
Coat: Long haired: medium length, soft texture. Smooth Coated: smooth, soft texture
Colour: Any
Lifespan: 14–18 years

Chihuahuas are big dogs in a little body. Bold and spirited, they are lively and playful and devoted to their owners. They are also friendly to others, although naturally wary of boisterous children or dogs much larger than themselves.

Long-haired variety

ORIGINALLY BRED
to be a companion.

SPECIAL CHARACTERISTICS
The Chihuahua is playful and likes human company.

EXERCISE REQUIREMENTS
Low. Enthusiastic about exercise.

COMMON ATTITUDE TO
OWNERS affectionate, devoted
CHILDREN puppies and adults may be injured by boisterous children
OTHER PETS good
STRANGERS reserved, shy
UNFAMILIAR DOGS friendly

PERFECT OWNER
Gentle, affectionate owner who will play with and take special care of this tiny dog.

Chinese Crested

Chinese Cresteds are bred in two varieties, the Hairless and Powder Puff. Chinese Cresteds are lively, affectionate pets that are devoted to their owners.

Size: 23–33 cm (9–13 in)
Weight: 2–5.5 kg (4½–12 lb)
Coat: Soft, supple skin with long silky hair on the head, feet and tail
Colour: Any
Lifespan: 15 years

Hairless

lively
affectionate
sensitive
fun-loving
stubborn

ORIGINALLY BRED
to be a companion.

SPECIAL CHARACTERISTICS
The Chinese Crested is friendly and likes to be with people.

EXERCISE REQUIREMENTS
Low.

COMMON ATTITUDE TO
OWNERS affectionate, devoted
CHILDREN puppies and adults may be injured by boisterous children
OTHER PETS good
STRANGERS friendly
UNFAMILIAR DOGS friendly if well socialized.

PERFECT OWNER
Sociable, affectionate owner who will happily perform daily skin care.

THINGS TO WATCH OUT FOR
May be difficult to housetrain and prone to territory marking, particularly if male.

⚠ A daily skincare routine is needed for the Hairless variety, which can be prone to skin complaints. It may have missing teeth and toenails. Some young Hairless dogs can go through a 'teenage' acne stage. They also suffer from cold temperatures and get sunburned easily.

Chinese Crested

Powder Puff

lively
affectionate
sensitive
fun-loving
stubborn

Size: 23–33 cm (9–13 in)
Weight: 2–5.5 kg (4½–12 lb)
Coat: Completely covered with
long, silky hair
Colour: Any
Lifespan: 15 years

ORIGINALLY BRED
to be a companion.

SPECIAL CHARACTERISTICS
The Chinese Crested is friendly
and likes to be with people.

EXERCISE REQUIREMENTS
Low.

COMMON ATTITUDE TO
OWNERS affectionate, devoted
CHILDREN puppies and adults
may be injured by boisterous
children
OTHER PETS good
STRANGERS friendly
UNFAMILIAR DOGS friendly if
well socialized.

PERFECT OWNER
Sociable, affectionate owner
who will perform daily coat care.

THINGS TO WATCH OUT FOR
May be difficult to housetrain
and prone to territory marking,
particularly if male.

⚠️ The Powder Puff variety
will need daily grooming
to keep its silky fur free of
tangles.

*The Powder Puff's face is usually
shaved for shows.*

English Toy Terrier (Black and Tan)

keen
alert
discerning
determined
tenacious
devoted

Size: 25–30 cm (10–12 in)
Weight: 2.7–3.6 kg (6–8 lb)
Coat: Thick, short and glossy
Colour: Black and tan
Lifespan: 12–13 years
*Also known as Manchester
Terrier (Toy)*

**English Toy Terriers look like a smaller
version of the Manchester Terrier, but have
pricked ears. Cat-like and clean, they are
active, lively and playful. Aloof with strangers,
they prefer to be with their owners.**

ORIGINALLY BRED
to hunt and kill rats, later
as a companion.

SPECIAL CHARACTERISTICS
This dog is alert, feisty
and playful.

EXERCISE REQUIREMENTS
Medium. Needs to be kept
entertained.

COMMON ATTITUDE TO
OWNERS affectionate, devoted
CHILDREN puppies and adults
may be injured by boisterous
children
OTHER PETS may be problematic
with small pets
STRANGERS wary, aloof
UNFAMILIAR DOGS good if
well socialized

PERFECT OWNER
Gentle, playful experienced
owner who can provide enough
activity to keep this active dog
entertained and who will enjoy
its rather independent nature.

THINGS TO WATCH OUT FOR
Tends to bark excessively. Lack
of exercise may lead to escapes.

Griffon Bruxellois (Brussels Griffon)

lively
alert
good-natured
tenacious
courageous
sensitive

Size: 18–20 cm (7–8 in)
Weight: 2.3–5 kg (5–11 lb)
Coat: Rough: harsh, wiry.
   Smooth: short and tight
Colour: Clear red, black or black
   and rich tan without white
   markings
Lifespan: 12–14 years

A possible descendant of the Affenpinscher, Griffon Bruxellois are lively and inquisitive. They have retained strong hunting instincts, make good watchdogs, are devoted to owners and friendly to strangers.

ORIGINALLY BRED
to kill rats, later as a companion.

SPECIAL CHARACTERISTICS
Alert and active, the Griffon Bruxellois likes company.

EXERCISE REQUIREMENTS
Low. Enjoys exercise and play.

COMMON ATTITUDE TO
OWNERS affectionate, devoted
CHILDREN puppies and adults may be injured by boisterous children
OTHER PETS may be problematic with small pets
STRANGERS friendly if well socialized
UNFAMILIAR DOGS friendly if well socialized

PERFECT OWNER
Gentle, sociable owner who will enjoy this playful, good-natured little dog.

THINGS TO WATCH OUT FOR
May bark excessively.

⚠ This dog's bulbous eyes are prone to injury. Its shortened nose can make breathing difficult and it is likely to snore. Some may be finicky eaters. Coat will need to be hand-stripped or clipped.

Havanese

lively
gentle
affectionate
responsive
friendly
sensitive
outgoing

Size: 23–28 cm (9–11 in)
Weight: 3–6 kg (6½–13 lb)
Coat: Soft, silky, wavy or slightly curled, full coated with an undercoat
Colour: Any
Lifespan: 14 years

Gentle and a little reserved with strangers, Havanese are responsive and devoted to their owners. Playful and outgoing, they are also sensitive and can be easily upset.

ORIGINALLY BRED
to be a companion.

SPECIAL CHARACTERISTICS
The playful Havanese likes to be with people.

EXERCISE REQUIREMENTS
Medium. Enjoys playing.

COMMON ATTITUDE TO
OWNERS affectionate, devoted
CHILDREN usually good
OTHER PETS good
STRANGERS reserved
UNFAMILIAR DOGS friendly

PERFECT OWNER
Gentle, affectionate owner who will enjoy grooming and playing with this sensitive, energetic little dog.

THINGS TO WATCH OUT FOR
May suffer from separation problems.

⚠ This dog's full coat will bring in mud and dirt from outside and requires daily brushing to prevent mats from forming. The long hair above the eyes needs to be clipped or tied up so that it can see clearly.

Italian Greyhound

elegant
affectionate
sweet-natured
sensitive
aloof

Size: 32–38 cm (12½–15 in)
Weight: 3.5–4.5 kg (8–10 lb)
Coat: Short, fine and glossy. Can be cold in winter
Colour: Black, blue, cream, fawn, red, white, or any of these colours broken with white
Lifespan: 14 years

Elegant, sweet-natured and sensitive, Italian Greyhounds like to be close to their owners. Like their larger relations, they exercise in short bursts of lightning speed so safe areas are needed for walks.

ORIGINALLY BRED
to be a companion.

SPECIAL CHARACTERISTICS
This dog likes to chase and enjoys company.

EXERCISE REQUIREMENTS
Medium. Full of energy.

COMMON ATTITUDE TO
OWNERS affectionate, devoted
CHILDREN usually good, but care needed with boisterous children
OTHER PETS good, may chase
STRANGERS reserved, discerning
UNFAMILIAR DOGS friendly if well socialized

PERFECT OWNER
Gentle, affectionate owner who can provide a safe area for this active dog to run off its energy.

THINGS TO WATCH OUT FOR
May display control problems on walks. May be hard to housetrain.

Japanese Chin

happy
gentle
good-natured
delicate
independent

Size: 23–25 cm (9–10 in)
Weight: 2–4 kg (4½–9 lb)
Coat: Profuse, long, soft, straight, of silky texture
Colour: Black and white or red and white
Lifespan: 12–13 years

Japanese Chins are friendly, good-natured and make affectionate, devoted companions. They are playful and friendly to visitors. Their long coats need regular grooming to keep them in good condition.

ORIGINALLY BRED
to be a companion.

SPECIAL CHARACTERISTICS
This playful dog enjoys company.

EXERCISE REQUIREMENTS
Low. Content with short walks.

COMMON ATTITUDE TO
OWNERS affectionate, devoted
CHILDREN puppies and adults may be injured by boisterous children
OTHER PETS good
STRANGERS friendly
UNFAMILIAR DOGS friendly if well socialized

PERFECT OWNER
Gentle, affectionate owner who will care for this delicate little dog.

⚠️ The profuse coat will bring in mud and dirt from outside and regular grooming is required to keep it in good condition. This dog's bulbous eyes are prone to injury. Its shortened nose can make breathing difficult and it is likely to snore.

The shortened face and high brow gives these dogs a startled appearance.

King Charles Spaniel

happy
reserved
gentle
sensitive
affectionate

Size: 25–27 cm (10–10½ in)
Weight: 4–6 kg (9–13 lb)
Coat: Long, silky and straight
Colour: Black and tan, tricolour,
Blenheim (white with chestnut-
red patches), ruby
Lifespan: 11–12 years
Also known as English Toy Terrier

Smaller and less popular than the Cavalier, the King Charles Spaniel has a shorter face and is less friendly to strangers. They are happy and devoted to owners, but reserved with people outside the family.

ORIGINALLY BRED
to be a companion.

SPECIAL CHARACTERISTICS
This is a playful dog that likes human company.

EXERCISE REQUIREMENTS
Low. Does not need too much in the way of exercise.

COMMON ATTITUDE TO
OWNERS affectionate, devoted
CHILDREN puppies and adults may be injured by boisterous children
OTHER PETS good
STRANGERS reserved
UNFAMILIAR DOGS friendly

PERFECT OWNER
Affectionate, gentle owner who lives a quiet life.

⚠ This dog's shortened nose can make breathing difficult and it is likely to snore.

Lowchen

happy
lively
independent
strong-willed
stubborn

Size: 25–33 cm (10–13 in)
Weight: 4–8 kg (9–18 lb)
Coat: Fairly long single coat of soft texture
Colour: Any
Lifespan: 13–14 years
In the 'Non-sporting' class in the USA

Show owners shave off the coat on the hind legs to make Lowchens resemble small lions. In character, they are wilful and stubborn. They are affectionate but independent with owners and are only friendly to strangers and other dogs if well socialized when young.

ORIGINALLY BRED
as a companion.

SPECIAL CHARACTERISTICS
This playful dog likes company.

EXERCISE REQUIREMENTS
Low. Enjoys play.

COMMON ATTITUDE TO
OWNERS affectionate, independent
CHILDREN usually good
OTHER PETS good, can be problematic with other dogs in the family
STRANGERS friendly if well socialized
UNFAMILIAR DOGS can be problematic

PERFECT OWNER
Affectionate, confident owner who will enjoy playing with and training this small dog with an independent spirit.

THINGS TO WATCH OUT FOR
Can be strong-willed and needs a determined owner.

Maltese

lively
alert
sweet-tempered
affectionate

Size: 20–25 cm (8–10 in)
Weight: 2–3 kg (4½–6½ lb)
Coat: Long, straight, of silky texture
Colour: White
Lifespan: 14 years

Lively, gentle and sweet-natured Maltese are sociable and enjoy company. They are willing to please but can be a little slow to learn what is required. They are happy and friendly to all and affectionate and devoted to owners. Daily grooming of the coat is essential.

ORIGINALLY BRED
as a companion.

SPECIAL CHARACTERISTICS
The playful Maltese enjoys company.

EXERCISE REQUIREMENTS
Medium. Loves exercise.

COMMON ATTITUDE TO
OWNERS affectionate, devoted
CHILDREN usually good
OTHER PETS good
STRANGERS friendly
UNFAMILIAR DOGS friendly

PERFECT OWNER
Affectionate, playful, gentle owner with plenty of time for grooming.

⚠ The long, silky hair will bring in mud and dirt from outside and the coat needs daily grooming or regular clipping to prevent mats from forming.

The hair on the head of the Maltese needs to be tied up out of the eyes.

Miniature Pinscher

confident
spirited
courageous
feisty
alert
lively
curious

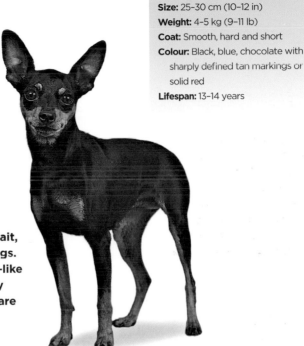

Size: 25-30 cm (10-12 in)
Weight: 4-5 kg (9-11 lb)
Coat: Smooth, hard and short
Colour: Black, blue, chocolate with sharply defined tan markings or solid red
Lifespan: 13-14 years

Miniature Pinschers have a distinctive gait, flexing at the knees more than other dogs. They are spirited and lively, with terrier-like instincts for hunting and a playful, feisty nature. Curious and independent, they are constantly busy and active.

ORIGINALLY BRED
to hunt rats and then as a companion.

SPECIAL CHARACTERISTICS
This alert dog enjoys company and has a playful nature.

EXERCISE REQUIREMENTS
Medium. Busy at home and outside.

COMMON ATTITUDE TO OWNERS affectionate, independent
CHILDREN puppies and adults may be injured by boisterous children

OTHER PETS may be problematic with small pets
STRANGERS friendly if well socialized
UNFAMILIAR DOGS friendly if well socialized

PERFECT OWNER
Active, affectionate, confident owner who will enjoy finding safe places to exercise and play with this active, independent little dog.

THINGS TO WATCH OUT FOR
May try to escape if bored.

Papillon

lively
friendly
alert
biddable

Size: 20–28 cm (8–11 in)
Weight: 4–4.5 kg (9–10 lb)
Coat: Long, fine, silky, without undercoat
Colour: White with patches or tricolour
Lifespan: 14 years

Papillons get their name from their dramatic ears, reminiscent of butterflies' wings. They are lively, responsive and devoted to their owners and can be wary of strangers and other dogs unless they are socialized well and early.

ORIGINALLY BRED
as a companion.

SPECIAL CHARACTERISTICS
Alert and playful, the Papillon enjoys company.

EXERCISE REQUIREMENTS
Medium. Busy at home and outside.

COMMON ATTITUDE TO
OWNERS affectionate, devoted
CHILDREN puppies and adults may be injured by young or boisterous children
OTHER PETS good
STRANGERS wary unless well socialized
UNFAMILIAR DOGS good if well socialized

PERFECT OWNER
Gentle, affectionate owner who will enjoy playing with, exercising and training this energetic little dog.

THINGS TO WATCH OUT FOR
Tends to bark excessively. Some suffer from separation problems.

⚠ The silky coat requires daily grooming to prevent mats from forming.

Pekingese

alert
courageous
loyal
calm
aloof
independent
stubborn

Size: 15–23 cm (6–9 in)
Weight: 4–5.5 kg (9–12 lb)
Coat: Long, straight with profuse mane and thick undercoat. Profuse feathering on ears, back of legs, tail and toes
Colour: All colours
Lifespan: 12–13 years

Pekingese were bred by ancient Chinese Royal Courts to have short, bowed legs so they could not wander far. Added to this, they have very thick coats, making them prone to overheating, and a shortened nose, that makes breathing difficult, so they do not enjoy exercise. Pekingese can be stubborn, aloof and independent.

ORIGINALLY BRED
as a companion.

SPECIAL CHARACTERISTICS
The Pekingese is an alert dog that enjoys company.

EXERCISE REQUIREMENTS
Low. The thick coat and breathing difficulties caused by its short nose sap its energy.

COMMON ATTITUDE TO OWNERS affectionate, loyal
CHILDREN puppies and adults may be injured by young or boisterous children

OTHER PETS good
STRANGERS aloof
UNFAMILIAR DOGS good if well socialized

PERFECT OWNER
Easy-going, gentle owner who will enjoy grooming and petting this independent little dog.

THINGS TO WATCH OUT FOR
Tends to bark excessively.

⚠️ This dog's long coat will bring in mud and dirt from outside and requires daily grooming to prevent mats from forming. Its bulbous eyes are prone to injury, and the shortened nose can make breathing difficult, so it is likely to snore.

Pomeranian

vivacious extrovert lively affectionate

Size: 22–28 cm (8½–11 in)
Weight: 1.8–2.5 kg (4–5½ lb)
Coat: Long, straight, harsh topcoat, with soft, fluffy undercoat
Colour: Any
Lifespan: 15 years

Pomeranians are lively, busy and extrovert. They are affectionate and devoted to their owners and are alert watchdogs, although early control is needed to prevent barking becoming excessive. Their coats are thick and need daily care.

ORIGINALLY BRED
to be a companion.

SPECIAL CHARACTERISTICS
The Pomeranian is alert and enjoys company.

EXERCISE REQUIREMENTS
Medium. Busy at home and outside.

COMMON ATTITUDE TO
OWNERS affectionate, devoted
CHILDREN puppies and adults may be injured by boisterous children
OTHER PETS good
STRANGERS good if well socialized
UNFAMILIAR DOGS good if well socialized

PERFECT OWNER
Active, gentle, affectionate owner with time to groom and play.

THINGS TO WATCH OUT FOR
Tends to bark excessively.

The head of the Pomeranian resembles a small ball.

⚠ This dog's long coat will bring mud and dirt in from outside and requires daily grooming to prevent mats from forming.

Pug

friendly
industrious
sociable
gentle
playful
obedient
busy

Independent, wilful and resolute, Pugs are forceful and determined. Distinctive and endearing, they are loyal, playful companions.

Size: 25–28 cm (10–11 in)
Weight: 6.5–8 kg (14–18 lb)
Coat: Fine, soft, short and glossy
Colour: Silver, apricot, fawn or black. Muzzle or mask, ears, moles on cheeks, thumb mark or diamond on forehead and trace as black as possible
Lifespan: 13–14 years

ORIGINALLY BRED
to be a companion.

SPECIAL CHARACTERISTICS
Alert and playful, the Pug enjoys company.

EXERCISE REQUIREMENTS
Low. Stocky but can move fast.

COMMON ATTITUDE TO
OWNERS affectionate, loyal
CHILDREN puppies and adults may be injured by boisterous children
OTHER PETS good
STRANGERS friendly
UNFAMILIAR DOGS friendly

PERFECT OWNER
Affectionate, gentle owner who will enjoy this friendly, independent little character.

THINGS TO WATCH OUT FOR
This breed has a small gene pool so health issues abound. Breathing difficulties and snoring are likely due to the shortened face.

⚠ This dog's shortened nose can cause breathing difficulties and it is likely to snore. Its bulbous eyes are prone to injury.

Toy Fox Terrier (American Toy Terrier)

bright
alert
courageous
playful
energetic
independent

Size: 24.5–25.5 cm (9½–10 in)
Weight: 2–3 kg (4½–6½ lb)
Coat: Smooth, short
Colour: Tricolour, tan and white, black and white
Lifespan: 13–14 years

Energetic and alert, Toy Fox Terriers are quick, energetic and playful. They like to be busy and are determined little hunters given the chance. Friendly and affectionate, they are easily aroused and need plenty of early socialization to keep them tolerant of others.

ORIGINALLY BRED
to hunt rats, then as a companion.

SPECIAL CHARACTERISTICS
The Toy Fox Terrier is alert and playful, and likes company.

EXERCISE REQUIREMENTS
Medium. Busy at home and outside.

COMMON ATTITUDE TO
OWNERS affectionate, devoted
CHILDREN puppies and adults may be injured by boisterous children

OTHER PETS may be problematic with small pets
STRANGERS good if well socialized
UNFAMILIAR DOGS good if well socialized

PERFECT OWNER
Active, affectionate owner who will enjoy exercising, playing with and training this lively, independent little dog.

Yorkshire Terrier

alert
spirited
friendly
courageous
stubborn

Size: 22.5–23.5 cm (9 in)
Weight: 2.5–3.5 kg (5½–8 lb)
Coat: Long, straight, fine, silky texture
Colour: Dark steel blue and bright tan
Lifespan: 14 years

Bred by miners to hunt rats, Yorkshire Terriers are feisty, courageous hunters despite their small size. Playful, tenacious and stubborn, these busy little dogs make good watchdogs. Excessive barking will need to be controlled and they require daily grooming sessions to de-tangle their long hair.

ORIGINALLY BRED
to hunt and kill rats.

SPECIAL CHARACTERISTICS
The Yorkshire Terrier is alert, playful and feisty.

EXERCISE REQUIREMENTS
High. Busy at home and outside.

COMMON ATTITUDE TO
OWNERS affectionate, loyal
CHILDREN puppies and adults may be injured by boisterous children
OTHER PETS due to a high prey drive and chase instincts, may cause harm to small pets; may injure cats unless raised with them

STRANGERS good if well socialized
UNFAMILIAR DOGS good if well socialized

PERFECT OWNER
Active, affectionate, gentle owner who can provide plenty of exercise and play for this lively little dog.

THINGS TO WATCH OUT FOR
Tends to bark excessively, especially if under-exercised.

⚠ This dog's coat will bring mud and dirt in from outdoors and requires daily grooming to prevent mats from forming. The long hair on the top of the head needs to be clipped or tied up out of the eyes so the dog can see clearly.

Akita

dignified
courageous
aloof
calm
independent
undemonstrative
stubborn

Size: 61–71 cm (24–28 in)
Weight: 34–50 kg (75–110 lb)
Coat: Medium-length, coarse,
straight topcoat with soft,
dense undercoat
Colour: Any
Lifespan: 10–12 years
In the 'Working' class in the USA

**Independent and aloof, Akitas are slow
to show their feelings. They are reserved
with strangers and need appropriate and
continued socialization with people and other
dogs to stay tolerant. Powerful, courageous
and determined, they are best suited to
experienced, strong-willed owners.**

ORIGINALLY BRED
to hunt large game, guard,
and fight other dogs.

SPECIAL CHARACTERISTICS
The Akita is determined, with
a powerful, muscular build.

EXERCISE REQUIREMENTS
Medium. Enjoys exercise.

**COMMON ATTITUDE TO
OWNERS** loyal, independent
CHILDREN will naturally guard
them, not tolerant
OTHER PETS will kill small
animals, will chase

STRANGERS reserved, territorial
UNFAMILIAR DOGS can be
problematic unless well
socialized

PERFECT OWNER
Experienced, strong-willed,
independent owner who can
provide plenty of socialization,
safe exercise and plenty of
games and activity.

THINGS TO WATCH OUT FOR
May be problematic with other
dogs. Can be strong-willed and
needs a determined owner.

American Eskimo Dog

alert
active
courageous
independent
affectionate

Size: Toy: 23–30 cm (9–12 in)
　　Miniature: 33–38 cm (13–15 in)
　　Standard: over 38 cm (15 in)
Weight: Toy: 2.5–4.5 kg (5½–10 lb)
　　Miniature: 4.5–9 kg (10–20 lb)
　　Standard: 9–16 kg (20–35 lb)
Coat: Profuse and long, with
　　dense undercoat
Colour: White
Lifespan: 12–13 years

American Eskimo Dogs come in three sizes. Alert and active, they make good watchdogs. They can be wary and shy with strangers and are loyal and independent with owners.

ORIGINALLY BRED
to be a companion.

SPECIAL CHARACTERISTICS
This lively and playful dog enjoys company.

EXERCISE REQUIREMENTS
High. Plenty of stamina.

COMMON ATTITUDE TO
OWNERS affectionate, loyal
CHILDREN usually good if raised with them
OTHER PETS good if raised with them
STRANGERS wary unless well socialized
UNFAMILIAR DOGS good if well socialized

PERFECT OWNER
Active, patient, calm owner who has plenty of time for grooming, play and activity.

THINGS TO WATCH OUT FOR
Tends to bark excessively. May be hard to housetrain.

⚠️ This dog's coat will bring in mud and dirt from outside and daily brushing is needed to prevent mats from forming. The thick coat also means that the owner should ensure the dog does not overheat in summer.

Boston Terrier

lively
determined
considerate
sensible
good-natured
outgoing

Size: 38–43 cm (15–17 in)
Weight: 6.8–11.5 kg (15–25 lb)
Coat: Short, smooth, fine
Colour: Brindle with white markings, black with white markings
Lifespan: 13 years

Very unlike other terriers in nature, the Boston Terrier would rather be with people than out hunting and getting into mischief. Sensible and considerate, they make friendly, good-natured pets.

ORIGINALLY BRED
as a companion.

SPECIAL CHARACTERISTICS
Alert and playful, the Boston Terrier enjoys company.

EXERCISE REQUIREMENTS
Medium. Undemanding.

COMMON ATTITUDE TO
OWNERS affectionate, loyal
CHILDREN usually good
OTHER PETS usually good
STRANGERS friendly if socialized
UNFAMILIAR DOGS friendly if well socialized

PERFECT OWNER
Gentle, good-natured owner who enjoys playing and socializing.

⚠️ This dog's bulbous eyes are prone to injury. Its shortened nose can make breathing difficult and it is likely to snore. Bitches may have trouble giving birth naturally due to the large heads of their puppies.

Bulldog

kind
courageous
tenacious
alert
bold
affectionate
stubborn

Size: 31–36 cm (12–14 in)
Weight: 23–25 kg (50–55 lb)
Coat: Fine, short, close, smooth
Colour: Whole colours or whole
colours with white
Lifespan: 8–9 years

Affectionate, resolute and courageous, Bulldogs are devoted to their owners. They are sociable with strangers, but they need careful socializing to be tolerant of other dogs. The design of their bodies causes them many difficulties and they are not very active or lively as a result.

ORIGINALLY BRED
for bull- and bear-baiting and dog-fighting.

SPECIAL CHARACTERISTICS
The Bulldog is alert and friendly.

EXERCISE REQUIREMENTS
Low. Restricted breathing and an ungainly body sap energy.

COMMON ATTITUDE TO
OWNERS affectionate, devoted
CHILDREN usually good
OTHER PETS good
STRANGERS friendly
UNFAMILIAR DOGS can be problematic

PERFECT OWNER
Affectionate, tolerant owner who will enjoy this characterful but slow companion.

THINGS TO WATCH OUT FOR
Tends to be problematic with other dogs if provoked.

⚠ The folds of skin above the nose and around the tail need regular cleaning. This dog's shortened muzzle may cause lack of saliva control and can make breathing difficult, especially in hot weather. It is likely to snore. Bitches cannot give birth naturally due to the puppies' large heads, so a Caesarean section is necessary.

Canaan Dog

**agile
alert
confident
vigilant
aloof**

Canaan Dogs are alert and make good watchdogs. With owners, they are aloof but responsive and willing to please. They are quick and able hunters, and do not find it easy to get on with strangers or other dogs.

Size: 50–60 cm (19½–23½ in)
Weight: 18–25 kg (40–55 lb)
Coat: Outer coat dense, harsh, straight, of short to medium length with close profuse undercoat
Colour: Sand to red-brown, white, black or spotted, with or without a symmetrical black mask
Lifespan: 12–13 years
In the 'Herding' class in the USA

ORIGINALLY BRED
to herd, guard and track.

SPECIAL CHARACTERISTICS
The Canaan Dog is alert, agile and curious.

EXERCISE REQUIREMENTS
Medium. Enjoys plenty of exercise.

**COMMON ATTITUDE TO
OWNERS** aloof, responsive
CHILDREN usually good if raised with them
OTHER PETS may be problematic with small pets, may chase cats
STRANGERS aloof, wary

UNFAMILIAR DOGS can be problematic without socialization

PERFECT OWNER
Experienced, active, independent owner who has plenty of time for exercise, training and play.

THINGS TO WATCH OUT FOR
Tends to be problematic with other dogs.

Chow Chow

aloof
independent
stubborn
strong-willed
quiet
loyal

Size: 46–56 cm (18–22 in)
Weight: 20–32 kg (44–70 lb)
Coat: Rough: profuse, abundant, dense, straight with soft, woolly undercoat.
Smooth: short, abundant, dense, straight
Colour: Red, black, cream, blue or cinnamon. Tongue is blue-black
Lifespan: 11–12 years

With its unusual blue-black tongue, the Chow Chow is a dog for the enthusiast. Independent, stubborn and reserved, they are not very tolerant or playful and will resist being handled unless they are used to it from a very early age. Their thick coats makes it likely that they will overheat on hot days, adding to their intolerance of others.

ORIGINALLY BRED
to hunt, herd, guard, pull sleds, also used for their meat and fur.

SPECIAL CHARACTERISTICS
The Chow Chow is quiet and independent, not a playful dog

EXERCISE REQUIREMENTS
Low.

COMMON ATTITUDE TO
OWNERS aloof, independent
CHILDREN not very sociable, intolerant, not playful
OTHER PETS may be problematic

STRANGERS suspicious, territorial
UNFAMILIAR DOGS can be problematic

PERFECT OWNER
Confident, experienced owner who likes a dog to be independent, no trouble and without much interaction or strong desire to please.

THINGS TO WATCH OUT FOR
Prone to overheating and can be irritable on hot days. May be controlling or intolerant

of handling, particularly by strangers. May guard food and possessions.

Chow Chows have a distinctive blue-black tongue.

Dalmatian

great endurance outgoing friendly exuberant

Size: 56–61 cm (22–24 in)
Weight: 23–25 kg (50–55 lb)
Coat: Short, hard, sleek
Colour: Ground colour pure white. Black-spotted, dense black spots or liver-spotted, liver-brown spots
Lifespan: 12 years

Distinctive, elegant, exuberant and agile, Dalmatians like to run and run. They are enjoyable pets providing they can get the exercise they need, and are friendly and affectionate. Good socialization is needed from an early age to ensure tolerance of other dogs.

ORIGINALLY BRED
to run alongside carriages.

SPECIAL CHARACTERISTICS
The Dalmatian loves running and has plenty of stamina.

EXERCISE REQUIREMENTS
High. Quiet at home, but needs long, energetic walks.

COMMON ATTITUDE TO
OWNERS affectionate, devoted
CHILDREN usually good if raised with them
OTHER PETS good, may chase
STRANGERS friendly if well socialized
UNFAMILIAR DOGS can be problematic

PERFECT OWNER
Active, energetic owner who will enjoy long walks with this dog.

THINGS TO WATCH OUT FOR
May display control problems on a walk due to a desire to run and exercise rather than stay with the owner, escaping if under-exercised. May be possessive over food.

French Bulldog

courageous vivacious affectionate responsive

Size: 30–31 cm (12 in)
Weight: 11–12.5 kg (24–27½ lb)
Coat: Fine, smooth, short
Colour: Brindle, pied or fawn
Lifespan: 11–12 years

Lively and affectionate, French Bulldogs are sweet-natured and make good companions. They are playful and alert and do not require too much exercise. Good socialization is needed with other dogs early on to ensure they are friendly with them later.

ORIGINALLY BRED
as a companion (from bull-baiting stock).

SPECIAL CHARACTERISTICS
This dog is alert, friendly and playful.

EXERCISE REQUIREMENTS
Low. Finds hot days hard going.

COMMON ATTITUDE TO
OWNERS affectionate, devoted
CHILDREN usually good if raised with them
OTHER PETS good
STRANGERS friendly
UNFAMILIAR DOGS friendly if well socialized

PERFECT OWNER
Affectionate, sociable owner who will enjoy this sweet-natured little dog.

⚠️ This dog's shortened nose can make breathing difficult, especially in hot weather, and it is likely to snore. The wrinkles on the face need to be cleaned daily.

German Spitz

German Spitz come in the Klein (Toy) and Mittel (Standard) varieties (there is also a giant variety too). All are feisty and reactive. Their profuse coats require daily care and they may be intolerant of this unless handled carefully. Potentially problematic with strangers and other dogs, they make good watchdogs.

Size: 23–29 cm (9–11½ in)
Weight: 8–10 kg (18–22 lb)
Coat: Long, harsh topcoat with soft woolly undercoat. Very abundant around neck and forequarters
Colour: Any
Lifespan: 14–15 years

Klein

active
alert
independent
confident
curious
bold

ORIGINALLY BRED
to be a watchdog and companion.

SPECIAL CHARACTERISTICS
The German Spitz is alert, reactive and lively.

EXERCISE REQUIREMENTS
Medium.

COMMON ATTITUDE TO
OWNERS affectionate, loyal
CHILDREN puppies and adults may be injured by boisterous children

OTHER PETS may be problematic
STRANGERS reserved, territorial unless well socialized
UNFAMILIAR DOGS can be problematic unless well socialized

PERFECT OWNER
Experienced, active owner who has plenty of time for grooming, play and exercise.

THINGS TO WATCH OUT FOR
May bark excessively.

⚠ This dog's long coat will bring in dirt from outside and needs daily grooming to prevent mats from forming.

German Spitz

Mittel

active
alert
independent
confident
curious
bold

Size: 30–38 cm (12–15 in)
Weight: 10.5–11.5 kg (23–25 lb)
Coat: Long, harsh topcoat with soft woolly undercoat. Very abundant around neck and forequarters
Colour: Any
Lifespan: 13–14 years

ORIGINALLY BRED
to work on farms, then as a companion.

SPECIAL CHARACTERISTICS
The German Spitz is alert, reactive and lively.

EXERCISE REQUIREMENTS
Medium.

COMMON ATTITUDE TO OWNERS affectionate, loyal
CHILDREN puppies and adults may be injured by boisterous children

OTHER PETS may be problematic
STRANGERS reserved, territorial unless well socialized
UNFAMILIAR DOGS can be problematic unless well socialized

PERFECT OWNER
Experienced, active owner who has plenty of time for grooming, play and exercise.

THINGS TO WATCH OUT FOR
May bark excessively.

⚠ This dog's long coat will bring in dirt from outside and needs daily grooming to prevent mats from forming.

Japanese Shiba Inu

**confident
lively
friendly
quiet
independent
spirited**

Size: 36.5–39.5 cm (14½–15½ in)
Weight: 8–10 kg (18–22 lb)
Coat: Hard, straight outer coat
with soft, dense undercoat
Colour: Red, red sesame, black
and tan, white
Lifespan: 12–13 years

Aloof and independent, Japanese Shiba Inus are reluctant to show their feelings. They are quiet and rarely bark, and can be reserved with strangers and problematic with other dogs unless they have been well socialized. With their owners, they are playful and enjoy company.

ORIGINALLY BRED
to hunt small game, then as a companion.

SPECIAL CHARACTERISTICS
This dog is alert and playful, and enjoys company.

EXERCISE REQUIREMENTS
Medium. Likes joining in activities.

COMMON ATTITUDE TO
OWNERS affectionate, aloof
CHILDREN usually good if raised with them
OTHER PETS good if raised with them

STRANGERS reserved, aloof
UNFAMILIAR DOGS can be problematic

PERFECT OWNER
Experienced, strong-willed owner who will enjoy training, socializing and playing.

THINGS TO WATCH OUT FOR
Can be strong-willed and needs a determined owner. Tends to be problematic with other dogs.

Japanese Spitz

affectionate
aloof with
  strangers
alert
bold
lively
independent

Size: 30–36 cm (12–14 in)
Weight: 5–6 kg (11–13 lb)
Coat: Straight topcoat with profuse, short, dense undercoat
Colour: White
Lifespan: 12 years

Lively and bold, Japanese Spitz make good watchdogs. They are affectionate and loyal to owners, but tend to be reserved with strangers.

ORIGINALLY BRED
as a companion.

SPECIAL CHARACTERISTICS
The Japanese Spitz is alert and playful, and enjoys company.

EXERCISE REQUIREMENTS
Medium. Busy in the house and outside.

COMMON ATTITUDE TO
OWNERS affectionate, loyal
CHILDREN usually good if raised with them
OTHER PETS good if raised with them
STRANGERS wary, reserved
UNFAMILIAR DOGS good if well socialized

PERFECT OWNER
Active, affectionate owner who has plenty of time for grooming, exercising, playing and training.

THINGS TO WATCH OUT FOR
Tends to bark excessively.

⚠️ This dog's coat will bring mud and dirt into the house and needs daily grooming to prevent mats from forming.

Keeshond

sturdy
sensible
good-natured
adaptable
bold
alert
friendly

Size: 43–46 cm (17–18 in)
Weight: 25–30 kg (55–66 lb)
Coat: Harsh, straight topcoat with soft, thick undercoat
Colour: Mixture of grey and black
Lifespan: 12–14 years

Keeshonds are alert and vocal and make good watchdogs. They are friendly, busy and adaptable and make good-natured companions if well socialized and exercised. Their thick coats require daily attention.

ORIGINALLY BRED
as a watchdog for farms and barges.

SPECIAL CHARACTERISTICS
The Keeshond is alert, vocal and excitable.

EXERCISE REQUIREMENTS
Medium. Busy at home and outside.

COMMON ATTITUDE TO OWNERS affectionate, loyal
CHILDREN usually good if raised with them
OTHER PETS good if raised with them

STRANGERS friendly if socialized
UNFAMILIAR DOGS friendly if socialized

PERFECT OWNER
Active, affectionate owner who has plenty of time for grooming, games and exercise.

THINGS TO WATCH OUT FOR
Tends to bark excessively.

⚠️ This dog's coat will bring mud and dirt in from outside and needs daily grooming to prevent mats from forming.

Lhasa Apso

assertive
alert
steady
confident
aloof with
strangers
stubborn

Size: 25–28 cm (10–11 in)
Weight: 6–7 kg (13–15½ lb)
Coat: Topcoat long, heavy, straight, hard with moderate undercoat
Colour: Golden, sandy, honey, dark grizzle, slate, smoke, particolour, black, white or brown
Lifespan: 12–14 years

Lhasa Apsos originated in Tibet and are alert and reserved with strangers. They make good watchdogs, but their tendency to bark needs to be controlled. Their coats need daily care and early handling is advisable as their tolerance for interference is low. Early socialization is needed for them to be tolerant of other dogs.

ORIGINALLY BRED
to be companions for monks.

SPECIAL CHARACTERISTICS
The Lhasa Apso is an alert and vocal dog.

EXERCISE REQUIREMENTS
Medium. Will cheerfully walk long distances.

COMMON ATTITUDE TO
OWNERS affectionate, loyal
CHILDREN usually good if raised with them
OTHER PETS good if raised with them

STRANGERS aloof, reserved
UNFAMILIAR DOGS can be problematic

PERFECT OWNER
Experienced, tolerant owner who has time for grooming and continued socialization and training with their pet.

THINGS TO WATCH OUT FOR
Tends to bark excessively. Can be strong-willed and needs a determined owner.

⚠ The long coat needs daily brushing to prevent mats from forming. Owners may prefer to have the coat clipped regularly. The hair needs to be trimmed or tied up out of the eyes so that the dog can see clearly.

Schnauzer

Lively and terrier-like, Schnauzers are inquisitive and persistent. They are friendly and playful and responsive and affectionate to owners. Barking is a favourite hobby and they make excellent watchdogs.

Size: 33–36 cm (13–14 in)
Weight: 6–7 kg (13–15½ lb)
Coat: Harsh, wiry with dense undercoat
Colour: All pepper and salt colours
Lifespan: 14 years
In the 'Terrier' class in the USA

Miniature

alert
reliable
biddable
inquisitive
eager
persistent

ORIGINALLY BRED
to hunt rats, then as a companion.

SPECIAL CHARACTERISTICS
Alert and playful, the Schnauzer enjoys company.

EXERCISE REQUIREMENTS
Medium. Busy at home and outside.

COMMON ATTITUDE TO
OWNERS affectionate, loyal
CHILDREN usually good if raised with them
OTHER PETS good if raised with them
STRANGERS friendly if well socialized
UNFAMILIAR DOGS friendly if well socialized

PERFECT OWNER
Active, confident, affectionate owner who enjoys playing, training and grooming.

THINGS TO WATCH OUT FOR
Tends to bark excessively.

Schnauzer

Standard

alert
reliable
calm
biddable
inquisitive
eager
persistent

Size: 46–48 cm (18–19 in)
Weight: 14.5–15.5 kg (32–34 lb)
Coat: Harsh, wiry with dense undercoat
Colour: Pure black or pepper and salt
Lifespan: 12–14 years
In the 'Working' class in the USA

ORIGINALLY BRED
to hunt rats and to guard, later as a companion.

SPECIAL CHARACTERISTICS
Alert and playful, the Schnauzer enjoys company.

EXERCISE REQUIREMENTS
Medium. Busy at home and outside.

COMMON ATTITUDE TO
OWNERS affectionate, loyal
CHILDREN usually good if raised with themn
OTHER PETS good if raised with them
STRANGERS friendly if well socialized, territorial
UNFAMILIAR DOGS friendly if well socialized

PERFECT OWNER
Active, confident, affectionate owner who enjoys playing, training and grooming.

THINGS TO WATCH OUT FOR
Tends to bark excessively.

⚠️ The wiry coat needs daily brushing to keep it tangle-free, and regular clipping.

Poodle

Poodles come in three varieties: Toy (small), Miniature (medium), and Standard (large). Lively, spirited and responsive, they are easily trained and reliable companions. Although their show clips can make them look frivolous, they are serious, willing and good-natured workers and make excellent companions for active owners. Their coats need to be clipped regularly. (The show clip is an exaggeration of a clip designed to protect joints in cold water. Pet owners, and dogs, may prefer the all-over puppy clips instead).

Size: 28–38 cm (11–15 in) (larger than the Toy Poodle)
Weight: 12–14 kg (26–31 lb)
Coat: Very profuse and dense. Does not shed
Colour: All solid colours
Lifespan: 14–15 years

Miniature

spirited
good-natured
biddable
affectionate
calm
dependable

ORIGINALLY BRED
as a companion.

SPECIAL CHARACTERISTICS
Alert and playful, this Poodle enjoys company.

EXERCISE REQUIREMENTS
Medium.

COMMON ATTITUDE TO OWNERS affectionate, responsive
CHILDREN usually good
OTHER PETS good
STRANGERS friendly if well socialized
UNFAMILIAR DOGS friendly if well socialized

PERFECT OWNER
Active, affectionate owner who will enjoy grooming, exercising, playing with and training this dynamic little dog.

Poodle

Standard

spirited
good-natured
biddable
affectionate
calm
dependable

Size: 37.5–38.5 cm (15 in)
Weight: 20.5–32 kg (45–70 lb)
Coat: Very profuse and dense. Does not shed
Colour: All solid colours
Lifespan: 11–13 years

ORIGINALLY BRED
to retrieve birds from water.

SPECIAL CHARACTERISTICS
Lively and playful, this Poodle loves people.

EXERCISE REQUIREMENTS
High. Enjoys racing about.

COMMON ATTITUDE TO
OWNERS affectionate, responsive
CHILDREN usually good
OTHER PETS good
STRANGERS friendly
UNFAMILIAR DOGS friendly

PERFECT OWNER
Active, affectionate owner who enjoys energetic walks, grooming, training and playing.

✓ Recommended for first-time owners especially if they are prone to allergies. Care is needed to find a healthy dog free of inherited disease.

Poodle

Toy

spirited
good-natured
biddable
affectionate
calm
dependable

Size: 25–28 cm (10–11 in)
Weight: 6.5–7.5 kg (14–16½ lb)
Coat: Very profuse and dense.
　Does not shed
Colour: All solid colours
Lifespan: 14–15 years

ORIGINALLY BRED
as a companion.

SPECIAL CHARACTERISTICS
This Poodle is alert and playful,
and enjoys company.

EXERCISE REQUIREMENTS
Medium.

COMMON ATTITUDE TO
OWNERS affectionate,
responsive
CHILDREN puppies and adults
may be injured by boisterous
children
OTHER PETS good
STRANGERS friendly if well
socialized
UNFAMILIAR DOGS friendly if
well socialized

PERFECT OWNER
Active, affectionate owner who
will enjoy grooming, exercising,
playing with and training this
dynamic little dog.

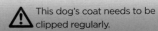
This dog's coat needs to be
clipped regularly.

Schipperke

lively
alert
amenable
responsive
loyal
inquisitive

Size: 22–33 cm (8½–13 in)
Weight: 5.5–7.5 kg (12–16½ lb)
Coat: Abundant, dense and harsh
Colour: Usually black, but other whole colours permissible
Lifespan: 12–13 years

Schipperkes are loyal and affectionate to owners, but wary of strangers. Their love of barking makes them excellent watchdogs, but this trait needs to be controlled if it is not to become excessive. Alert, busy and inquisitive, they need plenty of socialization with other dogs to remain tolerant.

ORIGINALLY BRED
as a watchdog on barges, later as a companion.

SPECIAL CHARACTERISTICS
The Schipperke is an alert, watchful and playful dog.

EXERCISE REQUIREMENTS
High. Busy at home and outside.

COMMON ATTITUDE TO
OWNERS affectionate, loyal
CHILDREN usually good if raised with them
OTHER PETS may be problematic with small pets
STRANGERS wary, territorial
UNFAMILIAR DOGS can be problematic

PERFECT OWNER
Active, affectionate owner who enjoys grooming and who can provide plenty of activity, exercise and training.

THINGS TO WATCH OUT FOR
Tends to bark excessively. May be difficult to housetrain.

⚠ The dense coat needs regular grooming to keep it in good condition.

Shar Pei

calm
independent
affectionate
wilful
aloof

Size: 46–51 cm (18–20 in)
Weight: 16–20 kg (35–44 lb)
Coat: Harsh with no undercoat
Colour: Any solid colours
Lifespan: 11–12 years
Also known as Chinese Shar Pei

Covered in distinctive folds of loose skin, many individuals of this breed pay the price for the fashionable excess of skin with painful eye problems and skin conditions. Good-natured and wilful, Shar Peis are independent and aloof and require early socialization to be tolerant of other dogs.

ORIGINALLY BRED
for dog-fighting and hunting.

SPECIAL CHARACTERISTICS
The Shar Pei is courageous and tenacious.

EXERCISE REQUIREMENTS
Medium.

COMMON ATTITUDE TO
OWNERS affectionate, aloof
CHILDREN usually good if raised with them
OTHER PETS may be problematic with small pets
STRANGERS friendly if well socialized

UNFAMILIAR DOGS can be problematic if not well socialized

PERFECT OWNER
Strong-willed, confident, affectionate owner who has plenty of time to care for and socialize this dog.

⚠️ Take care to find a healthy line whose dogs have not had to have their eyelids surgically altered.

Shih Tzu

active
alert
friendly
independent

Size: 25–27 cm (10–10½ in)
Weight: 4.5–7.5 kg (10–16½ lb)
Coat: Long, dense topcoat with good undercoat
Colour: Any
Lifespan: 12–14 years
In the 'Toy' class in the USA

Easily confused with the Lhasa Apso due to the similar appearance, Shih Tzus have a shortened face and a more amenable disposition. They are friendly with everyone if well socialized and playful and devoted to their owners.

ORIGINALLY BRED
as a companion.

SPECIAL CHARACTERISTICS
Alert and playful, the Shih Tzu enjoys company.

EXERCISE REQUIREMENTS
Low.

COMMON ATTITUDE TO
OWNERS affectionate, devoted
CHILDREN usually good if raised with them
OTHER PETS good if raised with them
STRANGERS friendly if well socialized
UNFAMILIAR DOGS friendly if well socialized

PERFECT OWNER
Active, sensible, affectionate owner who enjoys grooming, playing with and socializing their pet.

⚠ This dog's coat will bring in mud and dirt from outside and requires daily grooming to prevent mats from forming. The hair on the head should be clipped or tied up out of the eyes so that the dog can see clearly. The bulbous eyes are easily injured. The shortened muzzle can make breathing difficult and it is likely to snore.

Tibetan Spaniel

assertive
playful
alert
loyal
confident
independent

Size: 24–25 cm (9½–10 in)
Weight: 4–7 kg (9–15½ lb)
Coat: Silky topcoat, with fine, dense undercoat
Colour: Any
Lifespan: 13–14 years

Tibetan Spaniels are unlikely to have been used for hunting as the name implies, but instead are probably related to Pekingeses. Playful, lively and independent, they make good-natured pets. They are very vocal and this tendency needs to be controlled to prevent problems with excessive barking.

ORIGINALLY BRED
as a watchdog and companion for monks in Tibet.

SPECIAL CHARACTERISTICS
The Tibetan Spaniel is alert, curious and vocal.

EXERCISE REQUIREMENTS
Medium. Enjoys rushing around the garden or yard.

COMMON ATTITUDE TO OWNERS affectionate, loyal
CHILDREN puppies and adults may be injured by boisterous children

OTHER PETS good
STRANGERS friendly, will bark
UNFAMILIAR DOGS friendly

PERFECT OWNER
Active, sociable owner who enjoys energetic walks and playing games.

THINGS TO WATCH OUT FOR
Tends to bark excessively.

⚠️ The bulbous eyes are easily injured. This dog's coat will bring in mud and dirt from outside, and daily grooming is required to prevent mats from forming.

Tibetan Terrier

lively
loyal
outgoing
alert
aloof with
   strangers
persistent

Size: 36–41 cm (14–16 in)
Weight: 8–14 kg (18–31 lb)
Coat: Profuse, fine topcoat with fine, woolly undercoat
Colour: Any, except chocolate or liver
Lifespan: 13–14 years

A terrier in name only, this breed is lively, outgoing and affectionate with owners. They are reserved and aloof with strangers and make good watchdogs, although owners need to be careful about excessive barking.

ORIGINALLY BRED
to guard Tibetan monasteries and as a companion.

SPECIAL CHARACTERISTICS
This dog is alert, vocal and protective.

EXERCISE REQUIREMENTS
Medium. Nimble and energetic.

COMMON ATTITUDE TO
OWNERS affectionate, loyal
CHILDREN usually good if raised with them
OTHER PETS good if raised with them
STRANGERS aloof, reserved
UNFAMILIAR DOGS okay if well socialized

PERFECT OWNER
Experienced, strong-willed, active owner who enjoys grooming and has time for plenty of play, training and activity.

THINGS TO WATCH OUT FOR
May bark excessively.

⚠️ This dog's coat will bring in mud and dirt from outside, and daily grooming is required to prevent mats from forming. The hair needs to be clipped or tied up away from the eyes so that the dog can see clearly.

Alaskan Malamute

affectionate
loyal
devoted
aloof
dignified
stubborn

Size: 58–71 cm (23–28 in)
Weight: 38–56 kg (84–125 lb)
Coat: Thick, coarse guard topcoat
with dense undercoat
Colour: Light grey through
intermediate shadings to black,
or gold through shades of red
to liver, always with white on
underbody, parts of legs, feet
and part of mask markings
Lifespan: 12 years

Alaskan Malamutes are strong,
powerful and have plenty of stamina.
They are affectionate, but also aloof,
independent and unresponsive to requests
unless there is something in it for them.
Friendly and easy-going with humans,
they need plenty of socialization to
stay tolerant of other dogs.

ORIGINALLY BRED
to pull sleds in Antarctica.

SPECIAL CHARACTERISTICS
The Alaskan Malamute is a dog
with great stamina and power.

EXERCISE REQUIREMENTS
High. Needs a great deal
of exercise.

COMMON ATTITUDE TO
OWNERS affectionate but not
demonstrative
CHILDREN usually good if
raised with them
OTHER PETS good if raised
with them

STRANGERS aloof
UNFAMILIAR DOGS can be
problematic

PERFECT OWNER
Active, energetic owner who will
be able to find an outlet for this
dog's excess energy.

THINGS TO WATCH OUT FOR
Will need plenty of positive
associations to prevent
handling issues.

⚠ The thick coat will need
care to keep it in good
condition. When moulting, a
great deal of fur is shed that will
need to be removed.

Beauceron

versatile
bold
calm
courageous
biddable

Size: 63–70 cm (25–27½ in)
Weight: 30–39 kg (66–86 lb)
Coat: Short, rough and thick
Colour: Black and tan
Lifespan: 11–13 years
In the 'Miscellaneous' class in the USA

Beaucerons are calm, discerning, dependable and hard-working with plenty of energy. They are strong, playful and protective and need adequate socialization with people and other dogs when young.

ORIGINALLY BRED
to herd and guard livestock.

SPECIAL CHARACTERISTICS
This active and protective dog has a double dewclaw on its hind legs.

EXERCISE REQUIREMENTS
High. Enjoys plenty of activity.

COMMON ATTITUDE TO
OWNERS affectionate, protective
CHILDREN usually good if raised with them
OTHER PETS good if raised with them
STRANGERS friendly if well socialized
UNFAMILIAR DOGS friendly if well socialized

PERFECT OWNER
Experienced, strong-willed, active owner who can provide this intelligent dog with a job to do as well as plenty of games, activity and socialization.

THINGS TO WATCH OUT FOR
May be problematic with strangers if inadequately socialized.

Bernese Mountain Dog

confident
good-natured
friendly
courageous
protective

Size: 58–70 cm (23–27½ in)
Weight: 40–44 kg (88–97 lb)
Coat: Medium length, soft and silky, with bright natural sheen
Colour: Tricolour
Lifespan: 8–9 years

Good-natured and strong, Bernese Mountain Dogs are wilful and protective and need kind but firm ownership. In the right hands, they are friendly, happy and outgoing.

ORIGINALLY BRED
to pull carts.

SPECIAL CHARACTERISTICS
Strong and protective.

EXERCISE REQUIREMENTS
Medium. Enjoys exercise and play.

COMMON ATTITUDE TO
OWNERS affectionate, loyal
CHILDREN usually good if raised with them
OTHER PETS good if raised with them
STRANGERS good if well socialized
UNFAMILIAR DOGS good if well socialized

PERFECT OWNER
Experienced, strong-willed, physically strong, easy-going owner who can give this dog plenty of socialization, exercise and play.

THINGS TO WATCH OUT FOR
Dogs from some lines may display territorial aggression and other aggression problems.

⚠ The loose jowls of this breed lead to saliva control problems.

Greater Swiss Mountain Dog

confident good-natured friendly courageous protective

Size: 60–72 cm (23½–28 in)
Weight: 59–61 kg (130–135 lb)
Coat: Short, dense, glossy
Colour: Tricolour
Lifespan: 10–11 years

Strong and larger than the Bernese, Greater Swiss Mountain Dogs have a strong, protective nature. If well socialized, they are happy, gentle giants, but care needs to be taken with other dogs.

ORIGINALLY BRED
to pull carts.

SPECIAL CHARACTERISTICS
Strong and protective.

EXERCISE REQUIREMENTS
Medium. Enjoys exercise and play.

COMMON ATTITUDE TO
OWNERS affectionate, loyal
CHILDREN usually good
OTHER PETS good
STRANGERS good if well socialized
UNFAMILIAR DOGS can be problematic, care needs to be taken with unfamiliar dogs

PERFECT OWNER
Experienced, physically strong, easy-going owner who can give this dog plenty of socialization, exercise and play.

Bouvier des Flandres

wilful
amiable
calm
sensible
protective

Size: 59–68 cm (23–27 in)
Weight: 27–40 kg (60–88 lb)
Coat: Abundant, coarse, thick
Colour: Fawn, black, brindle
Lifespan: 11–12 years
In the 'Herding' class in the USA

Strong and robust enough to drive cattle and pull carts, the Bouvier des Flandres has a strong personality to match. They can be wary of strangers, territorial and problematic with other dogs unless well socialized and in the care of strong-willed owners.

ORIGINALLY BRED
to herd cattle and pull carts.

SPECIAL CHARACTERISTICS
This active and protective dog likes to chase.

EXERCISE REQUIREMENTS
Medium.

COMMON ATTITUDE TO
OWNERS affectionate, loyal
CHILDREN usually good if raised with them
OTHER PETS good if raised with them
STRANGERS wary, territorial
UNFAMILIAR DOGS can be problematic

PERFECT OWNER
Experienced, strong-willed, physically strong owner who has time and energy to train, socialize, play games with, groom and exercise this powerful dog.

THINGS TO WATCH OUT FOR
Tends to be problematic with strangers and other dogs unless properly socialized.

⚠ Fur around the eyes needs to be cut or tied back to help the dog see clearly.

Boxer

Size: 53–63 cm (21–25 in)
Weight: 25–32 kg (55–70 lb)
Coat: Short, glossy, smooth
Colour: Fawn or brindle with white markings
Lifespan: 10–12 years

Boxers are exuberant, energetic, playful and agile. They are good-natured and friendly to all, although proper socialization is needed to ensure they are tolerant of other dogs.

ORIGINALLY BRED
to hang on to the nose of large game until hunters arrived.

SPECIAL CHARACTERISTICS
The Boxer is tenacious, agile and playful.

EXERCISE REQUIREMENTS
High. Loves to do everything at speed.

COMMON ATTITUDE TO
OWNERS affectionate, devoted
CHILDREN playful, exuberant (may be too much for very young children)

OTHER PETS good if raised with them
STRANGERS friendly if well socialized
UNFAMILIAR DOGS can be problematic unless well socialized

PERFECT OWNER
Experienced, active, affectionate families who will enjoy an exuberant, responsive dog and who have enough time and energy for exercise, playing with and training.

THINGS TO WATCH OUT FOR
Tends to be problematic with unfamiliar dogs unless well socialized. These dogs like to use their paws and hold on with their front legs, so owners should discourage jumping up.

⚠ This dog's shortened nose can make breathing difficult and it is likely to snore. The loose jowls can lead to a lack of saliva control.

Bullmastiff

powerful
reliable
alert
loyal
stubborn

Size: 61–69 cm (24–27 in)
Weight: 41–59 kg (90–130 lb)
Coat: Short and hard
Colour: Any shade of brindle,
fawn or red with black muzzle
Lifespan: 10 years

Powerful and strong, Bullmastiffs require training and owners need physical strength if they are to stay in control. These dogs do not require very much exercise considering their large size, but they need careful socialization with other dogs to remain tolerant.

ORIGINALLY BRED
as a guard dog.

SPECIAL CHARACTERISTICS
The Bullmastiff is protective, strong and independent.

EXERCISE REQUIREMENTS
Low–Medium. Enjoys exercise but not over-demanding.

COMMON ATTITUDE TO
OWNERS affectionate, loyal
CHILDREN protective, can knock over small children
OTHER PETS good if raised with them
STRANGERS reserved unless well socialized

UNFAMILIAR DOGS can be problematic unless well socialized

PERFECT OWNER
Experienced, physically strong, strong-willed owner who will socialize and train this powerful dog well.

THINGS TO WATCH OUT FOR
Tends to be problematic with other dogs and to strangers unless well socialized.

⚠ This dog's shortened nose can make breathing difficult and it is likely to snore. Loose jowls can lead to lack of saliva control.

256 // Working

Canadian Eskimo Dog

alert
active
enduring
strong
independent
aloof

Size: 50–70 cm (19½–27½ in)
Weight: 18–40 kg (40–88 lb)
Coat: Thick, dense undercoat with hard, stiff guard hairs
Colour: Any
Lifespan: 12–13 years

Canadian Eskimo Dogs are energetic, independent hunters. Reserved and aloof with strangers, they have a strong sense of family and readily take on other dogs over food or territory. They are scavengers and will hunt, chase and may cause harm to smaller pets.

ORIGINALLY BRED
to pull sleds in the Canadian Arctic.

SPECIAL CHARACTERISTICS
This active dog has plenty of stamina.

EXERCISE REQUIREMENTS
High. Enjoys working (hunting or pulling sleds).

COMMON ATTITUDE TO
OWNERS affectionate, independent
CHILDREN best in adult household
OTHER PETS due to a high prey drive and chase instincts, may cause harm to small pets; may chase
STRANGERS reserved, aloof

UNFAMILIAR DOGS can be problematic

PERFECT OWNER
Experienced, strong-willed, active owner who wants a working dog, either for sled-pulling or hunting.

THINGS TO WATCH OUT FOR
Tends to be problematic with other dogs, both unfamiliar and within the household, and to be possessive over food and territory.

⚠ This dog needs daily grooming to prevent mats from forming in its thick coat. It will overheat easily in summer, so care needs to be taken in the warmer months.

Dobermann

bold
responsive
alert
strong-willed
loyal
obedient

Size: 65–69 cm (25½–27 in)
Weight: 30–40 kg (66–88 lb)
Coat: Smooth, short and glossy
Colour: Definite black, brown,
   blue or fawn only, with rust-red
   markings
Lifespan: 12 years
Also known as Doberman Pinscher

Dobermanns are strong in both body and mind. Easily trained, they make natural guards and are affectionate and loyal to their owners. They have abundant energy and they need careful socialization when young.

ORIGINALLY BRED
to guard.

SPECIAL CHARACTERISTICS
Strong-willed and protective.

EXERCISE REQUIREMENTS
High. Needs a great deal
of exercise.

COMMON ATTITUDE TO
OWNERS affectionate, loyal
CHILDREN will naturally guard
them
OTHER PETS good if raised
with them

STRANGERS reserved, territorial
UNFAMILIAR DOGS can be
problematic unless well
socialized

PERFECT OWNER
Experienced, strong-willed,
active owner who will socialize
and train this powerful dog and
find time to play, exercise and
keep it occupied.

THINGS TO WATCH OUT FOR
Dogs from some lines
may be problematic with
strangers and other dogs.
Can be strong-willed and
needs a determined owner.

Giant Schnauzer

bold
alert
reliable
calm
inquisitive
eager
persistent

Size: 60–70 cm (23½–27½ in)
Weight: 32–35 kg (70–77 lb)
Coat: Harsh, wiry with dense undercoat
Colour: Pure black or pepper and salt
Lifespan: 11–12 years

Exuberant and strong-willed, Giant Schnauzers are inquisitive and persistent. They are responsive, playful and protective towards owners. Barking is a favourite hobby and they make excellent watchdogs.

ORIGINALLY BRED
to herd and guard cattle.

SPECIAL CHARACTERISTICS
This alert and playful dog is a natural guard.

EXERCISE REQUIREMENTS
Medium.

COMMON ATTITUDE TO
OWNERS affectionate, loyal
CHILDREN will naturally guard them
OTHER PETS good if raised with them
STRANGERS guarding, territorial
UNFAMILIAR DOGS can be problematic

PERFECT OWNER
Experienced, active, strong-willed, affectionate owner who can give this active dog a job to do.

THINGS TO WATCH OUT FOR
Tends to display excessive territorial barking. Can be strong-willed and needs a determined owner.

⚠ The coat needs daily brushing to keep it tangle-free and also requires regular clipping.

Great Dane

independent
alert
powerful
exuberant
outgoing

Size: 71–76 cm (28–30 in)
Weight: 46–54 kg (100–120 lb)
Coat: Short, dense and sleek
Colour: Brindle, fawns, blue, black, harlequins (white with black patches)
Lifespan: 8–10 years

Great Danes are large and exuberant. They tend be clumsy and may knock delicate things flying. Usually they are gentle giants, but care should be taken to train and socialize them early due to their size.

ORIGINALLY BRED
to hunt large game.

SPECIAL CHARACTERISTICS
The Great Dane is inquisitive, exuberant and playful.

EXERCISE REQUIREMENTS
Medium–High. Enjoys exercise but can be quiet at home.

COMMON ATTITUDE TO OWNERS affectionate, independent
CHILDREN usually good if raised with them, may knock over young children
OTHER PETS good if raised with them, may chase
STRANGERS friendly if well socialized
UNFAMILIAR DOGS friendly if well socialized

PERFECT OWNER
Experienced, physically strong, strong-willed owner who will socialize this dog well and have homes and cars large enough to accommodate this giant.

THINGS TO WATCH OUT FOR
Dogs from some lines may be problematic with people and other dogs.

Greenland Dog

alert
active
enduring
strong
independent
aloof

Size: 51–68 cm (20–27 in)
Weight: 27–47.5 kg (60–105 lb)
Coat: Impenetrable undercoat, with outer coat of coarser longer hair
Colour: Any
Lifespan: 13 years

Greenland Dogs are very energetic and need a job to do. Their hunting instincts are strong and they may harm small pets. Reserved and aloof with strangers, they are likely to be difficult with other dogs unless controlled.

ORIGINALLY BRED
to pull sleds in the Arctic.

SPECIAL CHARACTERISTICS
This active dog has plenty of stamina and loves to hunt.

EXERCISE REQUIREMENTS
High. Enjoys working (hunting or sled-pulling).

COMMON ATTITUDE TO
OWNERS affectionate, independent
CHILDREN best in adult households
OTHER PETS due to a high prey drive and chase instincts, may cause harm to small pets; tends to chase

STRANGERS reserved, aloof
UNFAMILIAR DOGS can be problematic

PERFECT OWNER
Experienced, strong-willed, active owner who wants a working dog, either for pulling a sled or hunting.

THINGS TO WATCH OUT FOR
Tends to be problematic with other dogs, both unfamiliar and within the household, and to display possessive aggression.

Hovawart

watchful
agile
self-assured
playful
alert
biddable

Size: 58–70 cm (23–27½ in)
Weight: 25–40 kg (55–88 lb)
Coat: Medium length, with fine, light undercoat
Colour: Black/gold, gold, black
Lifespan: 12–13 years

Hovawarts look similar to Flat Coated and Golden Retrievers, but are very different in temperament. They make good guards, being naturally alert and protective as well as reserved with strangers. They are playful, responsive and devoted to their owners.

ORIGINALLY BRED
to guard homes and livestock.

SPECIAL CHARACTERISTICS
The Hovawart is alert and protective.

EXERCISE REQUIREMENTS
Medium. Does not demand a great deal of exercise.

COMMON ATTITUDE TO
OWNERS affectionate, devoted
CHILDREN usually good if raised with them
OTHER PETS good if raised with them
STRANGERS reserved, territorial
UNFAMILIAR DOGS friendly if well socialized

PERFECT OWNER
Experienced, active owner who will socialize this dog well and provide it with plenty of activity, games and exercise.

THINGS TO WATCH OUT FOR
Dogs from some lines tend to be aggressive to other dogs and to strangers.

Leonberger

amenable friendly self-assured playful

Size: 65–80 cm (25½–31½ in)
Weight: 34–50 kg (75–110 lb)
Coat: Medium length, with evident mane at throat and chest
Colour: Lion gold, red, reddish-brown, sandy (fawn or cream), always with a black mask
Lifespan: 9–11 years

Leonbergers are playful, good-natured and energetic. Since Newfoundlands played a part in their ancestry, they also like to swim.

ORIGINALLY BRED
to resemble the lion on the Coat of Arms of the Town Hall of Leonberg, Germany.

SPECIAL CHARACTERISTICS
Friendly and playful, the Leonberger likes to swim.

EXERCISE REQUIREMENTS
Medium. High when young.

COMMON ATTITUDE TO
OWNERS affectionate, loyal
CHILDREN usually good if raised with them, may knock over small children
OTHER PETS good if raised with them
STRANGERS friendly if well socialized
UNFAMILIAR DOGS friendly if well socialized

PERFECT OWNER
Experienced, active, affectionate, physically strong owners who will have plenty of time to socialize puppies and for activity, play, training and exercise when older.

THINGS TO WATCH OUT FOR
Dogs from some lines may be problematic with strangers and other dogs.

Mastiff

**powerful
courageous
calm
affectionate
protective**

Size: 70–76 cm (27½–30 in)
Weight: 79–86 kg (175–190 lb)
Coat: Short
Colour: Apricot-fawn, silver-fawn, fawn or dark fawn-brindle. Muzzle, ears and nose should be black with black around orbits and extending upwards between them
Lifespan: 9–10 years

Powerful and courageous, the Mastiff's sheer size alone would deter all but the most determined intruder. They are protective of owners and territory and require a great deal of time for early and continued socialization with both dogs and people.

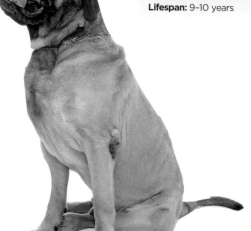

ORIGINALLY BRED
for guarding.

SPECIAL CHARACTERISTICS
The Mastiff is alert and protective.

EXERCISE REQUIREMENTS
Low–Medium. Enjoys exercise without being over-demanding.

COMMON ATTITUDE TO
OWNERS affectionate, loyal
CHILDREN protective, can knock over small children
OTHER PETS good if raised with them
STRANGERS reserved unless well socialized
UNFAMILIAR DOGS can be problematic unless well socialized

PERFECT OWNER
Experienced, physically strong, strong-willed owner who will socialize and train this powerful dog well and who has a large home and car to accommodate this giant breed.

THINGS TO WATCH OUT FOR
Dogs from some lines may be problematic with strangers and other dogs. Can be strong-willed and needs a determined owner.

⚠ This dog's shortened nose can make breathing difficult and it is likely to snore. Loose jowls will lead to saliva control problems.

Neapolitan Mastiff

**powerful
devoted
loyal
protective
courageous**

Size: 65-75 cm (25½–29½ in)
Weight: 50–70 kg (110–154 lb)
Coat: Short, dense, with good
sheen
Colour: Preferred black, blue, all
shades of grey, brown varying
from fawn to red
Lifespan: 9–11 years
*In the 'Miscellaneous' class in
the USA*

**Slow and ponderous, Neapolitan Mastiffs
are friendly, calm and devoted to their
owners. They are protective of owners
and territory and require a great deal of
time for early and continued socialization
with both dogs and people.**

ORIGINALLY BRED
to guard livestock, later for
dog-fighting.

SPECIAL CHARACTERISTICS
This dog is alert and protective.

EXERCISE REQUIREMENTS
Low–Medium.

COMMON ATTITUDE TO
OWNERS affectionate, loyal
CHILDREN protective, can knock
over small children
OTHER PETS good if raised with
them
STRANGERS reserved unless well
socialized
UNFAMILIAR DOGS problematic
unless well socialized

PERFECT OWNER
Experienced, physically strong,
strong-willed owner who will
socialize and train this powerful
dog well and who has a large
home and car to accommodate
this giant dog.

THINGS TO WATCH OUT FOR
Dogs from some lines may
be problematic with strangers
and other dogs. Can be
strong-willed and needs a
determined owner.

⚠ This dog's shortened
nose can make breathing
difficult and it is likely to snore.
Loose jowls will lead to problems
of saliva control.

Newfoundland

devoted
gentle
docile
calm

Size: 66–71 cm (26–28 in)
Weight: 50–69 kg (110–152 lb)
Coat: Medium length, with thick undercoat
Colour: Black, brown, Landseer (white with black markings)
Lifespan: 9–11 years

Newfoundlands love to swim and will try to rescue anyone from the water whether they are in trouble or not. Their thick coats can make them uncomfortable in summer or in heated houses. Calm and gentle, they need early training and socialization because of their large size.

ORIGINALLY BRED
to help fishermen by hauling in nets and pulling carts.

SPECIAL CHARACTERISTICS
The playful Newfoundland loves to swim.

EXERCISE REQUIREMENTS
Medium. Prefers to exercise in water.

COMMON ATTITUDE TO
OWNERS affectionate, devoted
CHILDREN usually good if raised with them, may knock over young children
OTHER PETS good if raised with them

STRANGERS friendly if well socialized
UNFAMILIAR DOGS friendly if well socialized

PERFECT OWNER
Experienced, physically strong, strong-willed owner who has enough space at home and in the car for these giant dogs and who can provide games and exercise, especially if it involves water.

THINGS TO WATCH OUT FOR
Dogs from some lines may be problematic with strangers.

⚠️ May overheat in summer. Will require regular brushing to keep coat in good condition. Loose jowls can lead to saliva control problems.

Pinscher (German)

lively
alert
courageous
tenacious
docile
biddable

Size: 43–48 cm (17–19 in)
Weight: 11–16 kg (24–35 lb)
Coat: Short, dense, glossy
Colour: All solid colours from fawn to stag red. Black or blue with reddish-tan markings
Lifespan: 12–14 years

Energetic, inquisitive and tenacious, German Pinschers are also responsive and biddable. They are easily aroused and need proper socialization with other dogs to prevent problems.

ORIGINALLY BRED
to hunt and kill mice and rats.

SPECIAL CHARACTERISTICS
This dog is feisty and playful, with an inquisitive nature.

EXERCISE REQUIREMENTS
High. Needs to burn off energy.

COMMON ATTITUDE TO
OWNERS affectionate, loyal
CHILDREN usually good if raised with them
OTHER PETS due to a high prey drive and chase instincts, may cause harm to small pets
STRANGERS friendly if well socialized
UNFAMILIAR DOGS dogs can be problematic unless well socialized

PERFECT OWNER
Experienced, active, strong-willed owner who has time to socialize, train and play with this energetic and lively dog.

THINGS TO WATCH OUT FOR
Can be strong-willed and needs a determined owner.

Portuguese Water Dog

energetic
self-willed
courageous
loyal
responsive

Size: 43–57 cm (17–22½ in)
Weight: 16–25 kg (35–55 lb)
Coat: Profuse and long
Colour: Black, white, brown
Lifespan: 12–14 years

Friendly and playful, Portuguese Water Dogs need plenty to do to use up their energy. Originally, the hair on their legs and part of the tail was clipped to reduce the drag while they were swimming.

ORIGINALLY BRED
to help fishermen.

SPECIAL CHARACTERISTICS
This playful dog loves being in water.

EXERCISE REQUIREMENTS
High. Full of energy and adores exercise, especially swimming.

COMMON ATTITUDE TO
OWNERS affectionate, devoted
CHILDREN usually good, can be too exuberant for young children
OTHER PETS good if raised with them
STRANGERS friendly if well socialized
UNFAMILIAR DOGS friendly if well socialized

PERFECT OWNER
Active, energetic owner who enjoys grooming and who will find plenty of time for activities, play and exercise to keep this exuberant dog occupied.

THINGS TO WATCH OUT FOR
May be destructive if under-exercised.

⚠ This dog's profuse coat requires regular grooming to prevent mats from forming, and regular clipping. Show breeders clip the coat on the back legs and tail, but there is no need for pet owners to do this.

Rottweiler

bold
courageous
confident
calm
biddable
protective

Size: 58–69 cm (23–27 in)
Weight: 41–50 kg (90–110 lb)
Coat: Short, thick and glossy
Colour: Black with clearly defined markings
Lifespan: 11–12 years

Rottweilers are strong, active and reluctant to show their feelings. They are naturally protective and will guard naturally. They are playful, responsive and affectionate with owners and require early training and socialization.

ORIGINALLY BRED
to drive cattle and guard.

SPECIAL CHARACTERISTICS
The Rottweiler is protective and courageous, but not very demonstrative.

EXERCISE REQUIREMENTS
High.

COMMON ATTITUDE TO
OWNERS affectionate, loyal
CHILDREN usually good if raised with them
OTHER PETS good if raised with them
STRANGERS aloof, territorial
UNFAMILIAR DOGS friendly if well socialized

PERFECT OWNER
Experienced, strong-willed, affectionate owner who has plenty of time to train, play with and exercise this large, powerful dog.

THINGS TO WATCH OUT FOR
Dogs from certain lines may display aggression to strangers. Can be strong-willed and needs a determined owner.

Russian Black Terrier

independent
courageous
calm
stubborn

Size: 63–75 cm (25–29½ in)
Weight: 40–65 kg (88–143 lb)
Coat: Short-haired and long-haired
   varieties. Harsh topcoat with
   thick woolly undercoat
Colour: Black
Lifespan: 10–12 years
*Also known as Black Russian
Terrier. In the 'Miscellaneous' class
in the USA*

Strong-willed and tenacious, Russian Black Terriers need experienced owners. Their drive to work and hunt is strong, and they require early and continued socialization with humans and other dogs to stay tolerant.

ORIGINALLY BRED
to be a guard/patrol dog for prison, police and army.

SPECIAL CHARACTERISTICS
This dog is active and alert.

EXERCISE REQUIREMENTS
High. Needs to work, but calm at home.

COMMON ATTITUDE TO
OWNERS loyal, affectionate
CHILDREN will naturally guard them
OTHER PETS due to a high prey drive and chase instincts, may cause harm to small pets; may injure cats unless raised with them
STRANGERS reserved, suspicious
UNFAMILIAR DOGS can be problematic

PERFECT OWNER
Experienced, strong-willed active owner who can control and take care with this powerful dog as well as provide it with a job to do or plenty of exercise, games and training to keep it occupied.

THINGS TO WATCH OUT FOR
Tends to be problematic with strangers. Can be strong-willed and needs a determined owner.

⚠️ This dog's coat requires regular clipping and grooming.

Siberian Husky

active
eager
gentle
alert
independent

Siberian Huskies are built for running. Since they are independent with a strong desire to hunt, they can only be let off the lead in secure areas. Owners need to be prepared to run or cycle several miles with this active breed every day as well as provide continued socialization with dogs and people.

Size: 51–60 cm (20–23½ in)
Weight: 16–27 kg (35–60 lb)
Coat: Thick, medium length with soft, dense undercoat
Colour: Any
Lifespan: 11–13 years

ORIGINALLY BRED
to pull sleds.

SPECIAL CHARACTERISTICS
This Husky likes to run great distances and to chase.

EXERCISE REQUIREMENTS
High. Full of energy and loves to exercise.

COMMON ATTITUDE TO
OWNERS aloof, independent
CHILDREN usually good if raised with them
OTHER PETS may be problematic with small pets, may chase
STRANGERS friendly if socialized
UNFAMILIAR DOGS friendly if socialized

PERFECT OWNER
Active, energetic owner who will be able to run or cycle with this dog for several miles every day.

THINGS TO WATCH OUT FOR
May display control problems on walks – may run off and not return. If under-exercised, may be destructive, dig and escape.

⚠ This dog will leave loose hair in the house. Its thick coat requires daily grooming to keep it in good condition.

St Bernard

steady
kind
courageous
trustworthy
benevolent

St Bernards are steady, reliable, very large and heavy. Affectionate and loyal to owners, they are naturally protective and early training and socialization are required.

Size: 61–71 cm (24–28 in)
Weight: 50–91 kg (110–200 lb)
Coat: Short, dense, thick
Colour: Orange to red with white patches
Lifespan: 8–10 years

ORIGINALLY BRED
to haul carts.

SPECIAL CHARACTERISTICS
This dog is strong and protective.

EXERCISE REQUIREMENTS
Low–Medium. Not very demanding.

COMMON ATTITUDE TO
OWNERS affectionate, loyal
CHILDREN usually good if raised with them
OTHER PETS good if raised with them
STRANGERS territorial unless well socialized
UNFAMILIAR DOGS friendly if well socialized

PERFECT OWNER
Experienced, physically strong, strong-willed owner who has time to socialize this powerful dog and who has enough space at home and in the car to accommodate its large size.

THINGS TO WATCH OUT FOR
Dogs from some lines can be strong-willed and need a determined owner.

Loose jowls often lead to lack of saliva control.

Tibetan Mastiff

**powerful
affable
aloof
courageous
protective
independent**

Size: 61–66 cm (24–26 in)
Weight: 64–82 kg (140–180 lb)
Coat: Long, thick topcoat, with heavy undercoat
Colour: Rich black, black and tan, brown, various shades of gold, grey and blue; grey and blue and tan
Lifespan: 10–11 years

Courageous and independent, Tibetan Mastiffs are easy-going and calm. Reserved with strangers, they are loyal and protective towards their owners and territory. Early socialization and training are essential for these gentle giants.

ORIGINALLY BRED
to guard livestock.

SPECIAL CHARACTERISTICS
This is a strong and protective breed of dog.

EXERCISE REQUIREMENTS
Medium. Enjoys exercise.

COMMON ATTITUDE TO
OWNERS affectionate, independent
CHILDREN natural guard
OTHER PETS good if raised with them
STRANGERS reserved, territorial
UNFAMILIAR DOGS can be problematic

PERFECT OWNER
Experienced, strong-willed owner who has the time to socialize this large dog and the space to exercise it adequately and safely.

THINGS TO WATCH OUT FOR
Tends to be problematic with other dogs. May be problematic with strangers unless properly socialized.

⚠ This dog will leave loose hair in the house. Its thick coat needs daily grooming to prevent mats from forming.

Health concerns

This section contains a glossary of some of the more common health problems seen in the breeds listed in this book. Most are caused by faulty genes that are concentrated in a breed or physical deformities as breeders attempt to breed a dog of the correct shape to fit the breed standard. Not all dogs of a specific breed will develop the problems listed below. Always check with a vet about any health concerns.

Before buying a pedigree or crossbred puppy, get to know all of the possible inherited conditions and problems within it. Make sure the parents of any puppy you choose have been screened for these conditions and found to be healthy. Avoid buying puppies from lines where problems occur frequently.

COMMON HEALTH PROBLEMS

Bloat – a life-threatening condition where the stomach swells up with gas or fluid. If the stomach twists it can develop into gastric torsion, which will require an immediate live-saving operation. It is most common in large dogs with deep, narrow chests, especially if they have a nervous or anxious temperament.

Cataracts – the lens of the eye becomes opaque leading to loss of functional vision. With problem breeds, this happens early in life rather than in old age as is more normal.

Congenital deafness – puppies with this condition are born deaf. It is most common in white, merle and piebald dogs.

Congenital heart disease – malformation of the heart and large blood vessels supplying the heart.

Ectropion – the eyelid is everted or rolled out, leading to increased exposure of the delicate membrane lining the eyelid. This can lead to infections or damage due to drying out.

Elbow dysplasia – an inherited fault in the elbow joint that causes arthritis, pain and debilitation. Elbows of breeding dogs can and should be X-rayed to check for normality.

Entropion – an inward rolling of the eyelid edges leading to discomfort, pain and scarring of the eye surface.

Epilepsy – an unpleasant condition where the dog has fits or seizures due to uncontrolled electrical activity in the brain.

Hip dysplasia – an inherited condition where the ball and socket joints of the hips do not fit well, leading to arthritis, pain and debilitation. Severe hip dysplasia can lead to the dog being unable to walk in later life. Dogs cannot be tested until they are two years of age, but hips of breeding dogs can and should be X-rayed and scored. A perfect score is 0:0 (one score for each hip). To be as sure as you can that your puppy will not get hip dysplasia, find a line where all your puppy's relatives have very low scores (less than 3).

Hypothyroidism – a disease of the thyroid that can be genetic in origin and usually appears in affected dogs between the ages of two and five years.

Legg-Calvé-Perthes – an inherited disorder of the hip joint leading to stiffness and pain, commonly seen in puppies of miniature and toy breeds.

Osteochondritis dessicans – a disorder of the immature long bones, which can lead to cracks and damage at the joints causing pain and discomfort, particularly in the hind legs.

Patellar luxation – the kneecap on the hind leg pops out of position causing pain and lameness. It is an inherited condition and is common in very small or very large breeds. The physical symptoms may not be seen in puppies even if the deformity is present so all breeding stock should be checked for this condition.

Progressive retinal atrophy – an inherited disease that causes the retina of the eye to degenerate, leading to partial or total blindness. Age of onset varies, but once it begins, it is slow and progressive and cannot be cured.

Sebaceous adenitis – an inherited disease leading to inflammation of the sebaceous glands that causes excessive dandruff or scaling, hair loss, lesions and a musty odour.

Von Willebrand's disease – a disorder where a vital clotting agent is missing in the dog's blood, leading to excessive bleeding on injury.

GUNDOGS

American Cocker Spaniel Cataracts, progressive retinal atrophy, hip dysplasia, Legg-Calvé-Perthes, luxating patellar, thyroid disorders, autoimmune conditions, skin problems, epilepsy, liver shunts, cherry eye

American Water Spaniel Patellar luxation, progressive retinal atrophy, detached retina, cataracts, epilepsy, hypothyroidism, heart disease

Braque Italian None known at present

Brittany Hip dysplasia, glaucoma, spinal paralysis, seizures, heart and liver problems

Chesapeake Bay Retriever Hip and elbow dysplasia, cataracts, osteochondritis dessicans, progressive retinal atrophy

Clumber Spaniel Cataracts, entropion, spine problems, hip dysplasia

Cocker Spaniel (English) Patellar luxation, progressive retinal atrophy, detached retina, cataracts, epilepsy, hypothyroidism, heart disease

Above: Making sure a purebred puppy is free from inherited defects and diseases will save both you and your dog from many years of distress.

German Shorthaired Pointer Hip and elbow dysplasia, cataracts

German Wirehaired Pointer Hip and elbow dysplasia, cataracts

Golden Retriever Prone to obesity, skin conditions, eye problems, cataracts

Gordon Setter Hip dysplasia, thyroid disease, progressive retinal atrophy, bloat, hypothyroidism

Hungarian Vizsla Hip dysplasia, progressive retinal atrophy, entropion

Irish Red and White Setter Hip dysplasia, cataracts and other eye problems, gastric torsion

Irish Setter Hip dysplasia, progressive retinal atrophy, hypothyroidism, epilepsy, bloat

Irish Water Spaniel Von Willebrand's disease, hip dysplasia, autoimmune diseases, epilepsy, hypothyroidism

Italian Spinone Hip dysplasia, eye conditions, cerebellar ataxia, bloat, ear infections

Kooikerhondje Von Willebrand's disease, cataracts, patellar luxation, epilepsy, necrotizing myelopathy

Labrador Retriever Prone to obesity, hip and elbow dysplasia, osteochondritis dessicans, cataracts, progressive retinal atrophy

Large Munsterlander Hip dysplasia, cataracts, skin disorders

Nova Scotia Duck-tolling Retriever Hip dysplasia, progressive retinal atrophy and other eye diseases, heart defects, hypothyroidism, Addison's disease, epilepsy, autoimmune disorders

Above: All purebred parents should be screened for all conditions and diseases known in the breed and only healthy dogs should be bred.

Curly Coated Retriever Hip dysplasia, progressive retinal atrophy, entropion, cataracts, bloat, hypothyroidism, epilepsy

English Setter Hip and elbow dysplasia, cancer, hypothyroidism, deafness, eye disease, skin conditions

English Springer Spaniel Hip dysplasia, epilepsy progressive retinal atrophy and other eye conditions

Field Spaniel Hip dysplasia, progressive retinal atrophy, hypothyroidism

Flat Coated Retriever Prone to bone cancer, hip dysplasia, patellar luxation, progressive retinal atrophy, cataracts, entropion, hypothyroidism

Pointer Hip and elbow dysplasia

Spanish Water Dog Hip dysplasia, glaucoma, progressive retinal atrophy

Sussex Spaniel Eye problems, hip dysplasia, autoimmune diseases, heart defects, hypothyroidism

Weimaraner Bloat, hip and elbow dysplasia

Welsh Springer Spaniel Hip dysplasia, progressive retinal atrophy, cataracts, allergies, epilepsy, hypothyroidism, glaucoma

Wirehaired Pointing Griffon Hip dysplasia

HOUNDS

Afghan Hound Hip dysplasia, cataracts, hypothyroidism, autoimmune disease

Basenji Progressive retinal atrophy and other eye problems, malabsorption, anaemia, kidney problems

Basset Fauve de Bretagne None known at present

Basset Griffon Vendeen (Petit and Grand) Hip dysplasia, patellar luxation, eye problems, epilepsy, spine problems

Basset Hound Osteochondritis dessicans, patellar luxation, elbow dysplasia, spinal problems, eye problems

Beagle Eye problems, hypothyroidism, epilepsy, intervertebral disc disease

Black and Tan Coonhound Hip dysplasia, eye problems

Bloodhound Hip and elbow dysplasia, bloat, torsion, entropion, ectropion

Borzoi Eye problems, bloat, heart disease, bone cancer, anaesthesia sensitivity

Dachshund (all types) Spinal problems, elbow dysplasia, Legg-Calvé-Perthes, patellar luxation, progressive retinal atrophy, cataracts, diabetes, epilepsy, painful spinal problems

Deerhound Osteochondritis dessicans, bloat, cardiomyopathy, bone cancer, anaesthesia sensitivity

Elkhound Hip dysplasia, progressive retinal atrophy, cataracts, kidney problems, hypothyroidism

Finnish Spitz Cataracts

Foxhound (English and American) None known at present

Grand Bleu de Gascogne Hip and elbow dysplasia, bloat

Greyhound Progressive retinal atrophy, bloat, hypothyroidism, anaesthesia sensitivity

Hamiltonstövare None known at present

Harrier Hip dysplasia, eye disorders

Ibizan Hound Axonal dystrophy, cardiomyopathy

Irish Wolfhound Von Willebrand's disease, hip dysplasia, eye problems, bloat, bone cancer, cardiomyopathy

Lurcher Bloat, anaesthesia sensitivity

Norwegian Lundehund Intestinal lymphangiectasia, inflammatory bowel disease, enteropathy

Otterhound Hip dysplasia, bloat, seizures

Pharaoh Hound Mostly free of inherited diseases but sensitive to anaesthesia

Plott Hound Bloat and gastric torsion

Rhodesian Ridgeback Hip dysplasia, hypothyroidism, cancers, dermoid sinus

Saluki Hip dysplasia, glaucoma, progressive retinal atrophy, hypothyroidism, heart defects

Segugio Italiano Hip dysplasia, glaucoma, progressive retinal atrophy, hypothyroidism, heart defects

Sloughi Hip dysplasia, cardiovascular problems, epilepsy, progressive retinal atrophy

Whippet Eye conditions, sebaceous adenitis, heart defects

Above: Physical and temperament defects are known to run in certain lines and it is important to avoid puppies whose parents carry faulty genes.

PASTORAL

Anatolian Shepherd Dog Hip and elbow dysplasia, entropion, hypothyroidism

Australian Cattle Dog Eye defects, deafness

Australian Shepherd Progressive retinal atrophy, eye conditions, epilepsy, deafness

Bearded Collie Cataracts, Addison's disease, hypothyroidism, autoimmune disease

Belgian Shepherd Dog (Malinois) Progressive retinal atrophy, pannus, cataracts, epilepsy, hypothyroidism **(Groenendael)** Progressive retinal atrophy, pannus, cataracts, epilepsy, hypothyroidism **(Laekenois)** Progressive retinal atrophy, pannus, cataracts, epilepsy,

hypothyroidism **(Tervueren)** Elbow dysplasia, cataracts, epilepsy, hypothyroidism

Bergamasco None known at present

Border Collie Eye problems, progressive retinal atrophy, deafness, epilepsy

Briard Progressive retinal atrophy, bloat, hypothyroidism

Collie (Rough) Eye problems, deafness, hypothyroidism, heart problems

Collie (Smooth) Eye problems, deafness, hypothyroidism, heart problems

Estrela Mountain Dog Hip dysplasia

Finnish Lapphund Progressive retinal atrophy

German Shepherd Dog (Alsatian) Progressive retinal atrophy

Hungarian Kuvasz Progressive retinal atrophy

Hungarian Puli Progressive retinal atrophy, cataracts

Komondor Hip dysplasia, bloat, entropion, cataracts

Lancashire Heeler None known at present

Maremma Sheepdog Hip dysplasia, bloat, anaesthesia sensitivity

Norwegian Buhund Hip dysplasia, eye problems

Old English Sheepdog Eye disorders, cataracts, diabetes, deafness, hypothyroidism, Wobbler's syndrome

Polish Lowland Sheepdog Heart defects

Pyrenean Mountain Dog Hip and elbow dysplasia, patellar luxation, cataracts, entropion, bleeding disorders, spinal problems, anaesthesia sensitivity

Pyrenean Sheepdog None known at present

Samoyed Hip dysplasia, progressive retinal atrophy, cataracts, hypothyroidism, sebaceous adenitis, diabetes

Shetland Sheepdog Digestive disorders, eye conditions, hypothyroidism, epilepsy, prone to leg bone fractures, Legg-Calvé-Perthes

Swedish Vallhund Some eye conditions including progressive retinal atrophy

Welsh Corgi (Cardigan and Pembroke) Eye disorders, spine problems

TERRIERS

Airedale Terrier Hypothyroidism, bleeding disorders

American Staffordshire Terrier Cataracts, hypothyroidism, cruciate ligament ruptures, cancers

Australian Terrier Hip problems, patellar luxation, diabetes, Legg-Calvé-Perthes

Bedlington Terrier Cataracts, patellar luxation

Border Terrier Patellar luxation, cataracts, autoimmune problems, hypothyroidism, heart problems, Legg-Calvé-Perthes

Bull Terrier (English) Patellar luxation, eye problems, heart defects, deafness, kidney problems, skin inflammation

Bull Terrier (Miniature) Patellar luxation, eye problems, heart defects, deafness, kidney problems, skin inflammation

Cairn Terrier Hip problems, patellar luxation, progressive retinal atrophy, blood disorders, kidney problems, Legg-Calvé-Perthes

Cesky Terrier Ovarian cysts, painful spinal problems due to its long back, eye problems

Dandie Dinmont Terrier Glaucoma, Cushings, thyroid, painful spinal problems due to its long back

Fox Terrier (Smooth) Eye and heart defects, epilepsy, Legg-Calvé-Perthes

Fox Terrier (Wire) Eye and heart defects, epilepsy

Glen of Imaal Terrier Hip dysplasia, progressive retinal atrophy, skin allergies

Irish Terrier Hyperthyroidism, cataracts

Jack Russell Terrier None known at present

Kerry Blue Terrier Cataracts, blood disorders

Lakeland Terrier Hip and elbow dysplasia, cataracts, Legg-Calvé-Perthes

Manchester Terrier Hip dysplasia, Legg-Calvé-Perthes, progressive retinal atrophy, seizures, hypothyroidism, limbs break easily when young

Norfolk Terrier Patellar luxation, heart defects, epilepsy

Above: To find a healthy purebred puppy free from inherited conditions and defects you will need to discover how genetically healthy the parents are.

Norwich Terrier Patellar luxation, heart defects, epilepsy

Parson Russell Terrier Hip problems, patellar luxation, eye problems

Scottish Terrier Hypothyroidism, lymphoma, Legg-Calvé-Perthes

Sealyham Terrier Eye problems, spinal problems, heart defects, deafness

Skye Terrier Elbow dysplasia, bone growth problems, hypothyroidism, painful spinal problems due to its long back

Soft Coated Wheaten Terrier Progressive retinal atrophy, cataracts, kidney disease

Welsh Terrier Patellar luxation, eye conditions, Legg-Calvé-Perthes

West Highland White Terrier Skin conditions, hip problems, Legg-Calvé-Perthes, cataracts

TOYS

Affenpinscher Luxating patellar, hip problems, Legg-Calvé-Perthes, open fontanelles, thyroid problems, heart defects, eye problems, leg breaks while a puppy

Australian Silken Terrier Patellar luxation, Legg-Calvé-Perthes, hypoglycaemia, liver shunts

Bichon Frise Patellar luxation, Legg-Calvé-Perthes, progressive retinal atrophy, cataracts, epilepsy, gum disease

Bolognese Luxating patellar, eye conditions

Cavalier King Charles Spaniel Heart defects, patellar luxation, cataracts, retinal problems

Chihuahua (Longhaired or Smooth coated) Patellar luxation, Legg-Calvé-Perthes, eye defect, heart conditions, hypoglycaemia, tracheal collapse

Chinese Crested (Hairless and Powder Puff) Patellar luxation, several different eye conditions, closed ear canals and epilepsy

English Toy Terrier (Black and Tan, Toy Manchester Terrier) Hip problems, progressive retinal atrophy, hypothyroidism, seizures, limbs break easily when young

Griffon Bruxellois (Brussels Griffon) Patellar luxation, progressive retinal atrophy

Havanese Patellar luxation, cataracts, hypothyroidism

Italian Greyhound Patellar luxation, progressive retinal atrophy, autoimmune disease

Japanese Chin Patellar luxation, progressive retinal atrophy, cataracts, seizures, anaesthesia sensitivity

King Charles Spaniel Patellar luxation, cataracts, inguinal hernias, heart problems, anaesthesia sensitivity

Lowchen Patellar luxation, progressive retinal atrophy, cataracts

Maltese Patellar luxation, progressive retinal atrophy, entropion, glaucoma, hypothyroidism, hypoglycaemia, deafness, dental problems

Miniature Pinscher Patellar luxation, hip problems, Legg-Calvé-Perthes, progressive retinal atrophy, cataracts, pannus

Papillon Patellar luxation, eye problems, teeth problems

Pekingese Pastern and patellar luxation, Legg-Calvé-Perthes, dry eye, spinal problems,

Pomeranian Patellar luxation, Legg-Calvé-Perthes, progressive retinal atrophy, cataracts, entropion, hypoglycaemia, tracheal collapse, dental problems

Pug Hip problems, Legg-Calvé-Perthes, progressive retinal atrophy, cataracts, entropion, dry eye, epilepsy, liver disease, anaesthesia sensitivity

Toy Fox Terrier (American Toy Terrier) Patellar luxation, demodectic mange, hip problems, bleeding disorders, hypothyroidism

Yorkshire Terrier Patellar luxation, Legg Calvé Perthes, hypoglycaemia, liver shunts, dental problems, collapsed trachea

UTILITY DOGS

Akita Hip dysplasia, patellar luxation, progressive retinal atrophy, bloat, bleeding disorders, hypothyroidism, sebaceous adenitis, pemphigus, lupus, cancer

American Eskimo Dog Patellar luxation, progressive retinal atrophy, diabetes

Boston Terrier Patellar luxation, Legg-Calvé-Perthes, cataracts, epilepsy, heart problems, deafness

Bulldog Cataracts, ectropion, entropion, dry eye, elongated soft palate, heart defects, hypothyroidism, hip dysplasia, small trachea

Canaan Dog Hip dysplasia, hypothyroidism, eye problems

Chow Chow Hip dysplasia, patellar luxation, growth disorders of the joints, entropion, glaucoma, stenotic nares, hypothyroidism, kidney problems, some skin and hormone problems

Dalmatian Progressive retinal atrophy, glaucoma, diabetes, deafness, bladder stones

French Bulldog Elbow dysplasia, patellar luxation, cataracts, entropion, elongated soft palate, spinal problems, stenotic nares

German Spitz (Klein) Patellar luxation, progressive retinal atrophy, epilepsy, dental problems

German Spitz (Mittel) Patellar luxation, epilepsy, progressive retinal atrophy, dental problems

Japanese Shiba Inu Patellar luxation, hypothyroidism

Japanese Spitz Patellar luxation

Keeshond Patellar luxation, eye problems, hypothyroidism, epilepsy

Lhasa Apso Patellar luxation, progressive retinal atrophy, entropion, bleeding disorders, spinal problems

Poodle (Miniature) Hip problems, Legg-Calvé-Perthes, patellar luxation, progressive retinal atrophy, cataracts, glaucoma, deafness, heart defects, epilepsy (recommended for first-time owners, especially if they are prone to allergies – care is needed to find a healthy dog free of inherited disease)

Poodle (Standard) Eye defects, cataracts, Legg-Calvé-Perthes, entropion, epilepsy, bloat, sebaceous adenitis

Poodle (Toy) Patellar luxation, Legg-Calvé-Perthes, cataracts, progressive retinal atrophy, epilepsy, hypoglycaemia

Schipperke Hip problems, Legg-Calvé-Perthes, progressive retinal atrophy, cataracts, entropion, hypothyroidism, epilepsy

Schnauzer (Miniature) Juvenile cataracts, progressive retinal atrophy, Legg-Calvé-Perthes, epilepsy, pancreatitis, hypothyroidism, bleeding disorders, liver disorders, dental problems

Schnauzer (Standard) Hip dysplasia, hypothyroidism, cataracts, cancer

Shar Pei Demodectic mange, amyloidosis, hypothyroidism, bloat, malabsorption, autoimmune diseases, kidney problems, skin disease, entropion (find a healthy line who's dogs have not had to have their eyelids surgically altered)

Shih Tzu Kidney problems, blood disorders

Tibetan Spaniel Progressive retinal atrophy, patellar luxation

Tibetan Terrier Patellar luxation, progressive retinal atrophy, lens luxation, cataracts, hypothyroidism, bleeding disorders

WORKING DOGS

Alaskan Malamute Hip dysplasia, bloat, kidney problems, hypothyroidism, progressive retinal atrophy, bleeding disorders

Beauceron Bloat

Bernese Mountain Dog Hip dysplasia, elbow dysplasia, osteochondritis dessicans, progressive retinal atrophy, thyroid problems, tumours, bloat, kidney disease

Bouvier des Flandres Hip dysplasia, cataracts, glaucoma, entropion, torsion, hypothyroidism, laryngeal paralysis, cancer

Boxer Hip dysplasia, progressive retinal atrophy, heart problems, torsion, epilepsy, bleeding disorders, cancers, intestinal problems

Bullmastiff Hip and elbow dysplasia, eye problems, bloat and torsion, heart defects

Greater Swiss Mountain Dog Hip, elbow or shoulder dysplasia, osteochondritis dessicans, bloat, torsion, hypothyroidism, splenic torsion, dilated oesophagus

Dobermann Hip dysplasia, bloat, cancers, von Willebrand's disease, liver disease, hypothyroidism, heart defects

Giant Schnauzer Hip dysplasia, osteochondritis dessicans, progressive retinal atrophy, glaucoma, heart defects, epilepsy

Great Dane Hip and elbow dysplasia, cataracts, bone cancer, bloat

Greenland Dog None known at present

Hovawart Hip dysplasia, thyroid problems

Leonberger Hip dysplasia, bloat, cancer, hypothyroidism, osteochondritis dessicans, Addison's disease, cardiomyopathy

Mastiff Hip and elbow dysplasia, joint and bone problems, eye defects, hypothyroidism, heart defects, bloat, epilepsy

Neapolitan Mastiff Hip and elbow dysplasia, joint and bone problems, hypothyroidism, heart defects, entropion, bloat

Newfoundland Hip dysplasia, osteochondritis dessicans, bloat, heart problems, eyelid problems, hypothyroidism

Above: Some breed councils take elimination of inherited defects seriously and work tirelessly to eliminate faulty genes within the breed.

Pinscher (German) Hip dysplasia, eye problems

Portuguese Water Dog Hip dysplasia, progressive retinal atrophy

Rottweiler Hip and elbow dysplasia, osteochondritis dessicans, eye defects, heart defects, cancer, bloat, hypothyroidism

Russian Black Terrier Hip and elbow dysplasia, eye problems

Siberian Husky Hip dysplasia, eye defects, progressive retinal atrophy

St Bernard Hip dysplasia, osteochondritis dessicans, bloat, cancer, epilepsy, entropion, ectropion, heart problems

Tibetan Mastiff Hip dysplasia, hypothyroidism

Index

Acknowledgements

Picture credits

age footstock Andreas Gradin 259. **Alamy** Andreas Gradin 177; Chuck Franklin 71, 72; FLPA 5; Gwenllian Jones 87; H. Mark Weidman Photography 55; Juniors Bildarchiv GmbH 191; Life on white 86; Oleksiy Maksymenko Photography 75; Petra Wegner 141, 255, 270; Realimage 19; vario images GmbH & Co.KG 266. **Animal Photography** Barbara O'Brien 114 above, 194, 227; Sally Anne Thompson 130; Tetsu Yamazaki 105, 186, 190, 197, 241. **Ardea** Jean Michel Labat 37, 185; John Daniels 98, 149, 150 161. **Battersea Dogs & Cats Home** 49, 51. **Corbis** Ocean 189; Yoshihisa Fujita/MottoPet/amanaimages 56. **Dorling Kindersley** 245, 251, 257. **Getty Images** Christina Handley 34; Dave King 127, 272 above; Gerard Brown 73; Ken Weaver 26; Louise Nichol 67; Paul Vozdic 2; Tracy Morgan 74, 76, 100, 107, 125, 126, 135, 137, 143, 212, 240. **Ironbark ACD** Angela Cocker 144. **John Daniels** 133, 134, 159, 168, 171, 181. **Nature Picture Library** ARCO 187; Petra Wegner 193, 253, 267. **Octopus Publishing Group** Angus Murray 28, 30 above, 30 below, 31 left, 77, 78, 80, 81, 82, 88, 89, 92, 93 above, 94, 99, 101, 102 above, 102 below, 103, 104, 106, 109, 111 above, 111 below, 115 above, 115 below, 118, 120, 122, 123 above, 123 below, 124, 128, 129, 139, 142, 145, 146, 147, 148, 151, 155, 160 above, 160 below, 162, 165, 166, 167, 169, 170, 173, 179, 180, 184, 198, 199, 206, 206, 208, 209, 211, 214, 215, 216, 217, 218, 219, 220, 222 above, 222 below, 223, 226, 231 above, 231 below, 233, 235, 236, 239, 246, 248, 250, 252, 254, 256, 261, 263, 265, 271, 272 below, 273, 275, 280; Ray Moller 93 below, 153, 158, 196, 229, 260; Russell Sadur 8, 9, 10, 11, 12, 14, 15, 17, 18, 20, 22, 23, 25, 27, 32, 38, 39, 40, 41, 42, 43, 44, 45, 52, 61; Steve Gorton 29, 31 right, 85, 90, 95, 96, 97, 108, 110, 112, 113, 116, 117, 119, 121, 131, 132, 136, 140, 152, 154, 156, 157, 163, 164, 172, 174, 175, 178, 183, 188, 192, 195, 200, 201, 202, 203 above, 203 below, 204, 205, 210 above, 210 below, 213, 221, 225, 228, 230, 232, 234, 237, 238, 242, 243, 244, 247, 249, 268, 269, 276, 278, 283. **Shutterstock** chalabala 62; Eric Isselée 84, 176; Lerche&Johnson 264. **SuperStock** Garo/Phanie 16. **Thinkstock** Hemera 60; iStockphoto 6, 13, 35, 46, 57, 66, 79, 83, 91, 138, 258, 262; Jupiterimages 36, 224; Monkey Business 68; Zoonar 182. **WyEast Kennels** Jim & Kathy Corbett/ www.anypet.com/dog/wyeast.html (tel: ++1 503 649 2712) 114 below.

Publisher's acknowledgements

Thank you to the staff at Battersea Dogs & Cats Home who have contributed to this book.

Editorial Director: Trevor Davies
Managing Editor: Clare Churly
Art Director: Jonathan Christie
Designer: Jaz Bahra
Picture Library Manager:
  Jennifer Veall
Production Controller:
  Sarah Connelly